Primitivist Modernism

W. E. B. DU BOIS INSTITUTE

Series Editors

Henry Louis Gates Jr.
W. E. B. Du Bois Professor of the Humanities
Harvard University

Richard Newman
Research Officer
The W. E. B. Du Bois Institute
Harvard University

The Open Sore of A Continent
A Personal Narrative of the Nigerian Crisis
Wole Soyinka

From Emerson to King
Democracy, Race, and the Politics of Protest
Anita Haya Patterson

Primitivist Modernism
Black Culture and the Origins of Transatlantic Modernism
Sieglinde Lemke

The W. E. B. Du Bois Institute brings together leading scholars from
around the world to explore a range of topics in the study of African
and African American culture, literature, and history. The Institute
series provides a publishing forum for outstanding work deriving
from colloquia, research groups, and conferences sponsored by the
Institute. Whether undertaken by individuals or collaborative
groups, the books appearing in this series work to foster a stronger
sense of national and international community and a better understanding of diasporic history.

PRIMITIVIST MODERNISM

Black Culture and the Origins of Transatlantic Modernism

SIEGLINDE LEMKE

Oxford   New York   Oxford University Press   1998

Oxford University Press

Oxford   New York
Athens   Auckland   Bangkok   Bogota   Bombay
Buenos Aires   Calcutta   Cape Town   Dar es Salaam
Delhi   Florence   Hong Kong   Istanbul   Karachi
Kuala Lumpur   Madras   Madrid   Melbourne
Mexico City   Nairobi   Paris   Singapore
Taipei   Tokyo   Toronto   Warsaw

and associated companies in
Berlin   Ibadan

Copyright © 1998 by Sieglinde Lemke

Published by Oxford University Press, Inc.,
198 Madison Avenue, New York, New York 10016

Oxford is a registered trademark of Oxford University Press

Library of Congress Cataloging-in-Publication Data
Lemke, Sieglinde.
    Primitivist modernism : black culture and the origins of transatlantic modernism / by
Sieglinde Lemke.
        p. cm. — (W.E.B. Du Bois Institute)
    Includes bibliographical references and index.
    ISBN 0-19-510403-X
    1. Modernism (Art)—Europe. 2. Arts, European. 3. Modernism (Art)—United
States. 4. Arts, American. 5. Arts, Black—Influence. 6. Afro-American arts—
Influence. I. Title. II. Series: W.E.B. Du Bois Institute (Series)
NX542.L46 1997
700'.4112'08996—DC21   97-1352

9 8 7 6 5 4 3 2

Printed in the United States of America
on acid-free paper

To my friends and my parents
who taught me to love.
Without this fire,
this book would have
remained unwritten.

▣ CONTENTS

Primitivist Modernism

INTRODUCTION
Was Modernism Passing?

This book is concerned with exploring the formal connections between "white" and "black" cultures in early-twentieth-century art and literature. Instead of juxtaposing white modernism with a "black counter-modernism," as Houston Baker does in his important study, *Modernism and the Harlem Renaissance*, I have sought to trace how both are inextricably interrelated.[1] Nor is this book an attempt to define a pure, black aesthetics, as is Richard J. Powell's book *Blues Aesthetics, Black Culture, and Modernism*.[2] Rather than talking about interracial friendships, moments of political cooperation, or an historically ignored black modernism, my focus will be aesthetic collaboration.

Two quotations serve as epigraphs for this study. Both are passages from canonical texts of modern literature, and both present powerful images of black and white. The first is from Virginia Woolf's novel, *To the Lighthouse* (1927):

> James looked at the Lighthouse. He could see the white-washed rocks; the tower, stark and straight; he could see that it was barred with black and white; he could see windows in it; he could even see washing spread on the rocks to dry. So that was the Lighthouse, was it?
>
> No, the other was also the Lighthouse. For nothing was simply one thing. The other Lighthouse was true too. It was something hardly to be seen across the bay. (Woolf, 186)

Woolf's statement serves as a convenient commentary on the recent trend in American literary history of acknowledging works written by people of non-European descent. As a result of these debates, the canon is rapidly being reconfigured and students are taught that the textual body of American and European art, literary, and cultural history is "barred with black and white." Authors such as Woolf are taught in the same class with Ralph Ellison and Toni Morrison—a racial mix unthinkable until recently.

A passage from Ellison's novel, *The Invisible Man* (1952), describing the effect a few drops of black paint have when added to a bucket of white paint, further illustrates the point:

I measured the glistening black drops, seeing them settle upon the surface and become blacker still, spreading suddenly out to the edges. . . . "How is it coming?" he [Mr. Kimbro] said, standing with hands on hips.

"All right, sir."

"Let's see," he said, selecting a sample and running his thumb across the board. "That's it, as white as George Washington's Sunday-go-to-meetin' wig and as sound as the all-mighty dollar! That's paint!" he said proudly. "That's paint that'll cover just about anything!"

He looked as though I had expressed a doubt and I hurried to say, "It's certainly white all right."

"White! It's the purest white that can be found. . . ." (Ellison, 197)

The paint becomes "pure" white only by adding ten drops of black; while these drops remain invisible to the naked eye, they are nevertheless crucial to achieving a perfectly white hue. These drops work as a catalyst, as a necessary transforming element in effecting whiteness. This image is, I think, an apt metaphor for a phenomenon that has itself been "the invisible man" of cultural criticism: that black, or African-inspired, expressions have played a seminal role in the shaping of modernism. It is my intent to paint a picture of modernism that stresses a chiaroscuro effect, the interplay between black and white.

It is this injection of blackness that caused modernism to assume the precise form it took. I shall demonstrate that several key expressions of modernism assumed their shape only through the incorporation of black forms. "The other"—to use the fashionable term—has been an integral part of modernism from its origins. But this fact has not yet become a commonplace in critical accounts of modernism, as the black cultural critic and feminist Michele Wallace has recently pointed out.

Wallace calls attention to the fact that the impact blacks have had on modernism has not been adequately discussed, specifically referring to the famous black performer Josephine Baker, calling her the "Afro-American 'other' of Euro-American Modernism."[3] Wallace brackets the term "other" in quotation marks to signal that the term is problematic, yet indispensable. This apparently neutral term connotes devaluation or disrespect. Who would want to be called by this name? Even when used as a reference to "the exotic Other"—the nonwhite, nonsterile, nonweary, not-so-uptight person—the term remains an affront. Throughout postmodern criticism, it has been applied indiscriminately to numerous kinds of alterity, and its original referent is now vague. Its semantic field includes a wide range of related designations and synonyms: non-Western, black, non-European, or "primitive," a term commonly used in the first third of this century by Americans and Europeans to mean a variety of mutually exclusive things.

"The primitive" is a highly charged term; in the racist discourse of the nineteenth and early twentieth century, it was infused with negative connotations and indiscriminately applied to peoples and objects worldwide (as well as to African Americans, of course). But when referring to human conduct or manners, "primitive" was the antonym of discipline, order, rationality—the antithesis of "civilized." The racist imagination conflated these two versions of alterity and defined people of African descent as irrational, uncivilized, and not-yet-modern.

How does primitivism mesh with accounts of modernism? Of course, it is impossible to discuss the vast range of theoretical work concerning modernist aesthetics, and we will necessarily limit ourselves here to a few basic ideas. One of the more common critical assumptions of this era, one mentioned in most surveys and textbooks, is that modernism is the art of the Machine Age. This assumption is maintained, for example, by Lewis Mumford, Charles Beard, and Guy Wilson. More recently, Miles Orvell's book, *The Real Thing: Imitation and Authenticity in American Culture, 1880–1940,* has argued convincingly that the shift in the aesthetic paradigm was related to the emergence of the Machine Age.

This line of thought holds that at the turn of the century, many artists became disenchanted with received aesthetic conventions. Out of their dissatisfaction with realist aesthetics and a "culture of imitation" there emergenced "a culture of authenticity," which, Orvell claims, manifested itself in the modernist fascination with precision, mechanics, and movement.[4] Similarly, Cecelia Tichi argues that rationality, speed, and efficiency were key to American modernism. In her book, *Shifting Gears: Technology, Literature, Culture in Modernist America*, she makes the case for the interdependence of technology, the machine, and modern literature.

A recent book by Terry Smith entitled *The Making of the Modern: Industry, Art, and Design in America* (1993) also supports this view.[5] Smith situates the early phase of modernism in the context of Henry Ford's ideas. No doubt, Ford's production techniques were a determining force that shaped the way we work and had a profound impact on our lifestyles; indirectly, they are reflected in the art produced in this century. But while modernism certainly emerged at a time when mechanical reproduction and mass-production replaced a long tradition of craftsmanship, it is reductive to attribute the formulation of modern aesthetics to the sole influence of the machine age, even where they marched hand in hand.

The situation is complicated: modernist aesthetics and the assembly line were often conflated in the popular imagination. In the twenties, for example, American culture was exported to Western Europe in countless forms, but, curiously, the two things "American" that most fascinated Germans were Henry Ford and jazz. Ford symbolized progress, prosperity, and the American way of life: most of the desirable, mass-produced goods that swept through desolate, post–World War I Germany came from America. Envious of the fact that one in five Americans owned a car, Germans were eager to watch American movies and to listen to American music: jazz. A significant segment of the emerging middle class spent their spare time listening to jazz, and its influence was so pervasive by the early thirties that the National Socialists would come to feel that they had to ban jazz.

But in the Weimar Republic, especially in twenties, these gifts from America were well received and very popular. The exciting rhythms that black musicians provided and the prosperity that Ford's system of production promised were inseparable within a European perspective that forged a literal connection between the two. That the syncopated improvisation of jazz and the mechanized routine of the assembly line in fact suggested contradictory metaphors was overlooked. More important, the inextricably black face of jazz was subordinated and all too often ignored.

This project also parts from those who have proposed consumerism as the only key to understanding the logic of modernity. According to cultural historian T. Jackson Lears, it has "become a newly minted critical commonplace that modernism and capitalism are (wittingly or unwittingly) accomplices."[6] Frederic Jameson has suggested that we relate cultural productions in the late twentieth century to multinational consumer capitalism. For Jameson, the earlier phase of modernism is a reflection of national or transatlantic capitalism. Jameson's characterization of postmodern culture and our position in it echoes an ethos with which the majority of poststructuralist critics would agree. He claims that "we are *within* the culture of postmodernism to the point where its facile repudiation is as impossible as any equally facile celebration of it is complacent and corrupt."[7] Jameson dismisses the idea that we have a critical distance or antagonistic stance toward the postmodern and acknowledges the hegemony of consumer structures *interwoven* with the social world.

In *After the Great Divide: Modernism, Mass Culture, Postmodernism*, Andreas Huyssen makes a crucial connection, asserting that mass culture itself was the threatening other that haunted modernism: "Modernism and mass culture have been engaged in a compulsive *pas de deux*."[8] He adds gender to the mix by differentiating between the "masculine mystique of avant-garde aesthetics" on the one hand and the "mystique of mass culture as feminine," on the other. These are suggestive terms, especially when we recall that blacks, metaphorically, have been conflated with the feminine in centuries of racist discourse. On a symbolic level, our project will be to explore the racial dimension of modernism and define the *pas de deux* in which white and black cultures have engaged. Indeed, Josephine Baker's *danse sauvage* will even prove to be a *pas de trois*, a dance of mass culture, primitivism, and modernism.

This book suggests that looking at early modernism from a different angle reveals that the "other" of color was always within the culture of modernism. (I shall leave to the reader any extrapolations one might apply to the culture of postmodernism. But even a cursory glance at MTV attests that the Other is deeply embedded within contemporary culture as well.) The notion that modernism and primitivism are (wittingly or unwittingly) accomplices has, however, not yet become a critical commonplace of modernist scholarship.

To mark the beginning and the end of this study, we will claim the years 1906 and 1934 as symbolic touchstones. In 1906, artists in Paris introduced each other to African sculptures and masks and began to acquire personal collections of West African art. Among the French avant-garde, African art was a valorized and preferred source of inspiration. Pablo Picasso's encounter with African sculptures might be the best documented example of the fermenting effect that the cultural other can have on the transformation of style. But not only was black art instrumental in forming white modernism; white culture was also instrumental in shaping black expression.

That same year, Franz Boas, a German immigrant who became a pioneering figure in American anthropology, gave the commencement address at Atlanta University. W. E. B. Du Bois, a teacher there at the time, later recalled his reaction to the speech:

> [Boas said], "You need not be ashamed of your African past": and then he recounted the history of black kingdoms south of the Sahara for a thousand years. I was too astonished to speak. All of this I had never heard and I came then and afterwards to realize how the silence and neglect of science can let truth utterly disappear or even be unconsciously distorted.[9]

Du Bois, an African American, first learned about the traditions of his African ancestors from a German American. This sort of reception—learning about "oneself" through a cultural other—is by no means rare. But it has not received adequate critical consideration. Indeed, I believe that such incidents have all too often, to echo Du Bois, been distorted, especially when transmitted across the American color line.

The year 1934, in which *Negro: An Anthology* appeared, marks the endpoint of this investigation. It marks the birth of the Nègritude movement, a black neoprimitivist movement that started in Paris and ultimately became central to the process of decolonization and to the Francophone African independence movement.

My goal is to reveal the concrete ways in which intercultural exchanges shaped the formation of modernist aesthetics in four fields: fine arts, music, performance art, and nonfiction. I have focused on a representative example from each genre: Pablo Picasso's *Les Demoiselles D'Avignon* (1907); Paul Whiteman's symphonic jazz concert, advertised as "Experiments in Modern Music" (1924); Josephine Baker's *danse sauvage* (1925); Alain Locke's anthology *The New Negro* (1925) and Nancy Cunard's anthology *Negro* (1934). The concern of my analysis is to explore how "marginal" black cultures have shaped the center, and how the center has shaped those cultures in return.

Picasso's revolutionary painting *Les Demoiselles D'Avignon* will be our focal point: it is the primal scene of the aesthetic encounter between Europe and Africa and also a metonym of a broader movement among French artists at the time. The *vogue nègre* had a profound transforming effect on the dominant forms of European art. The contact with African masks and sculptures—works that did not attempt to represent "accurately" the social world or the portrayed object—helped European artists to modify their style of representation and experiment with a nonrepresentational aesthetic. I shall refer to this particular sort of exchange as primitivist modernism, the hyphen indicating that cultural hybridity is the sine qua non for this type of artifact. It will be important to remember that African American artists and African writers often emulated European artists and reappropriated primitivist-modernism; to that end, I will discuss the presence of "Africanism" in the works of modern black artists such as Loïs Mailou Jones, William H. Johnson, and Meta Warwick Fuller.

While the impact of Africa on the visual arts has received significant attention—for example, in the 1984 Museum of Modern Art exhibition "'Primitivism' in Twentieth Century Art: Affinity of the Tribal and the Modern" curated by William Rubin—the impact African American musical expression has had on the development of popular culture in this century is even more compelling. The fact that America was coming of age during a time commonly referred to as the "Jazz Age" suggests how crucial black cultural expression has been in the shaping of the larger American artistic and cultural identity. In chapter 3, I situate the emergence of jazz in the sociocultural climate of the twenties. Symphonic jazz managed to overcome the initial antipathy for this "vulgar" music. However, Paul Whiteman's "respectable" jazz remained formally quite distinct from black jazz. Primitivist modernism in music manifested itself in America in two ways: in compositions by white composers, such as George Gershwin's "Rhapsody in Blue," featured by Paul Whiteman at his Aeolian Hall concert, and in the marketing of race records.

The appropriation of black culture by whites took place on both an artistic and a commercial level. However, it also had a more personal manifestation. In New York, the number of Anglo-Americans who were curious about the night life in Harlem increased; the result was a "Nordic" invasion of Harlem's clubs. Eager to watch blacks performing firsthand, white "slummers" spent considerable time and money in places like the Cotton Club or the Savoy. But the interest in blacks and the symbolic appropriation of black culture was not unidirectional. Preeminent jazz musicians such as Duke Ellington, whose band played nightly at the Cotton Club, profited from the money white people brought to Harlem. Furthermore, Ellington freely appropriated European musical idioms and even consciously drew upon white stereotypes of blacks. In his famous "jungle-style" compositions of the mid-twenties, he flaunted pseudo-African idioms, mocking the peculiar vogue for things African.

Europeans were also drawn to American jazz and to all-black musical shows. When *La Revue Nègre* was performed in Paris, it was an instant success. Its young, black, female dancer, Josephine Baker, who performed the *danse sauvage*, became a star overnight. Initially celebrated as a "Black Venus" and as an ambassador from a primitive locus far from civilization, Baker became, in her later years, a stately performer who sang in classic French. She remained one of the most popular performers in Europe for fifty years; her extravagant and glamorous stage persona has made her one of the icons of twentieth-century dance. She embodied the dialectical interplay at the core of primitivist modernism. I argue that this American in Paris was the successor to the original *vogue nègre* at the turn of the century that had so captivated the Parisian avant-garde. Baker was the embodiment—in the truest sense of the word—of primitivist modernism on stage.

This persistent interest in African culture among Europeans had complex repercussions. The black philosopher Alain Locke, for example, sought to appropriate the trend for African Americans. For Locke, aesthetics were a means to "uplift the race." The kind of primitivism embodied in his anthology *The New Negro* (1925) was politically charged and central to the birth of the Harlem Renaissance, the first major display of the creative potential of black writers in American history. When Locke encouraged young black artists to imitate European primitivist modernism and to get in touch with their

"African" legacy, he did so to fight American racism by revealing the American Negro to be a producer of culture and deserving of political equality.

Black primitivist modernism was not limited to Locke's Harlem Renaissance: it reemerged in dramatically different form in the anthology *Negro* (1934). The book, edited by Nancy Cunard (an aristocratic member of the British Communist Party), is a prominent example of the interrelation between black and white culture. Enormous (almost nine hundred pages), it discusses issues concerning people of African descent in America, Africa, and Europe. The articles, written by prominent black and white intellectuals, often idealize African or African American lifestyles as socioeconomically repressed but psychically unfettered, infused with "spontaneous" art, and inherently "collective." Cunard's anthology uses accounts of the "essence" of African civilizations as models for an aesthetics of communist life in which black primitivism is a counterforce to the capitalist ethos. In her attempt to defeat everything she associated with the bourgeoisie (e.g., positivistic rationalism, Puritanism, capitalism), Cunard embraced black people and black cultures as a model for an organic Ur-Communism.

Recent efforts at locating the black relation to white culture have concentrated more on the contributions that "black" voices have made to American literature. Increasingly, literary critics have argued that canonical American literature—and America itself—owes many of its themes and structures to intercultural, interracial exchanges. Literary critics have begun to analyze race as a powerful force in American literary history, echoing Toni Morrison's call to uncover the "always choked representation of an Africanist presence" in texts written by American whites. In her analysis of the literary works of Willa Cather, Edgar Allan Poe, Mark Twain, and Ernest Hemingway, Morrison demonstrates that "Africanism" and "Americanness" are inextricably intertwined.[10]

This study partakes in this emerging critical endeavor to illuminate the presence of blackness, or "Africanism," in American culture and attempts to extend the argument to modernism in general. The term *primitive* was often used to describe the people, cultures, and objets d' art of African origin or descent. Thought of as the antithesis of "Western" or "modern," the use of the term "primitive" was both arbitrary and racist. My use of the term in the title of this book is in part ironic, but it is also intended to acknowledge the fact that marginalized and despised black cultures were pivotal in the creation of transatlantic modernism. Thus, wittingly or unwittingly, Euro-American modernism's identity has always been hyphenated, has always been hybrid, has always been biracial.

Primitivist Modernism attempts to provide a context for Woolf's and Ellison's metaphors of the ways in which "blackness" helped to create the "white" aesthetic that we today refer to as modernism. The assertion of the book is that any critical account of modernism that ignores the impact of black culture fails to grasp the complexity of modernity. A second assertion is that "black" and "white" influences have been engaged in the dialectical formation of an aesthetic and cultural identity we think of as American. This identity is necessarily new, is neither purely black nor purely white, and is (metaphorically) the defining aspect of modernism.

1

STUDIES IN
BLACK AND WHITE

There is, indeed, a much better hypothesis to explain the American temperament, and it lies in the fact that the United States are pervaded by the most striking and suggestive figure—the Negro.

—Carl G. Jung (1930)

The contributions of the Negro to American culture are as indigenous to our soil as the legendary cowboy or gold-seeking frontiersman.

—V. F. Calverton (1934)

In Hemingway's novel *The Garden of Eden*, the blonde protagonist Catherine tries to make herself darker and darker to attract her husband sexually and to distinguish herself from other white people. This kind of Africanism, Toni Morrison argues in *Playing in the Dark*, conflates blackness with sex, chaos, and madness. But the underlying function of imagining an "Africanist other" is really, according to Morrison, "an extraordinary meditation on the self." Fabricating an Africanist persona enables the white self (character, writer, and reader) to explore its most sublimated fears and desires. It does not matter whether or not the Africanist persona is represented as loyal, inferior, rebellious, or fearful. What matters is that the persona remain a projection of white desire and fear.

Aldon Nielsen's study, *Reading Race: White American Poets and the Racial Discourse in the Twentieth Century* (1988), detects in Anglo-American literature an "ongoing project of white literature of separating itself from that which it regards as being not-itself" (Nielsen, 31). This symbolic gesture of expulsion, of trying to separate oneself by ousting the "other" is, Nielsen claims, made in Gertrude Stein's *Melanctha*. Although Stein represented black characters sympathetically and in spite of the fact that she opened her home to black writers such as Claude McKay and Richard Wright, her sympathy with blacks is "the sympathy of romantic racism, and it is this that marks it as the signpost of modernism's discourse on the nonwhite" (Nielsen, 21). "Modernism's discourse on the nonwhite," then, is marked by a dismissive attitude that creates a schism between the self and the other. For Nielsen as well as for Morrison—who is mostly interested "in the way black people ignite critical moments of discovery or change or emphasis in literature not written by them" (Morrison, viii)—the misrepresentation of black people by white writers, or the dismissal of their language through parody, indicates America's deeply held, racist attitudes toward the other of color.

Morrison's interpretation of *Huckleberry Finn,* for example, stresses the tension between Huck and Jim: Jim's enslavement enables and reinforces Huck's autonomy. While Morrison's interpretation focuses on the distance between self and other, Shelly Fisher-Fishkin reveals that adopting the language of the "other"—as with his emulation of the voice of a black slave—shaped Twain's literary style. For her, Twain's "white" identity is "tainted" by the inclusion of a black voice, a biracial, double-voiced discourse.

In her book *Was Huck Black?* Fisher-Fishkin argues that Twain's vernacular style and his sense of social satire were directly indebted to his childhood encounters with a slave named Jerry, as well as to the language of minstrel shows. She quotes Twain's recollection of an encounter with a "bright, simple, guileless little darkey boy" who was so talkative that he listened "as one who receives a revelation." Twain's confession that "the boy's spirit would descend upon me and enter into me" indicates that here, the "other" is, to echo Twain, within the self.[1]

Fishkin argues persuasively that "Jim was an amalgam of authentic black voices, and white caricature of them" (Fishkin, 92). By extension, she claims that much of the vernacular voice in American literature, such as that which empowered the works of Twain, Hemingway, and Faulkner, "is in large measure a voice that is 'black.'" The quotation marks indicate that she thinks of this black voice as the construct of the writers who employ it and that she distinguishes it from spoken black dialects. Fishkin is convinced that a "black" voice fundamentally shaped American literature. This notion of "racial ventriloquism" is central to the important work of the literary critic Michael North.

In *The Dialect of Modernism: Race, Language, and Twentieth-Century Literature* (1994), North detects a black voice in Joseph Conrad's *Nigger of the "Narcissus,"* Gertrude Stein's *Melanctha*, and T. S. Eliot's *The Waste Land*. North extends the claim that a "black" voice informs much of what we identify as "American" in modernist literature and carefully shows that modernism owes much of its shape and quality to its engagement with black dialect.[2] He argues that whereas Twain adopted the language of slaves for its flamboyant brilliance, modernist writers embraced "black" English primarily because it was nonconformist.

According to North, the rise of modernism was connected to a counterinsurgency against a linguistic movement that started around 1880 and that stigmatized all regional and ethnic dialects in an attempt to create "pure English." The modernists' rebellion against linguistic standardization ignited their interest in socially disdained black dialect. In imitating black language or using minstrel instrumentation, as Eliot did in *Sweeney Agonistes*, white writers fought rigid linguistic and social conventions. This "racial ventriloquism" or "racial masquerade," to use North's terms, helped the modernists to assault old cultural and literary authorities so that they could emerge as a new and bold literary authority.

For North, the plot of *The Jazz Singer*, the first talkie, is paradigmatic of this process. The young Jakie Rabinowitz refuses to obey his father's order to practice "Kol Nidre"; instead, he spends his time in the beer garden "shufflin'" and playing jazz. In the 1927 version of the movie, Jakie was played by Al Jolson in blackface, which is deeply symbolic because Jolson's appearance illustrates that a black masquerade is pivotal in attaining a new and unconventional identity. North writes: "Jakie can throw off conventions to become himself by becoming 'black,'" and he suggests that Jakie personifies a broader movement because the use of black dialect enabled many modern writers to realize a new literary persona, as it did for Jakie. He writes: "In this way, Stein and Picasso act out twenty years in advance the other side of *The Jazz Singer*, the generational drama, donning the African mask to make a break with their own cultural past. . . . In this way, African figures become the totem of the avant-garde, that tiny tribe unified by its shared opposition to the rest of European society" (North, 66).

It is North's accomplishment to tie a critical trope in the discourse on modern aesthetics—that a break with the past is a necessary condition of modernism—to the question of race. A complex, iconoclastic impulse motivated modern writers to transgress racial boundaries. For the white modernist, both black dialect and African art proved enormously useful in breaking from established norms. The appropriation of the "other"—or rather his rejected and devalued idioms—enabled the avant-garde to free itself from the cultural past and to solidify itself by "its shared opposition to the rest of European society." The underlying notion suggests an oedipal structure in which the (white) self manages to break away from the tradition of his (white) artistic forefathers by embracing a black other. In couching the making of modernism as an interracial oedipal drama, North radically challenges standard definitions of modernism.

This phenomenon of insurrection through a "black" voice, North suggests, was not limited to literature: "The new voice that American culture acquired in the 1920s, the decade of jazz, stage musicals, talking pictures, and aesthetic modernism, was largely a black one" (North, 7). Having made this sweeping claim, North nevertheless focuses on literary modernism; with the exception of *The Jazz Singer* and a brief discussion of Pablo Picasso's use of African masks, he explores mostly the effects the "verbal mask" had on the shaping of Anglo-American modernism.

Overall, North and Fisher-Fishkin are both interested in the impact and presence of blackness, which they take to be "within whiteness." Like them, Eric J. Sundquist feels that the black and white traditions are both "one and separate" and that they will ultimately "form a single tradition." Sundquist's magisterial *To Wake the Nations: Race in the Making of American Literature* sets out to explore the ignored interracial tradition in the nineteenth century.[3] In a thorough reconsideration of the canon of the American Renaissance (Thoreau, Whitman, Emerson, Hawthorne, and Melville), Sundquist includes works written by black authors (Douglass, DeLany, Chesnutt, Du Bois) because he feels that to ignore their contributions would be a significant loss. He agrees with W. E. B. Du Bois that America should acknowledge black song, black toil, and black cheer as national gifts.

In fact, almost ninety years after Du Bois demanded that the African American had to be recognized as a "co-worker in the kingdom of culture," *To Wake the Nation* makes a similar plea. Sundquist's work acts as a call to literary critics to abandon a monocultural perspective, to explicate the African American presence within truly American texts, and to explore the interrelatedness of black and white cultures. Sundquist's acknowledgment of the works of black authors is an opening to the richness of American literary history in its cultural and textual heteroglosia.

But this profusion of voices is, almost by definition, not only literary. Music, painting, travel writing, performance art, and life styles are crucial areas of investigation when it comes to the black impact on modern culture. Simply put, the aim of *Primitivist Modernism* is to extend the "discovery" of the black voice in American fiction across borders of genre to the various manifestations of modernism (art, music, dance). In this attempt to illuminate a widespread black presence in modern culture, *Primitivist Modernism* is part of another trend, joining works by authors such as Marianna Torgovnick, Ann Douglas, and Paul Gilroy in assessing the broad impact nonwhites have had on modernity.

In *Gone Primitive: Savage Intellects, Modern Lives*, published in 1990, Torgovnick explores such narratives as the travel accounts of Henry M. Stanley, Edgar Rice Burroughs's *Tarzan* novels, Tobias Schneebaum's autobiography, and Joseph Conrad's *Heart of Darkness*. She also considers the representations of the primitive in the anthropological works of Margaret Mead, Bronislaw Malinowski, and Michel Leiris. Furthermore, she investigates the works of art historians such as Roger Fry and William Rubin. And she devotes one chapter to Sigmund Freud's works, specifically *Totem and Taboo* and *Civilization and Its Discontents*.

Gone Primitive covers several disciplines—anthropology, literature, psychoanalysis, art criticism—and a time span of more than one hundred years, starting with Livingston's travel accounts of Africa (1874) and ending in Manhattan with William Rubin's MOMA show on "Primitivism" (1984). Moreover, her investigation takes us to three continents—Europe, Africa, and America. The word "primitive" connotes various meanings and is used by the authors she discusses as synonymous with "primeval," non-Western, or physical. While Torgovnick does not distinguish among the differences in these primitivist texts, she discloses a common structure. Her study traces "a male-centered, canonical line of Western primitivism" and finds, not surprisingly, that the Western self shapes itself against the primitive other.

Here, she echoes what Nielsen and Morrison have argued about the literary technique of "othering." Torgovnick also stresses the contrast, the gap, between the white self and the "primitive other." She claims that Tarzan personifies this structure of defining himself in opposition to the "other," be it apes, blacks, or women. His famous line—"Me Tarzan, you Jane"—is indicative of the condescending attitude underlying this discourse on the other: it shows that the assertion of a superior masculinity depends on a process of subjugating women and blacks.

Torgovnick suggests that Freud's psychoanalytical work is equally dismissive since Freud equates "the primitive" non-European with children and the neurotic. While the Freudian concept associates "the primitive" with the Id and with a lack of self-control, it relates identity to mastery over oneself and others. If the self does not retain the upper hand, if the Ego loses that sense of control, it experiences an uncanny feeling of being overwhelmed by otherness.

While Torgovnik's book explores the impact of race on modern literary, nonliterary, and popular texts, she also focuses on political aspects of this phenomenon, especially gender. This is most pronounced in her reading of *Tarzan and the Ant Men* (1924), which depicts a tribe where women are in control and regard men as subordinate even to slaves. "The savage Alalus woman" is a threat to the opposite sex because she and her female friends hunt and kill men. It is only with the help of Tarzan that the Alalus males regain power, that the social order is restored, and that ultimately the women are treated as slaves.

Torgovnick argues that the novel reveals both Burroughs's personal problems with women and political problems in America at the time: "it seems designed as a cautionary tale in the wake of suffrage for U.S. Women" (Torgovnick, 67). Torgovnick's main argument is that Burroughs's images of the other are primarily projections of the self. The (mis)representations of blacks expose latent fears—not just a fear of the dominant female—as well as latent desires. They are attempts by the West to come to terms with itself. The most important point of Torgovnick's study is expressed in her epilogue, where she claims to have exposed

> . . . two alternating and yet complementary pulsations in our century's involvement with primitive societies and with the idea of the primitive: a rhetoric of control, in which demeaning colonialist tropes get modified only slightly over time; and a rhetoric of desire, ultimately more interesting, which implicates "us" in the "them" we try to conceive as the Other. (Torgovnick, 245)

While it is important that she moves from literary studies to cultural studies, Torgovnick often confuses, as in the passage above, "primitive societies" with the "idea of the primitive." There are important differences between anthropological texts *about* "primitive" societies or African cultures, for example, and texts that are concerned with the *idea* of the primitive, such as Freud's essays. The crucial difference is between a metaphoric and a metonymic relation to "the other."

Reinforcing Toni Morrison's exploration of the literary techniques of "othering," Torgovnick demonstrates how widespread the process has been throughout Western culture. Unfortunately, although Torgovnick does mention that the other is implicated in the self, her book too rarely explicates what she calls "the flip-side of 'othering.'" An example of this identification with the other that she does discuss is Tobias Schneebaum's account of a tradition of the Asmat tribe, the "bond friendship." Learning that "bond friends" overtly practiced homosexual love and that the Asmat community fully accepted this tradition fascinated Schneebaum. In his autobiography, he wonders: "Why did I have to go out of my country, out of my culture, out of my family, to find the kind of assurance and companionship necessary to my inner peace?" This rhetorical question is an example of how an identification with African customs can be helpful in discovering one's own desires. Torgovnick claims that "going primitive" meant to Schneebaum nothing else but "going home."

These two types of rhetoric (the other as alien, and the other as uncannily familiar) are opposite sides of the same coin; in both cases, "the primitive" remains a product of Western fantasy. Toward the end of her book, Torgovnick suggests that there are also more "positive forms of Western primitivism lurking behind the forms I have criticized" but she does not trace these alternative forms of Western primitivism. Her study is principally a reconsideration of modernity that considers how demeaning Western cultures have been to minorities. An alternative study on primitivism would then, perhaps, open up views on modernity that show in which ways marginalized cultures have been informed by the main stream and vice versa.

Paul Gilroy's *The Black Atlantic*, published in 1993, presents such a perspective. By looking at the cultural and intellectual history of the black diaspora, Gilroy reconsiders modernity from an intercultural perspective. The black experience in the modern world has always been transnational, Gilroy claims. Most early black intellectuals (for example, the freed slaves Frederick Douglass, William Wells Brown, Alexander Crummell, Martin R. Delany, and W. E. B. Du Bois) traveled to Europe. The crossing of national boundaries had a tremendous impact on their works. But even before that, crossing the Atlantic had been constitutive of the collective experience of the black diaspora, beginning with the Middle Passage. For Gilroy, any cultural analysis of black modernity is inextricably linked to Africa, to the Caribbean, and to the rest of the Americas.

Characteristic of black cross-Atlantic creativity is, Gilroy writes, a basic "desire to transcend both the structures of the nation state and the constraints of ethnicity and national particularity." This yearning to move beyond ethnic confines generates what Gilroy calls "a politics of travel and voluntary relocation" (Gilroy, 19). Traveling—in person or in the form of global dissemination of, say, black music—is intrinsic to the experience of the black diaspora. Gilroy deftly argues that black cultural expressions are necessarily "modern because they have been marked by their hybrid creole origins" (Gilroy, 73). By claiming that hybridity marks modernity, Gilroy makes an important contribution to conventional definitions of the "modern" condition.

The claim that modernity in America has to be thought of as a cultural hybrid is examined best in a study that explores the role of black Americans during the 20s, Ann Douglas's *Terrible Honesty: Mongrel Manhattan in the 1920s* (1995). Douglas takes the reader on an extensive tour; discussing a wide range of cultural and artistic expressions, she explores pockets of "mongrel America." Her book ranges from Henry Ford to Nancy Cunard, from the Ziegfeld Follies to a discussion of neoorthodoxy, from the blues diva Bessie Smith to William James, and draws on material such as advertisements, legal decisions, magazine articles, and, of course, historiography.

Douglas's intercultural collage leisurely juxtaposes fragments from white and black cultures, from Manhattan and Harlem. Her thesis is that a disenchantment among modern Americans, fed up with the false promises of their Victorian predecessors, inspired a yearning for change, an urge to get rid of hypocrisy. The ethos of the modern age was, Douglas suggests, "Terrible Honesty," a phrase that she quotes from a remarkable number of writers, including Hemingway, Fitzgerald, and even Wallace Stevens, who admitted, "We have been a little insane about the truth."

It was this imperative to honesty that made the straightforwardness of black music—specifically, the blues' explicit references to sexuality—appealing. According to Douglas, "slang was another version of 'the terrible honesty ethos' . . . Ragging or slanging was the American revolution all over again; in a stroke, British subjects became American rebels." Although Douglas does not refer to North, she seems to agree that black slang was a means to break with linguistic conventions.

Like Michael North, Douglas refers to the oedipal complex as a model for explaining intercultural dynamics. The moderns rejected the values and the concept of civilization they had inherited from the nineteenth century; this antagonism was the starting point for a keen fascination with blacks. Discussing matricidal impulses in Hemingway and in Crane, Douglas argues that the struggle against the Victorian matriarch brought about two tendencies: a masculinization of modern American culture and an interest in, and identification with, African Americans. Relating vernacularization to masculinization, Douglas argues that rebellious ragtime swept away Victorian sentiments and points to the fact that the minstrel shows literally excluded the female element, since all female roles were played by men.

Douglas's view of the role of blacks in this process culminates in the assertion that "the Negro, assigned the role of infantalized and brutalized child in the family romance of Victorian America, has become the father, even a Founding Father, of modern American culture" (Douglas, 272). Here, Douglas diverts from Torgovnick's account of race and gender in the context of modernity because blacks are not aligned with the female other. Rather, they fraternize with white men and are models to reinvigorate masculinity. Douglas argues that American modern culture has to be conceived of as bicultural. By symbolically slaying the powerful white mother (Victoria) and by embracing the black "infantalized" other, the modern collective self becomes, willingly or unwillingly, a mongrel.

It is impossible, of course, that people at the time could have agreed with Douglas's characterization of modern America as "mongrel." Given the racial ordering of the 1920s (i.e., Jim Crow segregation), a mixed cultural heritage could not possibly have been welcomed. Only now can we begin to understand how racially tangled America has been on a cultural level. One of the most striking discrepancies of American history is that black Americans were politically almost nonexistent (Oscar de Priest was the first black congressman in this century, elected in 1928) and economically marginalized, even while they were crucial to shaping Anglo-American culture.

Ironically, Anglo-American and Afro-American modernism came together in America at the height of segregation. During the Harlem Renaissance, close ties existed between the white artists of the Greenwich Village Renaissance, gathering around Mabel Dodge, and the artists who gathered around Alain Locke and James Weldon Johnson. Most critics of the New Negro movement have argued that the movement owed its very existence and shape to what Harold Cruse called "interracialism." They have, however, disagreed on the significance of that fact.

In *The Crisis of the Negro Intellectual*, published in 1967, Cruse dismisses the New Negroes for having been insufficiently "nationalist" because black artists depended on the awards given out at the interracial Civil Club dinners and on the alms of white patrons. Equally, the National Association for the Advancement of Colored People relied on white funding. Criticizing "racial integration mania," Cruse chides the Negro intellectuals of the preceding generation for trying to live up to white expectations. The result, he argues, was devastating. Cruse proclaims: "Integration [led] to cultural negation."[4]

He expresses his objections to integration in strong terms. In fact, he blames the "ludicrous attempt to integrate" for the three major shortcomings of the movement: its failure to institutionalize a lasting cultural movement; its failure to define a nationalist aesthetic philosophy; and its failure to follow through a true cultural revolution that would transform politics, economics, and culture. The New Negroes' failure to attain autonomy in all three areas was, to Cruse, their greatest shortcoming. In a devastating evaluation of the Harlem Renaissance, Cruse makes it a showcase of what a truly revolutionary struggle would avoid. Claiming that the left-wing Negro intellectuals who cooperated with white Communists were dominated by them, he implies that interracial contact should have been avoided at all costs.

The hypothesis that interracialism brought about a failure of the Harlem Renaissance recurs in Nathan Irvin Huggins's book, *Harlem Renaissance* (1971). He claims that intimacy with white artists is what stopped black artists from creating a renaissance of their own. Since the Negro artists were "bound up in a more general American [Anglo-American] experience," they failed to express a distinctly "black" aesthetic. He concludes that "the lesson it [the Harlem Renaissance] leaves us is that the true Negro renaissance awaits Afro-Americans' claiming their *patria*, their nativity" (Huggins, 309). Unfortunately, he avoids expounding on exactly what such an aesthetic homeland would comprise. According to Huggins, there was only one black artist, Langston

Hughes, who evaded the general trend of white-influenced elitism. Hughes was the exception because he was more interested in the common man and because he took black artistic expressions (such as jazz) seriously as formal art.

While both Huggins and Cruse are convinced that the Harlem Renaissance failed because black Americans interacted too closely with white Americans, Cruse holds that avoiding interculturalism would have led to true cultural autonomy, whereas Huggins believes that the interaction was unavoidable. He discusses this in a matter-of-fact tone: "White men and black men unknowingly depend in their work to shape American character and culture. Whenever Americans do come of age, they will have gained true insight into themselves by claiming of that dependence" (Huggins, 12). Once this "interplay between white and black in America" is acknowledged, once the interdependence between the self and the other is no longer ignored, Huggins predicts that America will come into its own.

Huggins devotes considerable attention to primitivism as a movement of the 1920s. He is interested in the allure that drew white New Yorkers to Harlem to listen to jazz and abandon themselves to alcohol and hot rhythms. Among the white pleasure seekers were white writers such as Carl Van Vechten, who was the most prominent of those notorious for what one could call "white" primitivism. But Huggins is also interested in what one might call "black" primitivism, and he discerns this trend in different fields such as minstrelsy and the visual arts.

At the core of Aaron Douglas's paintings, for instance, Huggins finds "the Negro, the primitive soul" (Huggins, 172). He also examines a number of black authors who expressed a belief that blacks were particularly "spontaneous" and "vital." Huggins detects primitivism in Claude McKay's novel *Home to Harlem*; in Du Bois's protagonist Zora in *The Quest of the Golden Fleece*; in Helga, the protagonist of Nella Larsen's *Quicksand*; in Countee Cullen's poem "Heritage"; and throughout Zora Neale Hurston's writings. In these works, primitivism served the purpose of empowering ethnic identity.

Surprisingly, Huggins then claims that "for the purpose of ethnic identity, primitivism is peculiarly limited. It is especially a male fantasy" (Huggins, 188). But it was one that ignited the imagination of men and women, African Americans and Africans, as well Europeans and Anglo-Americans. Huggins points to the constructed relation of black Americans' culture to African culture:

> The Negro intellectual's fascination with primitivism was filled with ironies. Contrary to assertions of the soul-community of blacks, the American Negroes had to *learn* to appreciate the value of African art and culture. Too often they were taught by Europeans for whom Africa had a powerful, but limited, significance. . . . No less ironic is the stimulating effect that American "primitives" had on Africans. If we are to believe the testimony of African intellectuals like President Leopold Senghor of Senegal, Harlem writers (particularly Claude McKay in *Banjo*) gave them a sense of direction. (Huggins, 187–188)

This passage is revealing because it points out a myriad of cultural interaction. For example, Aaron Douglas discovered his "authentic black style" through his European mentor, Winold Reiss, a German artist. In fact, the ideological base of the Harlem Renaissance follows this very pattern of finding one's identity through one's cultural other. That African intellectuals then learned from American blacks about their *own* cultural "roots" and were inspired by African Americans to invent *Nègritude* is a further example of the complex intercultural dynamic at the core of modernism.

The broader implications of these intercultural exchanges, however, have not been explored, either by Huggins or by other critics, black or white. In the early 1970s, the failure hypothesis and, consequently, its stigma remained the unchallenged critical assessment of the New Negro movement. It was only in the eighties that Houston Baker, Jr. challenged this view. In *Modernism and the Harlem Renaissance,* Baker objects to the idea that the era "failed to produce a vital, original, effective, or 'modern' art." In opposition to Cruse and Huggins, Baker argues that the Harlem Renaissance was remarkably successful in producing a modernism of its own.

Through the mastery of the minstrel mask and the appropriation of white minstrel structure or humor, black performers took a first step toward black modernism. "The mastery of form," according to Baker, which is based on an appropriation of (white) minstrelsy and on an imitation of the master's nonsense, was first realized in Booker T. Washington's *Up from Slavery.* Another model for "black discursive modernism" was Charles Waddell Chesnutt's *The Conjure Woman.* Transforming conventional views of black folklore, *The Conjure Woman* differed from the darky voice that white audiences had come to expect in minstrel shows and in vaudeville. The use of black dialect created a particular African American "sound," Baker argues.

This supposedly authentic black sound is essential to black modernism; Baker detects "a distinctively Afro-American *sounding*" (Baker's italics) presence in Du Bois's *Souls of Black Folks*, in Alain Locke's *New Negro,* and even in Aaron Douglas's graphics and "ancestral arts" photos. To Baker, the *New Negro* is "our first national book." Since it was the most radical critique of white America published to that time, *New Negro* was an example of "extreme deformation" and of "radical marronage." Claiming that black modernism had emerged out of the interplay of formal mastery—the appropriation of white standards—and the deformation or modification of received (white) forms, Baker's concept is predicated upon interculturalism. He does not, however, address the issue of interracial appropriation; rather he celebrates only those texts written by black poets that blend black folk sensibilities, a rebellious subversiveness, and mastery of black and white forms.

By way of example, Baker feels that Sterling Brown's poem "Ma Rainey," epitomizes "the essence of black discursive modernism" because it blends "*poetic* mastery" with a "deformative *folk* sound" (Baker, 93). If this implies, as I think it does, that black modernism emerged out of a fusion of white "*poetic* mastery" and black "*folk* sound," then it is important to point out that Baker does in fact occupy common ground with Cruse and Huggins, though he insists that black artists *consciously* fused Africanism and whiteness.

While Baker thinks of the Harlem Renaissance as a success, praising the achievements of a black modernism's incorporation of whiteness, David Levering Lewis's historical account of the Harlem Renaissance reserves judgment. But he, too, discovers interracial collaboration at the heart of the "Golden Age" of the Renaissance and acknowledges that the influence of whites on black artistic achievement played a pivotal role throughout the New Negro movement. He states (with all the parched detachment of a historian) that "white capital and influence were crucial to success, and the white presence, in the beginning, was pervasive, setting the outer boundaries for what was creatively normative" (Lewis, xxvii). Instead of blaming white patrons for the Renaissance's failure, Lewis claims that they functioned financially as catalysts and culturally as interlocutors. Black artists welcomed their admiration and their money. Lewis is convinced that "Locke's New Negroes very much wanted full acceptance by Mainstream America."

One last study of the Harlem Renaissance that I want to mention in this context is George Hutchinson's *The Harlem Renaissance in Black and White* (1995). Hutchinson explores how the renaissance was shaped by the broader American cultural field, and conversely, how American modernism, pragmatism, and cultural nationalism were influenced by the Harlem Renaissance. In its tracing of interracial friendships and institutional ties, the book does actually reveal what its dust jacket promises: "the truly composite nature of American literary culture." While Hutchinson's hypothesis is based on the traditional scholarship of the Harlem Renaissance, his book is remarkably even-handed and inclusive. He invites his readers to rethink American cultural history by acknowledging that "'white' and 'black' American cultures [are] intimately intertwined, mutually constitutive" (Hutchinson, 3). His investigation devotes considerable attention to literary institutions and magazines, including the *Nation,* the *New Republic,* the *Modern Quarterly, American Mercury,* the *Messenger*, and *Crisis*, to reveal how interrelated black and white cultural life were during the 1920s. Hutchinson's account of the Harlem Renaissance privileges personal encounters over formal exchanges. Far from subscribing to the failure hypothesis, *The Harlem Renaissance in Black and White* ends on an encouraging note, quoting James Baldwin: "It is precisely this black-white experience which may prove of indispensable value to us in the world we face today."

While agreeing with the other four Harlem Renaissance scholars that interracial collaboration was crucial to the awakening of black cultural self-assertiveness, Hutchinson does so approvingly, whereas the other scholars, and particularly Harold Cruse, would only grudgingly concede this condition. Having acknowledged that black modernism was the product of a cultural tête à tête between the Anglo-American other and Afro-American self—perhaps the first such formalized exchange in American history—these critics have been at the forefront of establishing the conviction that modernism, both black and white, owes much of its existence and shape to "racial injections" from the other of color.

Curiously, if one were to transfer the failure hypothesis of the Harlem Renaissance to white modernism, one would have to argue that white modernism's indebtedness to, say, black dialect indicates that whites failed to invent a modernism of their own as well. Ironically, critics of European and Anglo-American modernism did accuse modernism of failure (though for vastly different reasons), claiming that the modernists had not separated themselves from their artistic predecessors, had not distanced themselves enough from the modern world and mass culture, or had not thwarted the expectations of their readers. But while most accounts of modernism necessarily assume an other, its cultural background is that of the identity of the self; theoretical accounts have not yet addressed interculturalism as a constitutive feature of modernist aesthetics. It is not surprising, therefore, that discussions of modernism's shortcomings have also ignored the presence of the other of color. To discuss what I think of this denial, it is necessary, at least briefly, to discuss a few general theories of modernism.

A very thorough account of these theories is Astradur Eysteinsson's book, *The Concept of Modernism.* Eysteinsson maintains that "there is a rapidly spreading agreement that 'modernism' is a legitimate concept broadly signifying a paradigmatic shift, a major revolt, beginning in the mid- and late nineteenth century, against the literary and aesthetic traditions of the Western world" (Eysteinsson, 2). While Eysteinsson places its beginnings in the nineteenth century, I would side with John Barth, who suggests that "the first half of this century" marks the era of the "predominant aesthetic of Western literature" (Eysteinsson, 3). The association of modernism with the Western world is certainly another commonplace. While both Eysteinsson and Barth relate the concept of modernism to the Western world, Eysteinsson claims that modernism constituted itself *against* the traditions of the Western world and Barth asserts that it *was* the aesthetics of the Western world. Both critics are right, of course, but their respective assessments reflect the general tendency to ignore the impact that the non-Western world had on the shaping of modernism.

Art Berman's *Preface to Modernism,* published in 1995, is another case of neglect. Berman discusses modernism in the context of romanticism, idealism, empiricism, and commercialism, without once mentioning interracialism. To Berman, modernism was primarily concerned with counteracting the negative aspects of modernity: our inability "to yield a contented and equitable society." He sees a tension between aesthetics, on the one hand, and the modern world, of which it is a part, on the other hand. "Ultimately," Berman writes, "modernism capitulates to the opposition [to modernity]. . . . Modernism fails in its original mission."[5]

Raymond Williams is even more critical. He accuses modernism of having "lost its anti-bourgeois stance, and [of having] achieved comfortable integration into new international capitalism."[6] Since the avant-garde's initial anti-bourgeois attitude gave way all too quickly to a fusion between commerce and art, it did not live up to its claim that art could change social realities and create a more humane praxis. Williams's critique of modernism hinges on

capitalism. Reminding his readers of modernism's original mission to coun-
terbalance stifling social praxis, Williams echoes Theodor W. Adorno's theory
of aesthetics that claimed art could be redemptive only by being opposed to
the actual social world. It must represent a better world [*Statthalter einer bes-
seren Welt*]. Adorno saw art's preeminent function in its refusal to communicate with a world that is false, irrational, and "disgusting."

Wolfgang Iser, the prominent reader-response critic, finds modernism's potential in its ability to defamiliarize rote assumptions and to engage the reader
in a cognitive act of communication with the text itself. Stressing art's power
to communicate, Iser suggests that modernist texts thwart the reader's hori-
zons of expectation. In doing so, they animate the reader to make sense of the
nonsensical, to reflect his own ways of thinking: "the reader's enjoyment begins when he himself becomes productive, i.e., when the text allows him to
bring his own faculties into play."[7] Structurally, one could say that the text is
the other, with which the self, the reader, has to come to terms. The formalistic innovations of the avant-garde have the potential to alter the act of reading
and the self.

Although each of these critical accounts deserves a full discussion, I have
ventured just a cursory glance to demonstrate that, on a large scale, these approaches all juxtapose, implicitly or explicitly, the modernist project with the
past, social reality, or the reader. These critics have situated modernism in
what we could call a dialectic of negation in order to transform the respectable. But none of these theoretical accounts includes the other of color. What
would such an account consider? A brief explication of Albert Giacometti's
Spoon Woman (1926–1927) may help to elucidate this book's theses and meth-
odology (figure 1.1).

Spoon Woman exhibits several characteristics of avant-garde art. It does
not represent a woman in a way, say, that Auguste Rodin (either in his classical youth or in his impressionist-influenced old age) represented female
nudes. *Spoon Woman* is an example of abstractionism, and it seems unlikely
that this object could become pop art, even if mass-produced. Its minimalistic
and abstract form gives the object an enigmatic quality. Its height—the sculpture is life size—makes it monstrous: its frontal assault on the viewer is
shocking.

When I looked at this metal sculpture at the Museum of Modern Art, *Spoon
Woman* reminded me of Herman Melville's short story "Bartleby the Scriv-
ener" in which the protagonist persists in saying, "I prefer not to." Likewise,
this object prefers not to represent or even to "show" us what it represents.
This figure of a woman rejects the mimetic task of portrait painting. It is not
about something—or somebody—other than itself. This sculpture draws attention to itself as an art object. In its refusal to communicate, the art object
creates a distance between itself and us. Its self-referentiality urges us to
come to terms with its unconventional features and uniqueness.

Confronting *Spoon Woman*, particularly the original, one is intrigued, if
not dazzled, by its compelling aura. Its enigmatic quality piques our curiosity
and urges us to make sense of the object. It engages us in what Iser calls an act

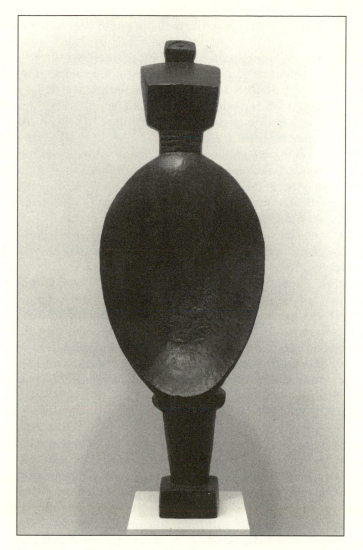

Figure 1.1   Alberto Giacometti. *Spoon Woman*. (1926–1927).
Courtesy of the Museum of Modern Art, New York. Acquired
through the Mrs. Rita Silver Fund in honor of her husband
Leo Silver and in memory of her son Stanley R. Silver, and
the Mr. and Mrs. Walter Hochschild Fund.

of communication. In contrast to the act of reading, a process that usually lasts
quite some time, this form of communication is likely to end after a few min-
utes, when the spectator moves on to another object. The sculpture will neither defamiliarize automated views nor actualize a "virtual constitutive horizon," as Iser claims modernist texts do. Nor does this sculpture help "to
organize a new life praxis from a basis of art," as Bürger argued. Although it

is "pure art" and has little to do with the lived experience of early twentieth-century Europeans, it is highly unlikely that it could be absorbed by the culture industry.

Spoon Woman is hardly a "governess of a better world," to paraphrase Adorno. *Spoon Woman* is a modernist manifesto of defiance. It rejects easily made assumptions about its nature. At the same time, it also defies some of the theoretical assumptions of modern aesthetics. In fact, its very title anticipates the issues at stake here. We might take this sculpture to be a representation of a woman—maybe even a pregnant woman—or we may take it to represent a spoon. Art historians have pointed out that *Spoon Woman* was modeled after West African wooden grain spoons that Giacometti encountered in 1923 in an exhibition at the Musée des Arts Décoratifs. If we look at it with this knowledge, Giacometti's art object is an ethnographic "ready-made," an aestheticization of an object of daily use, and an African object at that.

If we focus on the source of inspiration, the sculpture seems to be more about a *spoon* than a *woman*. What appears to be an abstract object becomes an oversized representation of a kitchen utensil, which makes it a semi-abstract representation. *Spoon Woman* integrates the two spheres of art and life that idealistic concepts of art attempt to separate. It is a monument to those incidents when European artists' attempts to transcend their traditions coincided with an incorporation of "Negro art." *Spoon Woman* embodies this peculiar, simultaneous cultural affirmation and symbolic incorporation of the other. Since *Spoon Woman* is, formally, the product of two cultures and two aesthetics, it disrupts monocultural accounts of modernism. She is a champion of the significance of cultural chiaroscuro.

The symbolic embrace of "Negro art"—as African art generally was called in the 1920s—is, of course, not limited to Giacometti. With surprising clairvoyance, the art critic Christian Zervos remarked in 1929 that "[Brancusi] has explored all the vistas that the Negroes have opened up to him, and which . . . permitted him to achieve pure form."[8] The fact that European artists were able to achieve pure (or abstract) art through the influence of "Negroes" and "Negro art" was best expressed by Madame Buffet-Picabia in the late 1920s: "Picasso had discovered his path with the aid of negro art."[9] If we were to agree with these observations, and if we were to assume that Picasso, Brancusi, and Giacometti were not the only artists who had benefited from encounters with "Negro art," we can extend this claim and argue that modernism owes much to its black culturoaesthetic alter ego.

In other words, to discuss *Spoon Woman* properly, it does not suffice to draw solely on the dialectic of negation. Though Giacometti certainly intended to negate and transcend the European premodernist tradition, the question remains: how did he succeed in doing so? What is most surprising, given the history of racism and colonialism, is that he chose "Negro art" as a catalyst to render obsolete the aesthetic traditions of the nineteenth century. From the current perspective, this symbolic embrace of the despised Negro is often seen, at best, as a harbinger of postcolonialism and, at worst, as a final upsurge of colonialist exploitation.

Even if we assess this act of cross-cultural appropriation merely as an act of theft—as many "politically correct" commentators do—we still have to consider the implications of an underlying dissonance: objects that nineteenth-century Europeans had dismissed as "curios" or "fetishes" suddenly became crucial to twentieth-century artists searching for new forms. This transformation—its completeness and swiftness—is astonishing. It did not go unnoticed, even in America: Alain Locke, the African American philosopher of art, observed as early as 1925 that "African art has influenced modern art most considerably."[10]

Before we explore the main venues of interculturalism at the center of modernism, it is necessary to discuss the term so often employed to denote intimacy between black and white peoples, just as it has been applied to denote the affinity between non-Western and Western art. This term, *primitivism*, is both semantically and politically problematic. Its politically offensive connotation has to do with its derogatory and condescending use in describing non-Western customs, traditions, social practices, and the arts— especially those of people of color. While the "ism" tries to cast an air of objectivity or neutrality, the European legacy of demeaning accounts of "the primitive"—a legacy that extends from Kant to Hegel to Gobineau—resonates deeply.

The term *primitivism* wears countless hats: primitivism in modern art differs from primitivism in modern literature, and both differ from primitivism in intellectual history. It is often used synonymously with exoticism, implying an admiration of the noble primitive. This is a relic of nineteenth-century romanticism, suggesting that white people admire a person or people of color (albeit in a remote way) because they feel that blacks are uninhibited, dynamic, and free. When the term is used in that sense, people of color, the other, are implicitly opposed to the modern world's self-control, discipline, and shame.

Constitutive of this structure of adulation is that blacks are essentially different from whites. The Southern writer Julia Perkins, for example, claimed that African Americans were more "colorful" than whites. She confessed, "I write about Negroes because they represent human nature obscured by so little veneer."[11] In American literary history, there are countless examples of this fascination with blacks. Among the primitivist novels written in the 1920s are Waldo Frank's *Holiday* (1923) and Carl Van Vechten's *Nigger Heaven* (1926). In poetry, there are Vachel Lindsay's "Congo" (1914) and Hart Crane's "Black Tambourine" (1921). In drama, there are Eugene O'Neill's *Emperor Jones* (1920) and DuBose Heyward's *Porgy* (1925). In short fiction, there are, of course, Gertrude Stein's "Melanctha" (1909) and Sherwood Anderson's "I Want to Know Why?" (1920), which includes the statement "I wish I was a nigger."[12]

Another kind of primitivism, which also stresses its contrast with the modern, does not refer to people so much as it refers to a darker strain of romanticism mostly associated with Nietzschean philosophy. This usage is best illustrated by a statement by Franz Kuna, who asserts that "beneath the surface of modern life, dominated by knowledge and science, Nietzsche discerned vital energies that were wild, primitive and completely merciless."[13] In equating "the primitive" with a tragic, irrational force that opposes civilized teleology, Kuna makes the term signify "unreason." In this case, *primitive* connotes blackness in a metaphorical, not a metonymical, sense.

Two further senses of primitivism are expressed and analyzed by Arthur Lovejoy and George Boas in their *Documentary History of Primitivism and Related Ideas in Antiquity*.[14] In this book, which is part of a series entitled *Contributions to the History of Primitivism*, Lovejoy and Boas examine the belief that "the most excellent condition of human life" must have occurred in the distant past or in distant places. They call this "chronological primitivism." "Cultural primitivism," on the other hand, is based on the belief that "existing primitives, or so-called 'savage' peoples" live a better life; it is synonymous with exoticism because it shares the "love of strangeness and the revolt against the familiar." According to Lovejoy and Boas, the yearning for primeval simplicity, the conviction that the "savage" is superior to the "modern," can be traced back to classical European antiquity. They suggest that primitivistic forms of exoticism started with Homer's idealization of the Lotus Eaters in the *Odyssey*.

Keeping in mind these different points of reference, we can distinguish among four kinds of primitivisms: "Chronological primitivism" denotes the belief that ancient or prehistoric times were superior to modern times. "Cultural primitivism" is the romanticization of non-Western peoples, usually idealizing their instincts, sexuality, and their proclivity to the natural. "Spiritual primitivism" appeals to the dark-irrational mystic powers and to Dionysian ecstasy. The fourth form we might think of as "aesthetic primitivism." It is based on the assimilation of non-European art forms.

This typology is necessarily reductive; one can easily make further distinctions. As we will discuss in chapter 2, Robert Goldwater suggests that there are several trends even within aesthetic primitivism. Or, considering the wide range of "primitivisms" in European intellectual history, we could set Jean-Jacques Rousseau, who praised the innocent, uncorrupted, natural "noble savage" (a fusion of cultural and chronological primitivism), apart from Friedrich Nietzsche, who identified with Dionysian vitality. Or we could distinguish the ideas of George Bataille, who valorized the bestial self (a fusion of a sinister cultural primitivism with spiritual primitivism), from those of Michel Leiris, who was fascinated by the primitive qualities he discovered in black music and entertainment. Expressing his discontent with European shows, Leiris wrote in 1929:

> We're tired of all-too-insipid shows that aren't inflated by any potential or actual revolt against sacred 'politeness'—the politeness of the arts, which we call 'taste'; . . . We've had enough of all that, which is why we would so much like to get closer to our primitive ancestry. . . . And so this [Negro] music and this dancing don't stop at our skin but put down deep organic roots in us, roots whose thousand ramifications penetrate us; and though this surgery is painful, it gives us stronger blood.[15]

Leiris combines cultural primitivism with chronological primitivism; he yearns for vitality and sturdiness. Having admitted the anemia afflicting European culture, he called for an injection of strong black blood. The imagery is remarkable: other versions of primitivism are based on the assumption of a cultural gap between the self and the other. Here, Leiris hopes to be penetrated by blackness.

This aspiration for symbolic amalgamation is motivated by the belief that a fusion with the other will result in a transformation, or revivification, of the self. This is most pronounced in "aesthetic primitivism" because for African art to function as a catalyst in changing European art, non-European art forms have to be absorbed. Thus, "primitive" is no longer the antonym of "modern." Both—the modern white self and the black primitive other—become one and the same.

In this respect, aesthetic primitivism differs significantly from chronological, cultural, and spiritual primitivism. The latter three versions aspire to invert the conventional view that the primitive is inferior; they are in agreement with the 1934 *Webster's Dictionary* definition that identified "primitivism" as "the belief in the superiority of the primitive." In the case of cultural primitivism, this resulted in a number of "positive" stereotypes, such as that of the "noble savage," the "suffering bondsman," and the "happy-go-lucky-darkie." Instead of undermining racial polarization, these variants of exoticism reconfirm a binary opposition.

Since these versions of primitivism fail to acknowledge the emotional and intellectual complexity of black people, they amount to a variant of racism that we might call, to cite George M. Frederickson's useful expression, "romantic racism." It is only in aesthetic primitivism that this either/or mentality—either "the primitive" is valorized and idealized for *being* different, or it is denigrated and humiliated *because* it is different—is transcended. Here, the fusion of black and white forms results in an implosion of the binary structure of racism.

So, having made these distinctions, the question remains as to how critics have accounted for the presence of primitivism in modernism. Do they portray it as chronological, cultural, spiritual, or aesthetic? In "The Culture of Modernism" (1963), Irving Howe argues that the fascination with the primitive was a crucial element of modern literature. He distinguishes between two kinds of cultural primitivism (though with a spiritual impulse as well):

> One of the seemingly hopeful possibilities is a primitivism bringing a vision of new manliness, health, blood consciousness, a relief from enervating rationality. A central text is D. H. Lawrence's story, "The Woman Who Rode Away" . . . But within the ambiance of Modernism there is another, more ambiguous and perhaps sinister kind of primitivism: the kind that draws us not of health but of decay, the primitive as atavistic, an abandonment of civilization and thereby, perhaps of its discontents. The central fiction expressing this theme is Joseph Conrad's *Heart of Darkness*. . . . In this version of primitivism, which is perhaps inseparable from the ennui of decadence, the overwhelming desire is to shake off the burdens of social restraint, the disabling and wearisome moralities of civilized inhibition.[16]

But how do healthy and sinister primitivism differ if both have a revitalizing effect? No matter if one suffers from "the burdens of social restraint" or "from enervating rationality," primitivism functions as an antidote that frees, relieves, or invigorates the self. The desire to abandon civilization and its discontents leads the weary Westerner to embark on imaginary journeys to Indian tribes like the woman in Lawrence's novel, or into the African jungle. The other helps the self (e.g., Kurtz, the white woman, the reader) to move away from stale rationalism, and to experience "real life." According to Howe, the moderns were primarily disenchanted with "the whole apparatus of cognition and the limiting assumptions of rationality." We must note, though, that when he claims that the "mind comes to be seen as an enemy of vital human powers," he is suggesting that "the primitive" represents the other side of rationality and is dabbling with racist stereotypes.

Lionel Trilling went as far as to claim that "nothing is more characteristic of modern literature than its discovery and canonization of the primal, non-ethical energies."[17] Asserting that no book had a greater effect on modern literature than Sir James Frazier's *The Golden Bough,* Trilling constructs a modernist tradition in which the mythical "primitive imagination" is the center. In this tradition, he includes Joseph Conrad, Thomas Mann, Friedrich Nietzsche, and William Blake, because each is ambivalent about civilization and each embraces "Dionysian rapture." Trilling quotes Nietzsche to argue that frenzy, orgiastic displays of lust, and sexual promiscuity prevail throughout the best modern literature. In our terminology, Trilling is concerned with "spiritual primitivism" and has very little to say about the other versions.

What Trilling suggests in his essay, "On Teaching the Modern Element"— that modernism brought about a valorization of the "primal, non-ethical energies"—is also addressed in one of the classic textbooks used to define the modernist era. Richard Ellmann and Charles Feidelson, Jr.'s *The Modern Tradition: Backgrounds of Modern Literature* (1965) refers to the "primitive" in several places; one chapter discusses "Myth in Primitive Thought" and another "Primitive Survivals," referring primarily to "spiritual primitivism."[18]

In his essay "Towards a Definition of American Modernism" (which appeared in an issue of the *American Quarterly* devoted to considerations of American modernism), Daniel J. Singal outlines a "modernist embrace of natural instinct and primitivism." But the primitivism Singal discusses is fundamentally different from that of Howe, Trilling, Ellmann, and Feidelson. Singal compares modern trends of "overthrowing the last vestiges of conventional sexual mores, and [of] creating in acid rock a music of pounding sensuality," to trends in intellectual thought. He quotes Susan Sontag's condemnation of a "hypertrophy of the intellect at the expense of energy and sensual capacity."[29] Singal does not approve of this upsurge of vitality and sensuality. Extending Trilling's account of the primitivist tradition within modernism, Singal's version of primitivism extends from Blake to Conrad, to rock and roll, and to feminism. He draws no distinctions between different variants, but uses the term as a metaphor for liberation, sexual and otherwise. In doing so, Singal implies that (spiritual) primitivism is a subtext for the twentieth century.

The Heath Anthology of American Literature succinctly states:

> Modernism had always cultivated its fascination with what it saw in the primitive. . . . The Native American had fascinated many writers, from Thoreau and Cooper to William Carlos Williams, as representing an anti-cultural figure. . . . Part of the anti-cultural impulse in the movement took the form of a high valuation of the life forms of people who had not been thoroughly industrialized, or even "civilized" in the modern sense.[20]

According to this passage—from an anthology that includes the work of African American, female, and Native American authors in an attempt to re-define the canon—the fascination with the nonwhite and nonmodern was always a fundamental part of modernism. Arguing that primitivism was one of the modernists' main concerns, the editors propose that the modern writers were primarily fascinated by what differed fundamentally from their daily lives: the "life forms of people who had not been thoroughly industrialized, or even 'civilized.'" Claiming that "this fascination goes back to Wordsworth," the editors imply that primitivism is another manifestation of romanticism. In the process, they conflate Wordsworth's romantic yearning for the mysterious aspects of life with Mabel Dodge Luhan's fascination with Native Americans, entirely ignoring the negrophilic aspects of modernism.

Sadly, the majority of critics of modernism have not commented on primitivism at all (much less the aesthetic primitivism that is our project), but it is safe to argue that primitivism has been a prominent feature in much of twentieth-century Western art and literature. By constructing a black *alter ego*, the Western primitivist sought either to strengthen his cultural Ego or to unleash his Id. Implicit in either process is a Western self projected onto a people remote in time, place, or character. By exploring this terra incognita, the primitivist (cultural, spiritual, chronological) discovers the vitality and sensuality of which he feels deprived. The primitivist is drawn to the black other: either figuratively to the mythical other, or literally to the "other of color."

The primitivist fascination with black art or black people had enormous political implications, even if they were not developed at the time. One of the first texts to address primitivism as a broad cultural force was Wyndham Lewis's book of essays, *Paleface* (1929). Lewis feared that "the passion for the primitive"—"negretic hysteria"—could have dangerous results. He warns his readers that primitivism leads to aesthetic relativism; that it is a Trojan horse for black power. Borrowing a quotation from W. E. B. Du Bois's novel *Dark Princess*, he states that the "Congo is flooding the Acropolis" and prophesies that the American Negro might assume cultural supremacy. The only chance to stop this process was to contain primitivism of *any* sort: it was necessary to prevent an insurgency of the (white) "primitivists" (e.g., Anderson and Lawrence) as well as the (black) "primitives" (specifically, Alain Locke).

In this book, I am not concerned with the fear (hysteric itself) that one culture is ascendant over another or that one culture could ever undermine or infiltrate another. In our search for an undiscovered history of aesthetic primitivism, we are chiefly interested in the collaborative moments in Western aesthetic history when white artists transcended the color line to borrow from black cultures, when black idioms were put to white ends, and when artists "went primitive"—formally—to become modern. I want to explore the role African and African American art and culture have had in the making of European and Anglo-American modernism, as well as the role of Europeans and white Americans in the making of African and African American modernism.

Since I am concerned with those occasions when black art becomes a constitutive element in the formation of modern aesthetics, this is not a study of white artists' idealizing black peoples and cultures or of their own romantic-primitivistic projections. I am less interested in showing that "the primitive" is socially constructed than in what kinds of cultural work it performed and the effects, repercussions, and ironies this entails. In contrast to other recent trends in American studies, I shall not focus on literature but will concentrate on the fine arts, music, popular entertainment, and nonfiction.

Carl G. Jung asserted in 1930 that the primitive was always within the American psyche: "Since the Negro lives within your cities and even within your houses, he also lives within your skin, subconsciously."[21] Jung referred to this as a "racial infection." Although this statement is as befuddled, in its way, as Wyndham Lewis's about the Congo flooding America, it reveals the range of possible attitudes, from the romantic debasing of "the primitive" to declaring American culture a true hybrid, as black as it is white, as African as it is European. This notion of the black other within the white, collective American self was an uncanny idea at the time.[22] Indeed, it remains unsettling almost seventy years later, and it is this ironic, uncanny, and unseen history that we will explore in the chapters that follow.

PICASSO'S "DUSTY MANIKINS"

L'art nègre? Connais pas!

—Pablo Picasso (1920)

In being modernistic they are indirectly being African.

—Alain Locke (1936)

Pablo Picasso's *Les Demoiselles d'Avignon* is a striking composition of five nude figures, only a few of which are obviously feminine (figure 2.1). The figure in the center has her arms lifted and crossed above her head; her dark eyes stare straight ahead with a blank expression. She and the figure immediately to her left flaunt their nudity, but the leftmost figure is a more staid observer of the scene. The fruit dish in the foreground, filled with grapes, an apple, and a slice of watermelon, is depicted in so flat a manner as to underscore the two-dimensionality of the image. Both fruits and bodies hardly resemble their natural counterparts.

The angular body shapes of the two figures at the right are crucial innovations in the representation of the female nude. The figures are obscure; their masklike faces are mysterious and gloomy. They are sexually indeterminate and "uncanny" in the Freudian sense: they are both familiar and strange. If we look at the head of the rightmost figure with its *quart-de-brie* nose, we can hardly discern whether it is that of a woman or a man. But its green striations and the black ellipse of an eye direct our attention, and the face looms from the background. In fact, the figure literally protrudes from the canvas. Its ghostly presence is heightened by a swirling impasto noticed only when inspecting the original canvas at an angle.

Below this cryptic figure is another, equally strange and perhaps more abstruse. The face is represented from a frontal perspective. One eye is blue, the other white. Both are tilted. The nose is a flat plane and the mouth a small slit

Figure 2.1   Pablo Picasso. *Les Demoiselles d'Avignon.* Paris
(June–July 1907). Courtesy of the Museum of Modern Art,
New York. Acquired through the Lillie P. Bliss Bequest.

at the far left of the face. The body of the figure, though, has its back turned to
us, which places it in an impossible contortion. Like the figure above, its attitude to the viewer is ambivalent. Certainly they are both disturbing: their
faces are distorted and neither has the open stance of the three other figures.
In fact, there seems to be a visual fault line bisecting the left from the right
side of this painting.

The visual break within *Les Demoiselles d'Avignion* is a break in art history. The left-hand side is closer to nineteenth-century realism, whereas the
right-hand side departs from such a realistic representation of human anatomy. If we look at the bestial, masklike faces on the right, it is evident that
the image does not strive for loyalty to the object it represents. Instead of displaying a reliable reproduction of the represented object, the image purposefully distorts, calling attention to its own production. Its formal devices become the subject matter of the painting.

In this shift toward an autodeictic mode, the oversimplified, geometric, and
fragmented forms assume visual centrality. Far from concealing its own construction, far from passing for the real, the image displays its semi-abstract
composition and flaunts its own construction. Obviously, the exhibitionist aspect of the image and its proto-cubist features are most pronounced in the

two right-hand figures. It is my contention that modernism emerged out of this visual divide; since the two halves relate to two phases in the painting of the canvas, we will discuss the peculiar genealogy of the work.

In his first sketches for this painting, created in 1906, Picasso included two male figures. In the center, a sailor sitting on a chair holds a skull (death), and to his left a medical student stands with a book (reason) under his right arm. This arrangement pushed the nude female figures to the margins. The image is apparently a scene in a brothel; the title refers to an Avignon Street located in the red-light district of Barcelona. William Rubin has suggested that the skull is a metonym of syphilis and that the image depicts a dreadful interplay between Eros and Thanatos.

Rubin proposes another, more interesting point when he argues that the first version was painted in an anecdotal and narrative mode that all but told the viewer the scene takes place in a bordello, whereas the final version of *Les Demoiselles* is painted in an "iconic" mode. This iconic mode is, Rubin claims, "more frontal, more spatially compressed, and comparatively abstracted from time and place."[1] The iconic mode of representation directs one's attention to the image's formal features. The image rejects "telling," but flaunts its independence and exposes its symbolic potency. On the right-hand side, a visual boldness and density prevail. In its immediacy and fierceness, it assumes an extraordinary intensity whose style, Rubin insinuates, has almost phallic qualities. Though Rubin does not extend the argument, we can induce the following hypothesis: Picasso's fear that sexual intercourse might be fatal is stylistically eliminated by the formalistic resurrection of iconic potency.

Rubin refers also to a well-established distinction between the two sides of the painting. The left side, painted in the so-called Iberian style (inspired by the art of his native country), is generally contrasted with the right side of the final version, painted in the so-called African style. This demarcation goes back to a visit that Picasso made to the Musée de Trocadéro. He had the habit of visiting the wing that housed the Greek sculptures, but one Sunday afternoon, probably in June 1907, he decided to take a look at the wing of the building that housed African sculptures and masks.

It is true that some art historians believe that Picasso visited the Trocadéro only after finishing *Les Demoiselles*. But a close look at the image itself betrays the influence. If we compare the upper right-hand figure with masks from the Ivory Coast (the Bakota and Fang peoples), we cannot but notice the striking similarity. However, according to Rubin, "not one of the types of masks that art historians have through the years proposed as possible models for Picasso could, in fact, have been in the Trocadéro or—experts insist—found on the Parisian market as early as 1907." Nevertheless, Rubin is convinced that "the Trocadéro visit [was] a turning point"[2] (figure 2.2).

Perhaps we should turn to Picasso's own assertions on the role African art played for him. Fascinating here is the marked difference between Picasso's early coyness and subsequent pride. When asked about *art nègre* in the 1920s, Picasso answered boldly: "L'art nègre? Connais pas!" ["African art? Don't know it!"] This famous claim, published in *Action* in April 1920, was an out-

Figure 2.2　Pablo Picasso. *Detail of Les Demoiselles d'Avignon*. Paris (June–July 1907). Courtesy of the Museum of Modern Art, New York. Acquired through the Lillie P. Bliss Bequest.

right distortion of the truth. In 1910, the American writer and journalist Gelett Burgess reported on the Parisian avant-garde and remarked that "all the Fauves have been ransacking the curio shops for negro art."[3] His article, "The Wild Men of Paris," includes one photo of *Les Demoiselles* and another of Picasso sitting in his studio before two big African sculptures. Burgess was shocked by the recent developments in Paris: the fauves no longer painted women in a style attractive to him, but insisted on representing the female as "ugly." When Burgess describes Picasso's "pyramidal women, his sub-African caricatures, figures with eyes askew, with contorted legs" (408), he implicitly refers to Picasso's source of inspiration.

Furthermore, even if we assumed that Picasso had executed *Les Demoiselles* before he visited the museum, he could have hardly not known about African art by 1920. Matisse had always insisted that it was he who had introduced Picasso to African art in 1906 when he purchased an African mask and brought it to a dinner party at Gertrude Stein's home. This is impossible to prove, but several of Picasso's friends, such as Max Jacob, a frequent visitor to Picasso's studio, vividly remembered Picasso's connection to Negro art: "Fascinated by the black idols, he had been working all night. Cubism had been born" (Seckel, 233).

Another close friend, Françoise Gilot, remembered in her book *Life with Picasso* a visit with Picasso to Gertrude Stein's apartment. Alice Toklas, wearing an enormous hat, opened the door and led the two guests to Stein, who was sitting in a large armchair under a portrait of herself that Picasso had painted in 1906. A few hours later (shortly after Stein had asserted that "without [me], there would be no American literature as we know it"), she cross-examined Gilot on cubism. Gilot remembered, "I replied with whatever seemed the apropriate observation on analytic Cubism, synthetic Cubism, the influence of Negro art, of Cézanne, and so on" (Gilot and Lake, 69). Gilot, in other words, knew about the influence of Negro art and mentioned it in Picasso's presence.

It is helpful here to investigate the role that Paul Guillaume, an art critic and dealer, played. There is reason to believe that in his 1918 exhibit "Matisse et Picasso" he included *Les Demoiselles* in his selection, displaying the large canvas on the sidewalk because it would not fit through the door of his gallery (in a too literal manifestation of the painting's metaphoric power). Guillaume organized the first exhibit where African art and European art were displayed together. He copublished *Primitive Negro Sculpture* (1926) with Thomas Munro. He also published "African Art at the Barnes Foundation" in 1924 and "The Triumph of Ancient Negro Art" in 1926—both articles appearing in *Opportunity* magazine. In May 1924, one month after the Civil Club dinner, Guillaume stated clearly:

> The modern movement in art gets its inspiration undoubtedly from African art, and it could not be otherwise. Thanks to that fact France wields the artistic sceptre, because since Impressionism no manifestation in art could be shown that is not African in essence. The work of the young painters such as Picasso, Modigliani, Soutine, for example, is to a certain extent, the work of African emotion in a new setting. In the same way the sculpture of Archipenko, Lipchitz and of Epstein is impregnated with Africanism. The music of Bernard, Satie, Poulenc, Auric, Honegger—in short, all that which is interesting since Debussy, is African. One can say as much also of the poetry since Rimbaud up to Blaise Cendrars and Reverdy, including Apollinaire.[4]

Modernism is impregnated with Africanism, Guillaume pronounces, stressing that the French could not have held artistic hegemony had it not been for African art.

Picasso was not the only artist who pretended that he had nothing to do with colonized art and who refused to admit his debt to African art idioms. Jacques Lipchitz stated that "it would be mistaken that our own art would be mulatto. It is quite white."[5] Quite white, indeed. This negation, in the Freudian sense of the word, is a revealing slip. Picasso's and Lipchitz's distortions are alarming and intolerable. The fact that Picasso imitated African art should not, of course, be held against him or simply dismissed as cultural imperialism; however it is ironic that Picasso was anxious about admitting something so obvious as the formal impact *art nègre* had on *Les Demoiselles.*

Even more alarming than Picasso's reticence is the fact that many art critics have also denied this influence. Christian Zervos, for example, accepted completely Picasso's version: "at the time [Picasso] was painting *Demoiselles d'Avignon*, he was unaware of the art of black Africa. It was only somewhat later that he had the revelation" (Seckel, 216). Zervos became one of the early spokespersons for those arguing that African art had nothing to do with this revolutionary painting. Kahnweiler also denied any "influence of this kind"— that is, African influences—because he wanted to believe that Picasso "created Cubism through an internal development of his own work" (Seckel, 239).

Many art historians have recognized Picasso's protestations as disingenuous. In 1939, Alfred Barr contributed an article to the catalog of "Art in Our Time" that discussed *Les Demoiselles* in a passage entitled "The Negro Period." Surprisingly, the American press was unambiguous about the African influence. On November 6, 1937, when the painting was first exhibited to the American public, the *New York World Telegram* noticed that "the right hand side is peopled with figures more patently derived from negroid sculpture. Their grotesque heads are like African masks." That same day, the *New York Post* remarked that *Les Demoiselles* was filled "with a jungle of figures (based on African Negro sculpture)," and they detected in it "a rhythm, more like the wild beat of the tom-tom." Two weeks later, the *New Yorker* claimed that "this pivotal picture . . . marks the end of the period in which Negro masks were the artists' strongest influence."[6]

Curiously, it was only at this time of international acceptance that Picasso finally spoke directly about what had happened at the museum. In a conversation with André Malraux in 1937 (though not published until 1974—after Picasso's death—in Malraux's *La Tête d'obsidienne*), Picasso referred to the visit to the ethnography museum and the epiphany that triggered his creativity in an unprecedented manner. The passage is revealing:

> Everybody always talks about the influences that the Negroes had on me. What can I do? We all of us loved fetishes. Van Gogh once said, "Japanese art—we all had that in common." For us it's the Negroes. . . . When I went to the old Trocadero, it was disgusting. The Flea Market. The smell. I was alone. I wanted to get away. But I didn't leave. I stayed. I stayed. I understood that it was very important: something was happening to me, right?
>
> The masks weren't just like any other pieces of sculpture. Not at all. They were magic things. . . . I always looked at fetishes. I understood; I too am against everything. I too believe that everything is unknown, that everything is an enemy! Everything! Not the details—women, children, babies, tobacco, playing—the whole of it! I understood what the Negroes use their sculptures for. Why sculpt like that and not some other way? After all, they weren't Cubist! Since Cubism didn't exist. It was clear that some guys had invented the models, and others had imitated them, right? Isn't that what we call tradition? But all the fetishes were used for the same thing. They were weapons. To help people avoid coming under the influence of spirits again,

to help them become independent. Spirits, the unconscious (people still weren't talking about that very much) emotion—they're all the same thing. I understood why I was a painter. All alone in that awful museum, with masks, dolls made by the redskins, dusty manikins. *Les Demoiselles d'Avignon* must have come to me that very day, but not at all because of forms; because it was my first exorcism painting—yes absolutely. (Malraux, 10–11)

His choice of the word "exorcism," though curious, is apt here. Picasso wanted to free himself from possession by artistic predecessors who believed in the complete divide between life and art. The immediate outcome of this encounter with the "dusty manikins" was that he abandoned the Iberian style, revised his early version of *Les Demoiselles,* and experimented with proto-cubist features. Although Picasso had drawn many sketches before "that day at the museum," the encounter with "Negro art" triggered his creativity and he managed to reinvent himself artistically.

After that day at the museum, Picasso was no longer interested in representing objects in the traditional style of still-life painting. He hoped to capture the expressive power of the masks and instill it in his own work. "The masks weren't just like any other pieces of sculpture," or any other piece of art. "They were magic things," Picasso proposed. To him, these magical masks contained something that contemporary European art lacked; they were potential weapons for exorcising the old style. So strong was their influence that Picasso had to remind himself that "they weren't Cubist." They were, however, tools to work out the new style of representation later referred to as cubism. With the help of "dusty manikins," Picasso reinvented himself and his art.

This transformation was so complete that thirty years later it was still possible to witness the trauma of its birth. The passage reveals Picasso's aesthetic struggle with his own revulsion for the forms of African art (and, by extension, the traditional revulsion of the West to African aesthetic conventions generally). Picasso vividly describes the encounter with the uncanny. His evocative description of "the smell," followed by the realization that he was alone, and his initial desire "to get away," which, however, he managed to resist—"But I didn't leave. I stayed. I stayed."—are symbolic. Thirty years later he was still haunted by what he remembered as a tormenting odor. The unpleasant sensations are metaphors for Picasso's anxiety and the sublimity of this encounter with the black uncanny.

This famous quotation has been reprinted many times to illuminate the dynamics of primitivism and modernism. Because it is one of the few incidents where Picasso explicitly talks about *l'art nègre*, coupled with the fact that it is so cryptically rendered in general terms (the exorcism of "women, children, babies, tobacco, playing—the whole of it"), this passage has become the mysterious urtext of primitivist modernism.

There exists, however, another account of Picasso's explanation of why he was drawn to African art. This statement, which is less ambiguous and was published ten years before the passage cited above, is reported by Françoise Gilot. She remembers Picasso's saying:

When I became interested, forty years ago, in Negro art and I made what they refer to as the Negro Period in my painting, it was because at that time I was against what was called beauty in the museum. At that time, for most people a Negro mask was an ethnographic object. When I went for the first time, at Derain's urging, to the Trocadéro museum, the smell of dampness and rot there stuck in my throat. It depressed me so much I wanted to get out fast, but I stayed and studied. Men had made those masks and other objects for a sacred purpose, a magic purpose, as a kind of mediation between themselves and the unknown hostile forces that surround them, in order to overcome their fear and horror by giving it a form and image. At that moment I realized what painting was all about. Painting isn't an aesthetic operation; it's a form of magic designated as a mediator between this strange, hostile world and us, a way of seizing the power by giving form to our terrors as well as our desires. When I came to that realization, I knew I had found my way.[7]

Opposed to the ideal that emphasized detachment as the preeminent feature of aesthetics, Picasso wanted to bridge the gap between art and life. He tried to produce an art that mediated between the people and the "unknown hostile forces that surround them." Picasso's goal was to expel the tradition that urged art to assume a distance from the social world.

Without previously knowing anything about African art, Picasso claimed to know that its function was to free people from spirits and make them independent. The power of his insight was such that, even as he achieved a formal breakthrough, Picasso realized that art should not be produced merely for art's sake; rather, it should help people come to terms with their fears and desires. The profoundly personal nature of this insight was natural since it so obviously applied to Picasso himself: the threatening spirits were, metaphorically, his own artistic antecedents.

Most critics have concentrated on the purely formal aspect of this insight. Pierre Daix dates "the beginnings of modern art as we understand it from *Les Demoiselles d'Avignon*."[8] Danielle Boone argues that *Les Demoiselles d'Avignon* is one of the "few real revolutions in the history of art" and that "this painting is rightly regarded as the beginning of modern art."[9] The Picasso expert, Alfred H. Barr, Jr., claims that *Les Demoiselles'* dynamic power was unsurpassed in European art and that it represents a "transitional picture, a laboratory, a battlefield of trial and experiment" because it triggered a radical shift in the history of Western painting: "Les Demoiselles d'Avignon may be called the first cubist picture, for the breaking up of natural forms, whether figures, still life or drapery, into a semi-abstract, all-over design of tilting shifting planes, compressed into a shallow space, is already cubism."[10] It represents, Barr notes, a leap in European art toward a mode of representation almost completely dissociated from the represented object. The fragmented forms, compressed into a shallow space, draw attention to the composition itself. It is not the mimetic accuracy but rather the performative nature of the painting that is the true subject matter of *Les Demoiselles*.

Picasso began his first sketches of *Les Demoiselles* when many of his colleagues were working on multifigure nude paintings. But Henri Matisse's

Three Bathers (1907), André Derain's *Bathers*, and Maurice de Vlaminck's *Bathers* (1908) were all colorful and idyllic images of outdoor scenes. Color and light permeate these fauvist paintings, whose subject matter and style is pleasant and harmonic. Picasso's *Les Demoiselles*, in contrast, is boldly deviant. The cubic noses, cylindrical eyes, and abstract geometric shapes convey a ferocity that parts from a romantic harmonious sentimentality. *Les Demoiselles* evokes a wildness lacking in Derain, Vlaminck, and Matisse.

Les Demoiselles was disturbing to most spectators, and even (or particularly?) to other artists. Georges Braque, who was introduced to Picasso by Guillaume Apollinaire, compared Picasso's image to "drinking kerosene and eating flaming tow."[11] More recently, Varnedoe confessed that the image had given him the shivers. These exclamations of horror and loathing replicate Picasso's own description of his encounter with African art. For Apollinaire, it was precisely this grotesque quality that attracted Picasso and others to "Negro statuettes":

> Negro statuettes taught modern European artists a "moral lesson." They helped them formulate artistic aims. Early twentieth-century painters and sculptors read into primitive art the qualities which they themselves wished to attain in their own works: simplicity, unsophistication, "barbarism" . . . crudeness and grotesqueness.[12]

This attempt to capture "simplicity, unsophistication, 'barbarism'" and incorporate them into their art to achieve a "crudeness and grotesqueness" is very much a wish-fulfilling strategy. In large part, the artists were projecting desired metaphors onto the art of the other.

This fascination with *art nègre* became an obsession; people referred to it as the *vogue nègre*. It was a badly informed curiosity; even artists had little concern over the cultural or historical origins of this art and indiscriminately referred to African, Oceanic, and Native American art as *art nègre*. They did not differentiate among contemporary African art, "primitive art," and "Negro art." Artists were not interested in African art *sui generis*; rather they were intrigued by the objects because the majority of their contemporaries considered them horrific artifacts of a heathen world and because they saw in them the potential to overcome the aesthetic quandry they were groping with at the time. Nobody expressed the desperate moment French artists were in at the time better than A. Browness when he wrote: "Nobody in France was able to go forward into radically new kinds of art until 1905."[13]

What started in Paris was soon to spread to modern artists in other European countries. German Expressionists such as Erich Nolde and Paul Klee became interested in *Negerkunst*; Giacometti and Brancusi felt equally drawn toward these strange objects. It hardly seems coincidental that European art underwent a significant revision of its modes of representation around the same time that European artists began to incorporate the barbarous forms of *l'art nègre*, *Negerkunst*, or "Negro art."

What were these barbarous forms? Several statements may elucidate. The first is by Paul Guillaume, who, after stating that "in a living human face, an eye is an eye, a mouth a mouth," writes, "the negro mask-maker" had the freedom to "select from the given data to emphasize a certain recurrence, and eliminate whatever would not fit in with it" (Guillaume and Munro, 41–42). The second is from the ethnographer Franz Boas. In *Primitive Art* (1927), he stresses that African masks are entirely different from human physiognomy because "there are no ears; the eyes are slits with geometrical ornaments; the mouth a circle enclosing a cross."[14]

The third is a comment Picasso made to Leo Stein about representing a head: "A Head," he said, "was a matter of eyes, nose, mouth, which would be distributed in any way you like—the head remained a head."[15] Picasso's farewell to loyal representations and stylistic consistency signify on European academic conventions. In painting a diamond-shaped nose and a mouth as a diagonal slit, as he did in *Les Demoiselles*, Picasso became the harbinger of an artistic movement whose artists eliminated whatever they thought did not fit.

Paul Guillaume understood the nature of this revolution completely:

> If the negro sculpture is to be enjoyed at all, it will probably be through its plastic effects. . . . These effects would be impossible in a representation of the human figure if natural proportions were strictly adhered to. . . . They can be attained only by abandoning both these considerations utterly and freely distorting the natural shape of body into arbitrary forms, emphasizing and enlarging here, diminishing there, rounding, flattening or elongating at will.
>
> Any observer can see at once that a negro statue is far from both nature and the human ideal. . . . One comes to regard the statue not as a distorted copy of a human body, but as a new creation in itself.[16]

The encounter with the cultural other enabled the Europeans to discover a new aesthetic law in which the art object became a "creation in itself," as Guillaume puts it—or in which the art object became, to use Miles Orvell's term, the "real thing."

What is at stake here is not just a growing interest in African art and the direct borrowing from this art; what matters is its seminal role as a catalyst in shifting the aesthetic paradigm. The European interest in black art cannot be reduced to apparent similarities. Nor is it enough to assume a natural affinity between modern and "primitive" art. Although there was direct borrowing, the contribution that black art made was to initiate a paradigm shift in European art history. The intercultural encounter—or rather the discovery of non-European art in European institutions—caused European artists to experiment, transform, and regenerate their own styles.

Guillaume talked about the fermenting influence African art had on the emergence of the new aesthetic paradigm, suggesting that it would spread to other art forms, such as poetry and music. Guillaume extends the list of Africa-inspired artists from the fine arts to other fields and argues that the "hideous little idols" had a broad and pervasive impact on the shifting of the paradigm from a tired, old aesthetic order. Guillaume even comments on this sense of weariness and wish for aesthetic renewal. In *Primitive Negro Sculpture,* he reports people's lamenting that "the plastic arts were exhausted," and in *Opportunity*, he asserts that European art "exhausted its energies, and was dying of a slow anaemia."[17]

Guillaume ends his book with a succinct statement: "negro art has brought creative forces that may prove to be inexhaustible" (Guillaume and Munro, 134). He makes it sound as if European art had received an energizing injection. His construction, "negro art has brought creative forces" to European art, distorts the fact that French artists had made a deliberate effort to capture this creative force. They realized, consciously or unconsciously, that impregnating their style with Africanism could revitalize their art. When Europe became weary of the "old" style—the overly refined and overladen aesthetics of nineteenth-century art—formerly discredited objects, such as a Fang mask, became appealing.

This ferment of Africanism manifested itself directly through Picasso and his imitators, but it also appeared in the works of other modernists (across disciplines and genres), who learned from *art nègre* that an art object can be a thing in itself. Critics of modernism (such as Miles Orvell in *The Real Thing*) who identify this self-reflective quality as a prime feature of modern art always fail to mention the link between artistic self-referentiality and African art. While abstractionism and self-referentiality are well-established tropes in debates on modernism in literature and art history, the fact that this particular style was first conceived through a formal encounter with non-European art is still not common critical discourse.[18]

Central to modernist aesthetics (and not only in painting but also in music and fiction) is exactly this sort of abstract conceptualism. Edward F. Frey, after quoting Picasso's remark about representing a head, adds that this "mode of thought [was] analogous to the method of composition by tone-row in the music of Schoenberg and other twelve-tone composers."[19] Frey sees an affinity between Picasso's African-inspired conceptualism and Schoenberg's twelve-tone compositions. To Gertrude Stein, a sentence "exists in and for itself, there is no relation of it and therefore there is no element of completion, it is a thing that exists by internal balancing, that is what a sentence is."[20]

That this innovation sprang whole out of the influence of the primitive is ignored. Even though critics of modernism were aware of the importance of formalistic difference, they shied away from including "the other" in their discussions. In *Concepts of Modernism*, Astradur Eysteinsson states: "What makes modernism 'different' is the way in which it is aware of and acts out the qualities of 'différance'."[21] Considering modernism's fascination with displacing signifiers and deferring meaning, Eysteinsson, however, neglects the pivotal role that cultural difference has played.

Les Demoiselles could never have been conceived but for an act of cultural transgression. Visiting these heterotopias—to use a term coined by Michel Foucault to describe areas within the cultural landscape that depart from the norm—represented a transgressive act that enabled Picasso's act of aesthetic transformation. Mocking philistine notions of decency by allying himself with what the bourgeois ethos considered taboo—prostitutes and African masks—Picasso exorcised that ethos and its underlying concept of art. Picasso symbolically utilized despised objects—whores and fetishes—that were

conventionally seen for their use-value alone and employed them symbolically in terms of subject matter and form.

Among the first art historians to analyze the importance of this "primitive"
influence in modern art was Robert Goldwater, who published his pioneering
study, *Primitivism in Modern Painting,* in 1938. Goldwater dismissed the assumption that modern art is antithetical to non-European art. Decades before
the emergence of postcolonial criticism, Goldwater's book reacted against, as
he put it, "the generally disdainful opinion of primitive peoples which prevailed throughout the nineteenth century, and which, if it originated in the
theory of evolution, was influenced by and useful to colonial programs."[22]
The colonialist myth of the "white man's burden," Goldwater states with dis-
dain, "affected even the arts." Goldwater must have sensed that the best argument against racism is to demonstrate that the allegedly inferior race is not
entirely "other," but congruent with the "self."

The subtext of modernism, Goldwater argues, is primitivism, of which he
distinguishes four types: "the primitivism of the subconscious," "romantic
primitivism," "emotional primitivism," and "intellectual primitivism." The
first of these categories comprises dadaist and surrealist works because they
are freely associative, express paranoia or fantasies, and represent "personal
primitive elements."

Fauvism, and particularly the work of Paul Gauguin, fall under the category of "romantic primitivism." Gauguin's colorful images of Tahitian life reflect his romantic yearning for innocence and gaiety. While Gauguin idealizes
the exotic lifestyle of the South Seas, the preferred subject matter of other fauvists was nude women surrounded by verdant northern European fauna.
Looking at these simple, colorful, and sensual fauvist paintings is, as Matisse
once put it, like sitting in a "good armchair in which to rest from physical fatigue" (Goldwater, 98). This refreshing effect stems from the saliency of the
colors and the simplicity of the composition; the fauvists' attempt to "return
to naked simplicity" manifests itself in their use of pure color, the lack of perspective, and the broad, unfinished line. Since the fauvists were less concerned with nuance than with harmonious composition, Goldwater detects
anti-intellectual and anti-analytical tendencies in their images.[23]

Similarly, in "emotional primitivism," the creation of feelings is far more
important than an accurate depiction of the object that has produced this
emotion. In contrast to romantic primitivism's proclivity for the natural, "emotional primitivism" expresses the "jungle" life of the human psyche. Goldwater calls German Expressionist paintings, such as *Die Brücke* and *Die Blaue
Reiter*, "emotional" because in these images, psychological and highly subjec-
tive experiences are the subject matter. Instead of giving an impression of an
exotic world outside, "emotional primitivism" refers to the primitive elements within. Accordingly, the *Brücke group* was drawn to children's art, as
well as to the more violent manifestations of human nature.

In "intellectual primitivism," the structure and compositional arrangement
of the aesthetic object are far more important than the content. Furthermore,
intellectual primitivism provided the impetus to move away from mimetic

modes of representation toward abstraction. The elimination of details leads to quasi-geometric, highly stylized compositions. Picasso is an exemplary artist of "intellectual primitivism" because African art is noticeable not so much in his content as in his form.

In Goldwater's account, emotional primitivism is imbued with the exotic nostalgia for a "golden harmonious day," whereas intellectual primitivism is informed by the geometric, rhythmic forms of African sculpture. Although he writes that the latter group is more rational than the former, Goldwater describes it as "ferocious primitivizing," which suggests that intellectual primitivism might be emotionally charged as well. It is readily apparent that Goldwater's terms for the various modes of primitivism in modernism are problematic because his categories are not mutually exclusive. Nevertheless, these two main impulses in modern European art history—the twin trends of intellectual abstraction and emotional subjectivity—are the two vectors of European modernism derived from primitivism.

Goldwater's early study of primitivism in art history is, in many ways, more progressive than the controversial 1984 exhibition at the MOMA, "Primitivism in Twentieth Century Art." Its curator, William Rubin, begins his written introduction to the exhibition on a bold note: "No pivotal topic in twentieth-century art has received less serious attention than primitivism," implying that he will give the heretofore ignored topic the treatment it deserves. After this opening blast, he defines what he means by primitivism and declares that it signifies "the interest of modern artists in tribal art and culture, as revealed in their thought and work." According to this definition, primitivism, or modernist primitivism, as he also calls it, has nothing to do with the art of "primitive" peoples. For Rubin, primitivism is a "Western phenomenon."

If the show's principal aim was to present the "affinity of the tribal and the modern," in doing so it ignored the cultural context of African art, as well as the complex repercussions this intercultural nexus has had in the West.[24] By pairing off the right-hand figure in *Demoiselles* with an Etoumbi mask, and by confusing art history with anthropology, Rubin produced striking resemblances but lost the point.[25]

Yve-Alain Bois rightly assesses that the curators "overestimated the purely formal affinities" and ignored the metaphoric side of primitivism.[26] This metaphor is discussed only when Rubin compares Picasso's *Guitar* with a Grebo mask. Here, Rubin detects a relationship he calls "conceptual," and Bois suggests that by looking at masks, Picasso first "understood something about the arbitrariness of the sign, in much the same way that structural linguistics came to understand it at roughly the same time" (Bois, 185). Here lay much of the radical potential of the show, but it was an opportunity missed.

When Rubin pronounces that "modernist primitivism" denotes the "affinity between the modern and the tribal," he fails to specify what he means by "affinity." Is it a genuine interest among Western artists to overcome the colonialist rejection of non-Western art? Is this proclivity motivated by a sense of identification with despised cultural outsiders? Is it a formal resemblance, a convergence of two styles?

The questions remain unanswered. Instead of analyzing the nature of the encounter, Rubin celebrates the Western appropriation of primitive art, rejoicing that "we [Europeans and Americans] respond to them [African art objects] with our total humanity." To praise "tribal art" because "we" can relate to it is dangerously close to the colonialist attitude that Goldwater worked against. It is surprising that an exhibit about non-European art in 1984 failed to shed eurocentric biases that Rubin must have been aware of. Unfortunately, Rubin's benevolently humanist stance reveals only a paternalistic and condescending attitude; we are not surprised to read his brash claim: "These guys [African sculptors] have to be as good as Picasso and Brancusi or they don't interest me."[27]

Concomitant with Rubin's blatant cultural arrogance is a gross ignorance of political and cultural contexts. When Rubin discovers in a New Guinean object a "mordant and truly hallucinatory quality," he announces that the object's "creator really believes in monsters."[28] In another instance, he argues that "these sculptors usually functioned within a framework of religious needs and values," repeating a common simplification in discussions of non-Western art. Rubin concludes cryptically that this religious framework "left them with the problem of plastic solutions" and snidely adds, "even though they had no concept for what such words [plastic solutions] mean" (Rubin, 19).

Of course, Rubin knew very little about the linguistic or cultural contexts of non-Western art forms himself; his judgments, ungrounded in scholarly expertise, are arrogant. Instead of admitting the limits of his knowledge, Rubin assumes the attitude Picasso took toward African art when he claimed, "Everything I need to know about Africa is in those objects" (Rubin, 19). If Picasso's curious claim can be justified as the pure formalism of an artist, Rubin, an art historian, cannot make a similar claim for the irrelevance of cultural context.

His exhibition was skewed by eurocentric bias. The absence of critical essays by experts in African art history undercut his attempt to combine art criticism and ethnography. Rubin's ambitious project set out to disclose that an African impulse had shaped the rise of modernism, but ultimately the show focused only on European art history and made the African influence a mere adjunct to the history of European modernism. Cultural myopia impinged on the MOMA show's ability to live up to its promise—that is, to unveil "the invisible man" of art history: "Modernist Primitivism."

The intersection between modern and primitive art was by no means unknown at the time Rubin wrote his introduction to the exhibition. Thirty years after Goldwater's pioneering study, Jean Laude had published *La peintre française (1905–1914) et l'art nègre* (1968) and there had been two important exhibits preceding the MOMA show: "Arts primitifs dans les ateliers d'artistes" (1967) at the Musée de l'Homme in Paris and "World Civilizations and Modern Art" (1972) in Munich. Working from the material at that exhibit, Charles Wentick published *Moderne und primitive Kunst* in 1974. The English translation, *Modern and Primitive Art* (1979) includes eighty illustrations arranged in pairs; this intercultural juxtaposition of European modernist images and non-Western or premodern art produced obvious and striking similarities. The nexus between the primitive and the modern, in other words, was by no means invisible. The MOMA show passed up the great opportunity to present to a broader public how culturally complex modernism was; the critical task of revealing the cultural hybridity at the core of modernism remained unperformed even in the late 1980s.

A recent attempt to uncover the breadth of the phenomenon of primitivism in art is Colin Rhodes's Ph.D. thesis, published in 1994 as *Primitivism and Modern Art*. Rhodes surpasses his predecessors by extending the scope of study to graffiti, child art, Bretonism (art by Paul Gauguin and Émile Bernard representing the noble peasant), neoprimitivism in Russia (e.g., Kazimir Malevich), shamanic imagery, and the esoteric tendencies of Jackson Pollock and Wassily Kandinsky. As a matter of course, he also discusses cubism, expressionism, dadaism, Gauguin's exotic images, and Jean Buffet's simple and naive paintings. The most recent art work that he discusses is Joseph Beuys's *Honey Pump at the Work Place* (1977), an installation in which an electric motor generates energy to pump honey through transparent tubes spread across the museum. Like blood through a body, the honey circulates through what Beuys calls the "social sculpture," suggesting that his intent may be to transform society into a work of art. This installation of tubes and mechanic devices is far removed from any "tribal art."

Paul Guillaume had understood the intrinsic, nonmetaphoric value of African art as far back as 1926. His *Primitive Negro Sculpure* includes forty-one illustrations of West African art taken from the Barnes collection. The figures range from the tenth to the nineteenth centuries. Guillaume's intention is to investigate the formal properties of Negro sculpture, what he calls its plastic qualities, and its relation to African life. Negro sculpture, Guillaume claims, "was an integral part of a certain mode of existence that had more or less been the same; the product of long days of dreamy indolence after furious activity, in a shade with a knife and a log of wood."[29] The dismissive tone is eurocentric, of course, but he also condemns European colonialism: "in destroying these things [African art objects], civilization destroyed the art itself." Guillaume, who considered himself a custodian of African art, must have objected to this act of destruction. His voice seems to be the first that values African art for itself, not just for its metaphoric uses.

The dismissive tone is a remnant of the ideology Guillaume set out to fight against and that, Guillaume suggests, was challenged by an increasing number of Europeans. "The Growth of Interest in African Art" is the heading of his introduction, which he begins with the following statement: "Scarcely twenty years ago, negro sculpture was known only to an occasional missionary, who would write home with horror of the 'hideous little idols' of the savages, and to a few explorers and ethnologists, who collected it among other phenomena of African art without suspecting that it might ever be taken seriously as art." While the missonary gazed at these "hideous little idols" with horror and dismay, "a few people in Paris," Guillaume writes, looked at these figures with awe and wonder. They felt, Guillaume argues, that these figures carved by "unknown artists from the jungle" were superior in many ways to the finished products of the academies.

This superiority is complex. The "dilemma" of primitivism, Rhodes claims, is that "the relevance of the primitive as a point of opposition in postmodern Western cultures is apparently given institutional sanction, while at the same time its difference to those cultures is re-emphasized" (Rhodes, 196). Creating (and appreciating) primitive art might once have been subversive, but today it is only postmodern playfulness. Or to put it in a chronological context, primitivist modernists who once undermined racist attitudes by appropriating aspects of primitive art initiated the new practice of absorbing and nullifying cultural difference.

This is one of the reasons that the MOMA show evoked a barrage of hostile responses. Hal Foster thought that the MOMA show and primitivism in general were reactionary. To Foster the "primal scene of modern primitivism," *Les Demoiselles d'Avignon*, which illustrates "a bridge between modernist and premodernist painting" indicates a "leap within the tradition" that coincides with "a step outside the tradition." But Foster "wonders if this aesthetic breakthrough is not also a breakdown, psychologically regressive, politically reactionary."[30] Picasso's appropriation of *art nègre*—his leap outside the tradition—led him to use the other for his own ends while not acknowledging African culture. Stating flatly that "the primitivist appropriation of the other is another form of conquest," Foster interprets *Les Demoiselles* as an example of cultural imperialism.

By extension, Foster implies that the MOMA show, which suppressed the necessary imperialist condition, was politically reactionary. On both levels, that of Picasso's appropriating black art and of Rubin's universalizing primitivism, there is "a recognition and a disavowal" of difference, and ultimately there was only a "domesticated otherness" (Foster, 60, 46). In spite of his harsh critique of their ethnocentric inability to radically transgress, Foster partakes in what he condemns because he, too, puts the other to his own ends. In his final paragraph, Foster asks "why not turn to vital others within and without—to affirm *their* resistance to the white, patriarchal order of Western culture?" (Foster, 69).

This desire to disrupt Western logocentrism leads Foster to define the other as a conduit for change. Foster seeks to valorize the otherness of the primitive by citing the works of Baudrillard, Todorov, Derrida, and Foucault as protagonists in the battle, hoping that he can do for Western intellectual history what Picasso had done for art history. His principal failing is that he chooses not to discuss the other side of this encounter: what European primitivism meant for the other of color.

Black Primitivist Modernism

The use and misuse of African art by European modernists triggered an unexpected development: the Americans most sympathetic to the new aesthetic were black. Alain Locke was at the forefront of the reception. In *The New Negro: An Interpretation* (1925), he asks, "If the forefathers could so adroitly master these mediums, why not we?" He realized that black artists could become the vanguard of American modernism by appropriating African forms: "the Negro may well become what some have predicted, the artist of American life" (Locke, *New Negro*, 256, 258). He felt that this reevaluation of African art could spread to other areas of social life and lead to a complete revision of the status of the Negro. What was possible for the Negro mask should be possible for the New Negro as well. The central irony, of course, was the fact that black American artists, the putative "New Negroes," discovered African art only indirectly through *art nègre*.

Jack Flam and Daniel Shapiro have termed this reciprocal process "incipient globalism." They argue that it "was to have an enormous importance for Africa and Africans as well as for Europeans." Though Flam and Shapiro avoid specific examples, they stress that the interest in African sculpture was "the first extra-African awareness of the voice of Africa, and even the awareness that Africa had a voice."[31] Sadly, this interest in African art created comparatively little interest in African politics and culture, but Flam and Shapiro are correct that the globalism still emerging at the end of this century has, for better or worse, its predecessor in primitivist modernism.

In the catalog of an exhibit created by Flam and Shapiro, *Western Artists/ African Art*, we find such an example of the ironies behind primitivist-modernism: Lorna Simpson's *Flipside* (1991) (figure 2.3). Simpson juxtaposes two black and white gelatine prints, one showing the neck and head of an African American woman, the other the back of an African mask. In the text accompanying the reproduction, Simpson says:

> I became interested in using the masks, funny enough, because of an exhibition I saw at the Center for African Art, at its old space uptown. . . . The impression I left with was not of the actual objects but of the same old difficulty of presenting such objects outside their context, while also ignoring the problematic of gallery or museum spaces and their relationship historically to these objects, which are based in ritual and participatory performance. (Flam and Shapiro, 87)

Simpson saw the displaced masks as potential solutions to the distance between the gallery in New York and the ritual performances they were once part of. She was also concerned with "how one does or does not have access to a particular cultural past." Was Simpson suggesting that this encounter made her think about a cultural past that she had turned her back on? I don't know. But *Flipside* certainly reverses the process of symbolic acquisition familiar to us in such works as *Spoon Woman*. Instead of a man, Giacometti, utilizing African objects such as grain spoons, we have an African

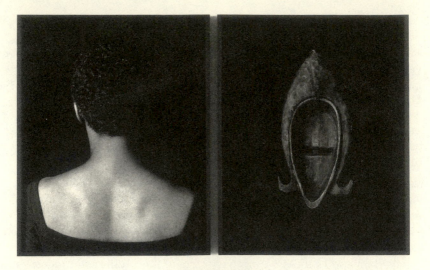

Figure 2.3   Lorna Simpson. *Flipside* (1991). Courtesy of the Sean Kelly Gallery, New York.

American woman (perhaps inspired by the male Picasso), using the most famous icon of modern European art as a matrix for her work. *Flipside* is an inversion of *Les Demoiselles d'Avignon*; it plays with the painting's parts—a black woman on the left and a mask on the right—even as it places us *behind* the mask.

To trace back the history of what I propose to call black primitivist modernism, it is necessary to take a closer look at those art objects produced by African American artists that reveal both formal influences from European modernism and visual references to Africa. Meta Warwick Fuller's life-size bronze sculpture, *Awakening of Ethiopia* (1914), is a good starting point in the endeavor to uncover this "legacy of the ancestral arts," to echo Alain Locke. Fuller finished the piece five years after returning from Paris, where she had lived during the height of the *vogue nègre*. She had studied under Auguste Rodin, who acknowledged and praised her work. Having witnessed the European obsession with African art, she had taken up the subject matter of Africa herself.

Art historians consider *Awakening of Ethopia* to be "among the earliest examples of American art to reflect the formal exigencies of an aesthetic based on African sculpture."[32] The sculpture pays homage to the art of Fuller's ancestors; it anticipated Locke's plea for an African-inspired art by a decade. Instead of emulating African styles of representation to create an abstract art, as Picasso had done, Fuller chose to sculpt in a realistic mode of representation closer to Rodin's work. Rather than mock mimetic art, as Giacometti's

Spoon Woman did, Fuller's life-size sculpture flaunts the beauty of an Ethiopian woman. The art world was not well prepared; in 1922, when *Awakening of Ethiopia* was shown at the "Making of America" exposition, it was evident that the label "Negro art," usually applied indiscriminately to African, Oceanic, and American art, had to be better specified.

In 1922, the American public was still trying to get used to European modernist art; only a few Americans would even have encountered African art when it had been exhibited in Stieglitz's New York gallery. The year 1922 was important for the history of black American art: that year the white patron William Elmer Harmon created a foundation to support black artists. Starting in 1928, the Harmon Foundation organized annual travel exhibits of the work of 150 black artists, and by 1933 these expressions of Negro art had been seen by 150,000 people.

A painting completed in 1932, *The Ascent of Ethiopia,* echoes the title of Fuller's sculpture (figure 2.4). In fact, Loïs Mailou Jones mentioned that her work had been inspired by *Awakening of Ethiopia* and that Fuller had encouraged her to grapple with the problem of representing the African legacy. But Jones's oil painting differs significantly from Fuller's bronze sculpture; while Fuller's sculpture is visually present in the painting, it has been transported into an urban setting; skyscrapers loom in the background. Whereas Fuller's sculpture refers only to its own form, this painting alludes to a long history; it illustrates a black ascent past pyramids into the Jazz Age. The painting depicts an easel, a theatrical scene, and a grand piano in order to symbolize black achievement. The well-formed face and impressive headdress of the figure on the lower right reminds us of a long legacy of dignity that has culminated in the artistic productions of the Harlem Renaissance.

While giving an impression of a monumental aesthetic that celebrates black cultures, past and present, the stylizations and collage-like composition also bear modernist features. Here, the visual tête-à-tête between the primitive and the modern manifests itself in terms of content and style, as Edmund Barry Gaither noticed. He asserts:

> She [Jones] has escaped being a mere illustrator of racial and cultural heritage. Rather, Jones has used her talent and rich experience to synthesize myriad influences encountered and digested over her lifetime. With cosmopolitan flair, she has woven American, African-American, Caribbean, African, and European formal and thematic strains into a visual language of deceptive directness and striking beauty.[33]

The Ascent of Ethiopia is, in other words, not only about the African cultural heritage; in its style of representation it reveals a European artistic influence.

The simultaneous exploration of African themes and formal experimentation with primitivist modernism is even more pronounced in Loïs Mailou Jones's painting *Les Fétiches* (1938) (figure 2.5). It represents a recognizably non-Western mask whose eyes and mouth are black ellipses of the same size; its nose is cubical. The mask is fierce; set against a gloomy background and surrounded by four other masks, it commands the eye. Painted in yellow,

Figure 2.4   Loïs Mailou Jones. *The Ascent of Ethiopia.* (1932). Courtesy of the Milwaukee Art Museum; Purchase, African-American Art Acquisition Fund with matching funds from Sue and Dick Pieper and additional support from Arthur and Dorothy Nelle Sanders.

ochre, and brown tones, with a red sculpture to its right and a brush-stroke of bright green on top, the mask assumes a gloomy, dismal magic. Its dark and saturated hues join in a swirling dance of colors.

Jones produced this image during her year (1937–1938) at the Académie Julian. This year was formative for her later career. Jones remembers, "When I arrived in Paris, African art was just the thing. All the galleries and museums were featuring African sculptures, African designs, and I sketched, sketched everything." When she showed the first sketches of *Les Fétiches* to the professors at the Académie Julian, she was criticized for abandoning still life painting for angular geometric composition. Jones also remembers how she responded to their critique of her art work: "I had to remind them of Modigliani and Picasso and all the French artists using the inspiration of Africa, and that

Figure 2.5   Loïs Mailou Jones. *Les Fétiches*. (1938). Courtesy of the National Museum of American Art, Smithsonian Institution; Museum purchase made possible by Mrs. N. H. Green, Dr. R. Harlan, and Francis Musgrave.

if anybody had the right to use it, I did. It was my heritage, so they had to give in."[34] This bold answer is interesting in several aspects. First, Jones reconfirms the widespread influence of African art that we discussed earlier, something Picasso apparently did not know of. Second, she tells us that the established art schools were reluctant to acknowledge an African-oriented art as art. Third, Jones's self-claimed entitlement to her African heritage convinced the French professors to let her finish the painting.

This meeting with Africa was a double encounter, with European primitivist modernism and African design; ironically, Jones discovered the legacy of her ancestors through her cultural other. Jones's reclamation of her legacy was mediated through European modernism. *Les Fétiches* flaunts the sources of influence for Jones's art and, simultaneously, parodies the *vogue nègre*. To clarify a statement made by art critic Jane Carpenter—that "in African masks and fetishes, she [Jones] had found powerful keys to infusing art with her an-

cestry's spirit and meaning"—we must add that Jones found those keys in
Paris, not Africa.[35]

Les Fétiches, a visual amalgam of African, European, and African American traditions, painted by a black artist, demonstrates the reappropriation of
European modernist primitivism. It is exactly this vision that was absent from
the MOMA exhibition "Primitivism in Twentieth Century Art." Even the critics of the MOMA show—Hal Foster, James Clifford, and Marianne Torgovnick
—who revealed Rubin's ethnocentric biases did not address this (flip) side of
primitivism in modern art. But it is in images such as these, images painted
by Negro artists, that the cultural dialectic underlying primitivist-modernism
manifests itself.

Of course, there were many Negro artists during the Harlem Renaissance
who depicted African motifs, but that in itself does not make them examples
of black primitivist modernism. Only those works by black artists who have
spent time in Europe fit this category. And even that criteria does not fully
suffice: Henry Ossawa Tanner, for example, lived in Paris most of his life,
but his works are premodern in style and their subject matter is mostly religious. Aaron Douglas's woodcuts or murals, for example, are replete with
visual references to Africa without revealing any formal influences from
Europe—or, if so, only those mediated through his mentor Winold Reiss.
One black artist who did manage to be both primitivist and modern was
William H. Johnson; his *Cafe* (1938) is an interesting example of the hybrid
style (figure 2.6).

The subject matter of *Cafe* is far removed from Africa; it presents a black
couple dressed in Western attire at a bistro. The man and woman are sitting
closely together at a round table on which we see two glasses, a bottle, and a
purse. The table is placed in a corner. The woman, who has thick lips and a
pointed nose, has her arm around her lover's shoulder; she looks at him
while he looks at us. His yellow hat matches the stripes on his brown suit,
while her purple hat is the same color as the two table legs, one of which she
is holding with her left hand. Their facial expressions are indeterminable, a
blend of boredom, devotion, and impatience. The bold colors, the clarity, and
the simplicity of this representation draw attention to the painting's subject
matter, as well as to its form.

The angular and flat forms suggest that *Cafe* is a cubist image, but its bold
colors and personal subject matter appear closer to an expressionist or social
realist aesthetic. If we were to apply Robert Goldwater's terminology, we
would consider this semi-abstract (but still representational) image an example of intellectual primitivism. Or, using William Rubin's distinctions, we
might consider it an example of an iconic mode of representation. Yet at the
same time, *Cafe* displays what Rubin called the narrative mode of representation: its geometric composition with its salient, saturated colors tells us
something about the couple while giving us few visual clues. *Cafe* seems
naive and simple, but its subject matter is ambiguous, and formally it is indeterminable—both cubist and figurative.

In 1930, Johnson was awarded the Gold Medal of the Harmon Foundation.

Figure 2.6   William H. Johnson. *Cafe.* (ca. 1939–1940). Courtesy of the National Museum of American Art, Smithsonian Institution; Gift of the Harmon Foundation.

The jurors, among whom were George Luks and Meta Warwick Fuller, justified their decision as follows: "We think he is one of our coming painters. He is a modernist. He has been spontaneous, vigorous, firm, direct; he has shown a great thing in art—it is the expression of the man himself."[36] The fact that Johnson is here acknowledged as "a modernist"—that Johnson was integrated into American art history—is surprising. One reason that he was recognized as such might have to do with the fact that his work was informed by European aesthetics.

Johnson had studied at the School of the National Academy of Design (1921–1926) under Charles Webster Hawthorne before moving to France for three years. By 1929, Johnson had developed a style that borrowed from realism and impressionism; he had expressed his admiration for the work of Van Gogh and Paul Cézanne. Johnson never tried to hide that his work was informed by an art tradition that was not "his own," but he was accused of "imitating white painters." An editorial that appeared in the *New York Amsterdam News* defended him by asserting that "Negro artists are no more imitative than other American artists. Can we name one eminent painter who is not saturated with European influence?"[37]

This rhetorical question has to be extended because many African American artists were also saturated with African influences. While this development was not mentioned in the editorial, Johnson himself commented on the impact African art had on him as an African American artist:

> Modern European art strives to be primitive, but it is too complicated. Now Modigliani believed he was "in Africa," but just look at his pictures: Raphael permeates them! All of the darker races are far more primitive—these are the people who are closer to the sun . . . [the sun] is closer to us dark people. . . .
>
> My aim is to express in a natural way what I feel, what is in me, both rhythmically and spiritually, all that which in time has been saved up in my family of primitiveness and tradition, and which is now concentrated in me.[38]

This self-proclaimed affinity to "people who are closer to the sun" and to the "family of primitiveness" is a veritable manifesto of black romanticism. It echoes Du Bois's messianic vision that the black race will be a complement to the cold Teutonic race. Moreover, it is a way to legitimize Johnson as a modernist superior to Modigliani. Johnson is better, so to speak, because he is "blacker"; as a black artist he is closer to the sun and has an innate "primitiveness."

Johnson advocated an essential difference between the races: "In reality colored folk are so different from the white race, Europe is so very superficial." Insinuating that blacks are less superficial because they have "primitiveness," Johnson expresses a cultural arrogance that is rather far-fetched considering that he lived in Europe for much of his life and was married to a Danish woman. When Johnson proclaimed his affinity to the Africans, he had not even visited the Dark Continent. It was only in 1932—a year after he first announced plans to go to Africa to find "the real me"—that he and his wife spent three months in Tunisia. It is likely that his essentialist claim to the African legacy was a strategic move to valorize his own cultural identity, a claim he would not have made had it not been for European primitivist modernism.

Despite his claim of affinity to African artists, Johnson had always been closer to European artists than to "people of the sun." In *Homecoming: The Art and Life of William H. Johnson,* the art historian Richard J. Powell argues that the sketches Johnson made from the 1935 MOMA catalog, *African Negro Art*, triggered a transition in his artistic development from landscape painting to figure painting. His sketch of an African sculpture, *Study of Bambara Figure*, led to experiments out of which "a new racial aesthetic" emerged (Powell). This immersion in figure paintings led Johnson to choose black Americans as the subject matter for his works *Street Life, Harlem*, and *Cafe*. Johnson's awakening desire to "paint his people" might have been motivated by a sense of racial solidarity or even by an innate sense of "primitiveness," but it also

Figure 2.7 Pablo Picasso. *The Frugal Repast.*
(1904). Courtesy of the Art Institute of Chicago,
Clarence Buckingham Collection.

was in agreement with the WPA's program. Johnson had taken on an assign-
ment with the WPA to teach art at the Harlem Community Center and was trying to comply with Alain Locke's demand: "We expect from the Negro artists a
vigorous and intimate documentation of Negro life itself."[39]

Cafe, then, is an amalgam of formal forces derived from Anglo-American
academicism (which originated in Europe), European modernism (including
its transformed African influences), African sculptures (mediated through
Sheeler's photographs in the MOMA catalog), social realism (propagated by
the WPA), and the appeal of the dean of Negro art, Alain Locke. Johnson fused
elements of European primitivist-modernism and transposed them onto an
African American urban scene; he created a black vernacular modernist style.

There is a further twist to this dynamic: if we agree with Powell that Johnson's couple in *Cafe* "resembles another famous male/female pairing in a bistro
scene from modern art: Picasso's 1904 etching, *The Frugal Repast*" (figure
2.7), we come to think of *Cafe* as signifying on Picasso. While not replicating
exactly the gaunt couple in Picasso's work, Johnson appropriates their ges-
tures, reverses them, and then transfers the scene. What *Cafe* reveals is not so
much the "rhythm and spirit" Johnson "has in him" but rather his thorough
knowledge of European art and his capacity to appropriate and signify on an

Figure 2.8   Robert Colescott *Les Demoiselles d'Alabama: Desnudas.* (1985). Courtesy of the Collection of the Greenville (S.C.) County Museum of Art; Museum purchase.

image Picasso made *prior* to his *period nègre.* Johnson reversed white modernist discourse and brought primitivist modernism home to Harlem. Johnson's use of Picasso mocks the accusation of primitivism as merely cultural imperialism; *Cafe* illustrates that cultural exchange goes both ways.

Among the more recent examples of this dialectic are Robert Colescott's *Les Demoiselles d'Alabama: Desnudas* (1985) and *Les Demoiselles d'Alabama: Vestidas* (1985). As the title indicates, these two images parody Picasso's famous primitivist modernist painting. But the title highlights the multinational identity of Picasso's work—the terms "Desnudas" and "Vestidas" refer to the Spanish and "Les Demoiselles" to the French influences—the reference to "Alabama" adds a third aspect to this hybrid.

Les Demoiselles d'Alabama: Desnudas (figure 2.8) represents five female figures positioned in exactly the same way as Picasso's figures. Colescott's canvas is the same size (96" by 92") as Picasso's canvas, but it is even more colorful than the original. The distinctive features of *Les Demoiselles d'Avignon,* its angularity, its two-dimensionality, and its flatness, are replaced by softer, rounded body forms. While the gender of the right-hand figures in *Les Demoiselles d'Avignon* is ambiguous, *Les Demoiselles d'Alabama* leaves no doubt.

The women's lascivious postures and gazes call to mind the first version of *Les Demoiselles d'Avignon*. Appropriately, the images are painted in a manner closer to the narrative, rather than the iconic, mode of representation, to use Rubin's terminology. But what exactly the image tells us remains unclear; it is devoid of obvious symbols such as Picasso's book and skull.

If we focus on the two right-hand figures, the visual differences between Colescott's remake and the original become more evident. In the case of the lower figure, an obscure "blackness" is replaced by a blond vamp. In the case of the upper figure, the scarification, the *quart-de-brie* nose, and the masklike qualities are transformed, reemerging as a brunette with dark skin and thick lips. The image has lost its gloomy qualities and taken on campy features that call to mind the mocking playfulness and gaudiness of pop art.

The visual presence of Africa, which had been so instrumental for Picasso in reinventing his artistic self, is symbolically abolished and replaced by a popularized and feminized "blackness." The sassy appearance of these figures is reinforced by their striking gazes. In fact, the two right-hand figures now stare at us. They face the spectator in a suggestive and provocative manner, soliciting our attention. In contrast to the figures in *Les Demoiselles d'Avignon*, these are neither shocking nor frightening; they are amusing, if not embarrassing.

The figure on the far left appears to be an observer of the scene. She is white, with sensuous body features. The contours of her feet are refined and closer to ideals of the female anatomy than Picasso's distorted original. The clarity of the foot is a gesture signifying on the distorted, out-of-focus foot that Picasso painted. This was a conscious effort by Colescott. His comment about the making of *Les Demoiselles d'Alabama* is revealing (it is hard to say whether the pun on "foot" is intentional):

> *Les Demoiselles d'Avignon* is about sources and ends. Picasso started with European art, producing "Africanism" but keeping one foot in European art. I began with Picasso's Africanism and moved toward European art, keeping one foot in Africanism. So the faces and bodies are derived from it. The irony is partly that what most people (including me) know about African conventions comes from Cubist art. Could a knowledge of European art be so derived as well?[40]

Colescott, I think, is suggesting that artists of African descent like him can learn a lesson from a culturally hybrid art such as cubism: they can take European primitivist modernist art as their source of inspiration and put it to their own ends.

Lowery S. Sims responded to Colescott's provocative question by stating, "In other words, Colescott asks, as an African-American, just who the primitive is." Echoing Locke, Sims comments on the discrepancy between the fact that non-Western art has served as a source of inspiration for Western art while non-Western artists "have remained 'undeveloped.'" Colescott intervenes in this process of one-way appropriation. Without mentioning other African American artists who have also signified on white artists, Sims writes:

Colescott retaliates by turning the tables on the appropriation model and re-infusing "ethnicity" into the "classical"—i.e. "Western"—matrix. But far from lapsing into nostalgic "nativism," he keeps the dialog about non-white participation in the contemporary art scene totally within a modernist (or, more precisely, post-modernist) context, and he does it so skillfully that the viability of this approach is immediately apparent. . . . As Colescott continues to champion the left-out parts of history and culture, he forces us to recognize, in spite of our petty tribalism, the greater and more profound truths that have persisted through the millennia and which will prevail despite momentary factionalisms indulged in by the human race. (Sims and Kahan, 9)

Colescott brings to our attention the deep and ironic truth about the history of primitivist modernism. He puts into practice what Alain Locke called for six decades ago. Colescott illustrates and confirms a point that Stuart Hall was to make in his seminal essay, "What Is 'Black' in Black Popular Culture?" In 1992, he wrote: "The rupture of primitivism, managed by modernism, becomes another postmodern event."[41] White primitivist modernism, unaware of the symbolic import the "dusty manikins" would have throughout the twentieth century, planted the seed of black postmodernism.

WHITEMAN'S JAZZ

Some may start with an enthusiasm for music of the jazz type, but they cannot go far there, for jazz is peculiarly of an inbred, feeble-stock race, incapable of development. In any case, the people for whom it is meant could not understand it if it did develop. Jazz is sterile. It is all right for fun, or as a mild anodyne, like tobacco. But its lack of rhythmical variety (necessitated by its special purpose), its brevity, its repetitiveness and lack of sustained development, together with the fact that commercial reasons prevent its being, as a rule, very well written, all mark it as a side issue, having next to nothing to do with serious music; and consequently it has proven itself entirely useless as a basis for developing the taste of the amateur.[1]

—War Department Education Manual (1944)

During the 1920s, jazz emerged out of the creative fusion of African and European musical forms. Borrowing from French quadrilles and marches, Protestant hymns, British ballads, West African rhythms, and African American spirituals—and, of course, the blues and ragtime—black musicians created an unconventional, hybrid form. By the time African sculptures and masks exerted their fermenting effect on Europe art, African music had long played an important role in America, at least in black America. We need to remember, however, that the conditions that the two art forms operated in were markedly different: African music arrived in this country on slave ships.

While European colonizers of Africa principally imported African resources and cultural artifacts to Europe, Americans appropriated African labor. Not only deprived of their belongings and families, the slaves were also deprived of their bodies. The peculiar aspect of the dissemination of African music in the West—as compared to that of African sculptures—was the fact that it was inextricable from the physical bodies of the African slaves. The black body was the vessel for the polyphony and polyrhythms of African

59

music and dance. Music and singing became a tactic for survival, a vent for frustration, and a reclamation of the body. Black musicians, who had to toil from day to night, used music as a means of communication and consolation. In America, as it had in Africa, the primitive manifested itself in the songs and dances of everyday life. This is a different course from what transpired in Europe, where, we remember, African art had to be exhibited in ethnography museums before European artists stumbled across the fetishes.

It is not surprising, therefore, that "the African element" essential to the birth of modernism in European art had a different (and problematic) status in the history of American modernism. An obvious sign of this uncertain position is that while it required only decades for European artists and art institutions to acknowledge art from Africa, it took several centuries for Anglo-American musicians and music critics to accept music influenced by African forms.

Among those American jazz critics who have acknowledged the complexity and artistry of African music is Gunther Schuller, a composer, conductor, and music critic. In his book, *Early Jazz; Its Roots and Development* (1968), he writes:

> There is a widespread misconception—in itself based on the false notion of African music as "primitive" (ergo, non-intellectual)—that early jazz could not have derived from African backgrounds, and therefore must have developed in the more "enlightened" environment of European civilization. . . . African music—whether in large formal designs or small structural units within these designs—is replete with highly civilized concepts. . . . To be sure, these forms are not abstract artistic forms in the European sense, nor are they intellectually conceived. They are irrevocably linked to everyday work and play functions.[2]

We saw an official example of this misconception in the quotation that opened this chapter, a statement published by the U.S. War Department dismissing jazz as a repetitive music lacking development and "having next to nothing to do with serious music." Those who did "mistake" jazz for an intellectual art form, Schuller implies, assumed it to be primarily a European one.

Schuller, however, disagrees with the attitude that associates jazz with the European tradition; he explains that the African element in jazz manifested itself in three ways: "(1) the so-called call-and-response pattern, (2) the repeated refrain concept, and (3) the chorus format of most recreational and cult dances" (Schuller, 27). While it is common critical knowledge that syncopation—the accentuation of weak notes and rhythmic displacement—is African, Schuller argues that jazz is actually a simplified version of more complex African musical structures. He argues that African and European music differ fundamentally, since European harmony is unknown in African music, and that the melodic repertoire of African music is primarily pentatonic as opposed to the diatonic structure of European music.

This difference did not prevent African slaves in America and around New Orleans particularly from incorporating European diatonic harmonic patterns into their music. "Acculturation took place," Schuller concludes, "but only to the limited extent that the Negro allowed European elements to be integrated into his African heritage" (Schuller, 62). Schuller obviously disagrees with the common dichotomy that jazz's complex rhythmic elements came from African traditions while its melodic and harmonic structures derived exclusively from European traditions. Schuller stresses the agency of black musicians, arguing that they chose to integrate extracultural forms while conserving their African heritage.

This fusion of African with European musical elements led to entirely new forms. The spirituals and blues, for example, are, according to Schuller, combinations of influences from German marching bands, Anglo-American hymns, and Afro-American funeral processions. Ragtime, on the other hand, came from the absorption of polkas, quadrilles, and jigs. Schuller suggests that jazz is not merely an inevitable cultural hybrid but rather the outcome of a conscious selective process. Black American musicians deliberately chose to reject overly intellectual music in favor of a music that was part of people's lives. Schuller writes:

> African native music and early American jazz both originate in a total vision of life, in which music, unlike the "art music" of Europe, is not a separate, autonomous social domain. African music even today, like its sister arts—sculpture, mural drawing, and so forth—is conditioned by the same stimuli that animate not only African philosophy and religion, but the entire social structure. . . . It is not surprising that the word "art" does not exist in African languages. Nor does the African divide art into separate categories. (Schuller, 4)

Although it seems doubtful that none of the African languages has an equivalent term for "art," Schuller's remark about the social embeddedness of art and music reminds us of Picasso's assertion that African sculptures and masks are intercessors that mediate between people's lives and the unknown. In other words, the affinity between African music and American jazz manifests itself not only in formal parallels but also in their social function. Jazz and the blues were a means for expressing emotions; they served as "weapons."

Through assimilation, a distinctly new musical form emerged. Jazz was profane, not sacred; it was urban, not rural. While the blues had strong ties to church songs and folk expressions, early jazz musicians played in bars and music clubs and improved their technique in record-cutting sessions. Jazz was a music increasingly based on improvisation, professionalism, and commercialism. By 1923, Schuller writes, musicians such as Jelly Roll Morton, Louis Armstrong, and King Oliver had started to record, and jazz became a popular entertainment commodity.

Are these early, black jazz musicians, then, in some way equivalent to the European primitivist artists? Both art forms were the result of intercultural exchange, and structurally there are striking parallels between European primitivist modernism and jazz. But there are important differences. The African idiom, as manifested in the European visual arts, was integrated and eventually effaced. Over time, the early African-inspired works were codified as masterpieces of modernism while their African sources became increasingly remote. The African idiom in jazz, however, remained visibly black but was not considered art. Most current critics of modernism would object to including jazz in the pantheon of modern art; its reputation in the 1920s was even worse. Few people praised jazz as an expression of modern art, and most resisted it vehemently.

Among the disdainful commentary was a curious article that reports a study on the origins and impact of jazz by "ethnologist" Walter Kingsley and Professor William Morrison Patterson of Columbia University. The essay, "Why 'Jazz' Sends Us Back to the Jungle. A Broadway Ethnologist Tells the Savage Origin of This 'Delirium Tremens of Syncopation',", was published in 1918 in *Current Opinion*. The writer quotes from Mr. Kingsley's "scientific" investigation:

> The word [jazz] is African in origin. . . . No doubt the witch doctors and medicine men on the Congo used the same term [jazz] at those jungle "parties" when the tom-toms throbbed and the sturdy warriors gave their pep and added kick with rich brews of Yohimbin bark. . . . "Jazz" music is said to be an attempt to reproduce the marvelous syncopation of the African jungle . . . its savage gift for progressive retardation and acceleration, guided by the sense of swing, reawakened in the most sophisticated audience instincts that are deep-seated in most of us.[3]

The statement is rather convoluted, but its course seems to be as follows: Jazz originated in an uncivilized country where it was played at "jungle parties." African men, "sturdy warriors," enjoyed listening to jungle music and drinking dark beer because it was stimulating. This stimulating effect—jazz's savage spirit—can revivify sophisticated modern listeners. The modern remake of "the marvelous syncopation of the African jungle" appeals primarily to the instincts; it could unleash "deep-seated" desires. It must remain dormant lest the sophisticated listener go back to the jungle, so to speak.

Kingsley was not the only scientist of his time who associated jazz with barbarism and savagery. Another professor proposed that jazz "is turning modern men, women and children back to the stages of barbarism," and yet another stated that "jazz is a relic of barbarism. It tends to unseat reason and set passion free."[4] The potential for jazz to "unseat reason" by setting sensuality free, along with its allegedly lascivious side effects, alarmed conservative Americans. Convinced that jazz represented a threat to the old social and moral order, traditionalists tried to keep jazz in its place and to impede its dissemination. Typically, their defamation of jazz began with a reference to its African or African American origins.

Anne Shaw Faulkner, for example, claimed that jazz is the "natural expression of the American Negroes and was used by them as the accompaniment for their bizarre dances and cakewalks." These dances were more than bizarre to Faulkner—they were sinful. In her article, "Does Jazz Put the Sin in Syncopation?," published in *Ladies' Home Journal,* Faulkner informs the reader of jazz's origins and detrimental effects:

> Jazz originally was the accompaniment of the voodoo dancer, stimulating the half-crazed barbarian to the vilest deeds. The weird chant, accompanied by

the syncopated rhythm the voodoo invokes, has also been employed by other barbaric people to stimulate brutality and sensuality. That it has a demoralizing effect upon the human brain has been demonstrated by many scientists.[5]

This passionate statement stigmatizes the music for the same reason that Kingsley objected to it: jazz was invented by the "half-crazed barbarian" and has the potential to "stimulate brutality and sensuality." Again, the fear is that the cultural other might draw out one's own other from within. But Faulkner paints an even more dramatic image by also suggesting that "the effect of jazz on the normal brain produces an atrophied condition on the brain cells of conception." This produces an inability to distinguish between good and evil. Jazz, Faulkner argues, is morally and physiologically detrimental.

Faulkner announces that "jazz disorganizes all regular laws and order; it stimulates to extreme deeds, to a breaking away from all rules and conventions; it is harmful and dangerous, and its influence is wholly bad." To avert this apocalypse, Faulkner calls for clergymen and physicians to join in a crusade against this symptom of "degeneracy." This line of argument was followed also by a commentator called William Earhard, who charged that jazz "represents, in its convulsive, twitching, hiccoughing rhythms, the abdication of control by the nervous system—the brain."[6] He promised that an overdose of jazz will cause an abdication of reason, destroy the individual's moral capability, and lead to deviance and chaos.

It is difficult to understand such overreaction, but these were certainly not the only extreme opponents to jazz. In an article published in *Ladies' Home Journal* in 1921, "Back to Pre-War Morals," John R. McMahon dismissed jazz on more "aesthetic" grounds as "a droning, jerky incoherence interrupted with the spasmodic 'blah, blah.'"[7] As the title of his article suggests, McMahon urges the American people to drop their new fad. "Unspeakable Jazz Must Go!," another article by McMahon, comments on the newly adopted motto of the National Dancing Masters' Association: "Don't permit vulgar, cheap jazz music to be played . . . jazz must go and leave room for clean, wholesome dancing" (Faulkner, 16).

While the Dancing Masters' Association had the power to prohibit jazz-inflected dancing in their schools and ballrooms, it was much more difficult to discourage the general public. The only realistic strategy was to demonize and criminalize syncopated music, as McMahon did in another *Ladies' Home Journal* article, "The Jazz Path of Degradation." Here, McMahon warns his readers that "jazz is lewd to the physiological limit. In many cases it leads to worse things; and in others it cannot lead to worse things—being a sufficient evil end in itself. Take alcohol. Some get drunk and others add murder to drunkenness. Those who only jazz but thoroughly and habitually, are sex troopers."[8] Distorted equations such as this are symptomatic of the surprisingly overheated and irrational debate. The anti-jazz movement made jazz—the "insidious sensuous poison," to use another McMahon phrase—into the 1920s symbol of evil.

In January 1924, an editorial in *Etude* observed that "respectable Americans are so disgusted that they turn with dismay at the mere mention of 'Jazz,' which they naturally blame for the whole fearful caravan of vice and near-vice."[9] As the number of self-acclaimed "respectable Americans" nauseated by the mention of jazz increased, they grew increasingly impatient; many became anti-jazz activists themselves. In 1923, as the headline of the *Musical Courier* reads, "Representatives of 2,000,000 Women Meet to Annihilate 'Jazz.'"[10] While this number seems exaggerated, we can not just dismiss the headline. In fact, as extremist and ludicrous as this movement seems, it had a powerful presence in the media, and the issue was discussed even in the most respectable newspapers.

Private citizens organized to make demands: a Mr. Guyon, for example, enjoined the government to "Abolish jazz music!," and a Mr. Bott "appealed to the music publishers to eliminate jazz music."[11] Both gentlemen created an association that enlisted the aid of the U.S. Health Service to stop "salacious dancing." Charts and booklets that showed "the correct positions and steps for the various approved dances" were distributed to high schools and public dance halls.

The U.S. Health Service was not the only federal institution that supported the jazz objectors; local politicians got in on the act too. In 1921 the mayor of Philadelphia appointed a policewoman to supervise the public dance halls. The ironically named Miss Walz, who supervised about seventy-five policemen in conducting the city's anti-jazz campaign, reported significant progress by the end of the first year: "There has been a marked improvement since this work began. The police class in censorship is told not to permit cheek to cheek dancing, abdominal contact, shimmy, toddle or the Washington Johnny, in which the legs are kept apart." In Philadelphia at least, censorship in the pursuit of jazz was fully acceptable.

Why was there such a strong resistance to syncopated music? Compared to contemporary black music such as rap, the early jazz tunes seem like lullabies. But at the time, people believed that jazz was the forerunner of the decline of Western civilization. The anti-jazz crusade was motivated by an apocalyptic fear. The anxiety that jazz was "endangering our civilization," as the populist William Jennings Bryant put it in the *New York Times* in May 1926, was the subtext to many of the negative voices. People felt, in other words, that the dawn of the Jazz Age heralded the decline of Western civilization. An assessment in the *New York Times* pronounced: "The consensus of opinion of leading medical and other scientific authorities, [is that jazz] is harmful and degrading to civilized races as it always has been among savages from whom we borrowed it."[12] Does this mean that the "civilized races" were able to colonize Africa because the "savages" were weakened by listening to degenerate music? Does it mean that by listening to jazz the "civilized races" might suffer a similar fate? Is it a manifestation of guilt, however slight, for enslaving the savages and perhaps even a suggestion that the now jazz-loving "civilized" race deserves to crumble itself?

This bizarre episode of American cultural history indicates the problems that many cross-cultural artifacts had in this country. Jazz was the proverbial tragic mulatto. Although we don't have exact numbers, it is safe to argue that around 1923, when jazz first emerged for the general public as a new music form, it was associated with the jungle and with brothels but hardly ever with serious music, much less counted among the ranks of modernist art. According to jazz critic James Lincoln Collier, "a substantial portion of the middle class did not like jazz—was indeed threatened by it—probably the majority tolerated it, and a large minority was excited by it."[13]

Now we turn to five critics who have given the opposition to jazz more serious attention: Morroe Berger, Neil Leonard, Alan P. Merriam, James Lincoln Collier, and Kathy J. Ogren. Berger's article, "Jazz: Resistance to the Diffusion of a Culture Pattern," published in *Journal of Negro History* in 1947, was the first such scholarly account.[14] His argument that many whites (and some blacks) denounced the music because it was played by members of a "low status group" stresses the issue of class over that of race or sex.

In *Jazz and the White Americans* (1962) Leonard draws a useful distinction between jazz opponents, whom he calls "traditionalists" because they upheld traditional values, and pro-jazz "modernists."[15] Glimpsing in jazz a joyful emotion, modernists discovered in it a conduit through which to leave artificial restraints behind. The modernists did not fear going back to the jungle since they yearned to end emotional repression. Moreover, they wanted to rebel against the traditionalists. To the question of why the pro-jazz camp, initially a minority, ultimately triumphed, Leonard provides two answers: First, he argues that it had to do with the breakdown of traditional values in the 1920s. Second, the emergence of a moderate version of jazz played by white musicians appealed to a broader public. As we will see, Paul Whiteman was crucial to this process because he fused European musical elements with jazz rhythms and created a gentle and hugely popular fusion, symphonic jazz.

Alan P. Merriam discusses the hostility to jazz in his book, *The Anthropology of Music* (1964), distinguishing among those who made jazz into an anti-Christian symbol; those who associated it with "crime, insanity, feeblemindedness"; those who made it a symbol of physical collapse; and, last but not least, those who regarded it as a "symbol of barbarism, primitivism, savagery, and animalism."[16] Merriam's typology is based on quotations taken form the popular press at the time, such as the following from the *New York Times*: "Jazz was borrowed from Central Africa by a gang of wealthy international Bolshevists from America, their aim being to strike at Christian civilization throughout the world."[17] This particular example combines an animosity to anti-Christian, communist, and African forces. Overall, Merriam's typology shows on what grounds the traditionalists rejected jazz.

In *The Reception of Jazz in America: A New View* James Lincoln Collier relates Anglo-Americans' increasing appreciation of jazz primarily to changes within the genre. Collier quotes the *New York Times Book Review and Magazine* pronouncement in 1921 that "jungle music is undergoing a refining process under the fingers of sophisticated art."[18] Collier suggests that this statement about the emergence of increasingly refined jazz rhythms was prophetic of a movement that culminated in Paul Whiteman's famous 1924 concert featuring symphonic jazz. As a result of this change, jazz became dissociated from its African roots. When it lost its "jungle" quality, the public was willing to accept it.

Jazz, though in its bleached version, soon became the national tune. After quoting another early jazz commentator, who stated in 1927 that "the ear-wracking hot jazz [that had] dominated the field for several years" was finally driven out, Collier concludes, "These comments are typical of dozens of others about the turn jazz had taken" (James Lincoln Collier, 17). But Collier does not expound on this musical turn. He simply states that once symphonic music had replaced hot—that is, black—jazz, the refined version gained acceptance by the Anglo-American mainstream.

One year after Collier's book was published, Kathy J. Ogren addressed the jazz controversy in her book *The Jazz Revolution* (1989). Like Collier, she refers to Paul Whiteman because he stylized and formalized jazz. Jazz became serious music when Whiteman turned to a symphonic—that is, European—style, which Ogren calls "sanitized jazz." Traditionalists could no longer stigmatize jazz as barbaric. The trade-off, however, was that once jazz became popular, it was dissociated from the African American tradition. Ogren states that "Whiteman's popular music became so closely identified with jazz that many Americans had no knowledge of its Afro-American origins."[19] This is a remarkable change from the racist statements that related jazz to voodoo and the Congo.

Ogren makes an important point when she suggests that jazz has to be discussed in the context of the cultural milieu of the 1920s and specifically in regard to the decade's vogue for primitivism. Ogren's thesis, that the jazz debate "provided a symbol for the transition to new values. The disaffected flocked to jazz clubs for a first-hand immersion in the primitive," presumes that jazz fans searched for hot rhythms and not "sanitized jazz" (Ogren, 146). Many white Americans were less than captivated by symphonic jazz. What made jazz popular was, Ogren argues, the belief that "primitivistic jazz could liberate overcivilized whites" and could "rejuvenate buried emotions or instincts, thus liberating an inner, and perhaps more creative, person."

Ogren does not mention how many whites became primitivistic jazz lovers, nor does she reconcile the apparent chasm between whitened or "sanitized jazz," as she calls it, and symbolically blackened "primitivistic jazz." Instead, Ogren relates the romantic idea—that blacks, and their cultural expressions, are more natural, emotional, spontaneous, and joyful—to the "twenties vogue of primitivism [that] began primarily among those young intellectuals exposed to modern artists like Picasso" (Ogren, 146). Those young intellectuals, Ogren tells us, included Gertrude Stein, Vachel Lindsay, e. e. cummings, Waldo Frank, Sherwood Anderson, and Carl Van Vechten.

Ogren's thesis, that Picasso's primitivism and Lindsay's primitivism were part of the same movement that popularized jazz, is germane to the thesis of this book. Had primitivist modernism budded a second blossom, this time in American popular culture? As tempting as it is to agree with Ogren and argue that we have in jazz another manifestation of the juncture of the primitive and the modern, it is more complicated than that. The myth that blacks will revivify the weary souls of white folks and the subsequent fascination with "the tune of 'Boomlay, boomlay, BOOM,'" to quote Lindsay, is utterly different from Picasso's formalistic incorporation of African-derived idioms. As I suggested in the first chapter, it is important to distinguish between exoticism and primitivist modernism. Although it is true that the pro-jazz fraction—whom Ogren calls "primitives" and Leonard calls "modernists"—rebelled against the "prudes" or "traditionalists," it is wrong to conclude that all jazz lovers were primitivist modernists. Most of them were merely slumming in the exotic.

To be considered an expression of modernism, jazz would have to be acknowledged as a form of art. But in the early 1920s, when jazz came of age, those who despised jazz certainly did not think of it as a modern art form; those who enjoyed jazz did so because it was exciting or "rejuvenating," as Ogren puts it. Ironically, the modernists (or those people Leonard refers to as such) did not think that jazz was art, much less an expression of modernism. As an exotic music, jazz had never even been considered a particularly American expression. LeRoi Jones observed that "Afro-American music did not become a completely American expression until the white man could play it."[20]

The "white man" who was the most important figure in making jazz a respectable and popular art form was the fortuitously named Paul Whiteman, already a famous dance-band maestro when he embarked on his mission to rehabilitate jazz. The mission, as he put it, was to "remove the stigma of barbaric strains and jungle cacophony from 'jazz.'"[21] His intention—to tame the jungle out of the music—led him to fuse jazz with classical forms. Although he reiterated the traditionalists' trope of jazz's barbarism, Whiteman himself welcomed jazz's vitality and tried to capture it in his arrangements. His own claim is telling: "Through it [jazz], we get back to a simple, to a savage, if you like, joy in being alive. While we are dancing, or singing or even listening to jazz, all the artificial restraints are gone. We are rhythmic, we are emotional, we are natural. We're really living to a pitch that becomes an intoxication."[22] Attempting to preserve this vitality while at the same time refining jazz's alleged vulgarity, Whiteman created the synthesis widely referred to as "symphonic jazz."

This blend debuted on February 12, 1924, at New York's Aeolian Hall as the "First American Jazz Concert." Advertised as an "Experiment in Modern Music," it drew a wide crowd to a venue usually consecrated to classical music—in a sense, Whiteman had triumphed simply by securing the hall. Featuring a blend of European symphonic music and "jungle-music," the band comprised saxophones, muted brasses, and percussion. The highlight of the evening was George Gershwin's new composition, "Rhapsody in Blue," undoubtedly the most famous piece of symphonic jazz. But the repertoire also included "Livery Stable Blues" and a composition by a British composer, Edward Elgar, called "Pomp and Circumstance."

The opening night was a success. Most reviews were sympathetic. Whiteman was able to convince the audience of what he had set out to demonstrate: that modern jazz was "different from its crude origins—that it had taken a turn for the better."[23] Whiteman's version of jazz, a synthesis that stressed European elements, enchanted critics, who lauded Whiteman for making jazz an art form. But it also appealed to the wider public, the majority of Anglo-Americans who might have agreed with the humorist George Ade's stamp of approval: "If the Paul Whiteman boys play 'jazz,' then I am in favor of that particular variety of 'jazz.'"[24]

Variety magazine noted that Whiteman "changed the entire system of jazz dance music from the blatant blare and roar to soft, symphonic harmony."[25] Most critics cherished its newly acclaimed sophistication, and the statement of a *Vanity Fair* commentator, who praised George Gershwin for having "exalt[ed] the idiom of Jazz into notable concert music," is indicative of the majority of reviews that interrelated notability and nobility.[26] A critic in the *Tribune* wrote that "Mr. Whiteman's experience was an uproarious success. This music conspicuously possesses superb vitality and ingenuity of rhythm, mastery of novel and beautiful effects of timbre" (Stearns, 112).

The reviews of the Aeolian Hall concert so enthusiastically praised the de-Africanized, harmonious European style that many other white jazz bands followed the trend. The big bands Whiteman himself had trained (approximately twenty bands in New York) were soon followed by many other imitators. "From the standpoint of popular music," argues Arnold Shaw, the director of the Popular Music Research Center at the University of Nevada, "no event of the 1920s, except for the introduction of the talkies, approaches in historical importance and musical significance 'The Experiment in Modern Music' presented by Paul Whiteman on February 12, 1924."[27]

Whiteman's new product, "sweet jazz" or "symphonic jazz," proved very lucrative in spite of financial losses at the concert itself. Whiteman's salary rose dramatically after 1924. In 1926, when his band played at the San Francisco Automobile Show, Whiteman received more than $3,000 a day. Rumor has it that he was paid as much as $10,000 for a single concert.[28] He eventually controlled twenty-eight bands, and his records sold millions of copies.

There is little disagreement among music critics that the Aeolian Hall concert was a revolutionary moment in American music history. Nobody has expressed the degree of Whiteman's newly acquired popularity better than Thomas A. DeLong in his *Pops: Paul Whiteman, King of Jazz*:

> Certainly by 1924 Whiteman's group was listened to and sought after more than any other musical organization in the United States.
>   Whiteman stood out as a music maker of gigantic proportions. He built an incredibly large and successful aggregation, which shaped the Jazz Age. He embraced virtually every facet of show business. A pioneer and an innovator, Paul Whiteman moved in the right direction at crucial moments in the rise and development of this century's forms of mass entertainment. His influenced was felt in recording studios, over radio, in theaters and concert halls, on movie sound stages, and on television screens.[29]

Whiteman's impact on popular music and mass entertainment was enormous; if DeLong is right that "Whiteman became the public symbol of jazz" (DeLong, 67), we might compare his impact on American music to Pablo Picasso's on modern European art. By 1924 Picasso was certainly acknowledged as a shaper of modernist art and is thus a potential counterpart to Whiteman, widely acclaimed as the "King of Jazz." Both artists owed a substantial part of their success to the modification of an African art form. Both managed to codify what had been dismissed as jungle forms, and both won considerable fame and fortune.

There are important analogies between Picasso's primitivist appropriation and Whiteman's fusion. In both cases, "the modern" emerged out of a synthesis of European and black traditions. Like Picasso, Whiteman realized the potential of black cultural expression, appropriated it, and modified it to achieve a formal breakthrough. In both cases, "Negro art" had a fermenting effect on other white artists and musicians. The process of primitivist acculturation and diffusion is, for both artists, based on three steps: discovery, appropriation, and modification.

Despite the fact that Whiteman called his concert "Experiments in Modern Music" and claimed to have created an expression of American modernism, Whiteman's primitivist modernism differs significantly from Picasso's; in many ways, they are the mirror image of each other. Whiteman felt that the best way to "rehabilitate" jazz was to "civilize" it. Turning down the African rhythms, he amplified the harmonies. This emphasis on the European tampered with the racial mix of jazz; attempting to undo its original hybridity, he created what we might think of as "whitened" jazz. Whiteman's version of interculturalism differed significantly from Picasso's encounter with *art nègre,* which amounted to a "darkening" of Picasso's canvas. The enigmatic "savage" character of those dusty masks enchanted Picasso; he attempted to capture the "crudeness" he found. Picasso's borrowings helped him to attain greater visual intensity and expressivity. In fact, he and the European avant-garde were weary of refinement and yearned for intensity. Since their appropriation of black art was motivated by the desire to attack bourgeois social mores and aesthetic values, they used colonized art as a weapon to instigate a formal iconoclasm.

While their motives were mostly formalistic, not political, Patricia Leighten argues in her article "The White Peril and *L'Art Nègre*: Picasso, Primitivism, and Anticolonialism" that the circles around Picasso were anticolonialist. Leighten implies, though, that this attitude was not so much motivated by a sense of solidarity with the colonized as it was by a rejection of the colonizers —the generation of their fathers, the bourgeois brokers of culture.[30] Indeed, Picasso turned to *art nègre* because he was "against everything," as he put it. His interest in "crude," "barbaric," and "primitive" expressions was motivated by his desire to strike a visual assault against cultural and artistic conventions.

Whiteman, however, created a smoother, more polite, harmonic style that pleased even some of the anti-jazz "traditionalists." His "sweet" or "symphonic" version was basically an aesthetic of appeasement. The difference between Europe's appropriation of African art and Anglo-America's appropriation of African American jazz is, in other words, that the European avant-garde used Africa as a conduit through which to critique its own bourgeoisie, whereas Whiteman modified an Africanized avant-garde form in a way that appealed to the bourgeoisie.

Curiously, Whiteman, who equated "refining" jazz with Europeanizing it, also thought of this process as "feminizing" jazz. In his autobiography, he asserts that he wanted to "make a lady of jazz." Whiteman was not the only one to conflate race and gender as metaphors for jazz. Walter Damrosch, the conductor of the New York Symphony Orchestra, announced in 1925 that:

> Lady Jazz . . . for all her travels and her sweeping popularity . . . has encountered no knight who could lift her to a level that would enable her to be received as a respectable member in musical circles. George Gershwin seems to have accomplished this miracle. He . . . has taken her by the hand and openly proclaimed her a princess to the astonished world.[31]

Underlying this statement is the assumption that unrefined jazz is "low" and ladylike, while whitened jazz is "high." Therefore, it takes a knight, a white male, to accompany her on the passage from lady to princess. The knight, then, magically transforms the lady into a princess. If Gershwin is the knight or the prince and Whiteman the king, then is jazz a princess from the jungle, the figure that Josephine Baker embodied?

As we have seen, this intersection of blackness and the female is a recurring theme in the discourse of primitivism. We encountered it in *Les Demoiselles*. That image, however, functioned in a very different way because Picasso used African forms to primitize his art. The right-hand figures of his painting are neither princesses nor ladies; they are more like Amazons. Nor are there knights or princes present since the medical student and the sailor—in fact, all the male figures—were exorcised in the final version of the painting.

Unlike Picasso, however, Whiteman never pretended that he did not know the black origins of his art. To the contrary, he expressed this clearly as early as 1926: "Jazz came in chains to America about three hundred years ago."[32] The history of the African's captivity and deprivation motivated him, he confesses, to give jazz the "respect" it deserved. In fact, Paul Whiteman's strategy of "musical uplift" elevated jazz to the realm of high art, which not only made it popular at home but also helped to attract artistic attention abroad. It is true, though, that in that respect, Whiteman suborned the black presence in jazz to a larger mission, the creation of a truly American music. Two months before Whiteman toured Europe to export symphonic jazz, he published an article in *Vanity Fair* entitled "The Progress of Jazz: Problems Which Confront the American Composer in His Search for a Musical Medium."

In this article Whiteman does not mention the words black, Negro, or African at all. He writes:

> In this country, we have been accustomed to following the dictates of Europe in music for so many years that we have begun only recently to think

and experiment in a modest way for ourselves. . . . [Now] we have independent ideas of strictly American origin, in these various professions and sciences—ideas that are to be held valuable abroad. And this is true of music, too, for our jazz has spread—the only item in American musical composition which has even attracted the slightest attention in Europe. The reason for this is simple enough—it is the only *original* idea we have produced. Europe had no interest in what was merely imitation of its own achievements (and usually poor imitation, at that). Jazz, an original invention, was sponsored immediately.[33]

This passage reads like a manifesto of denial; jazz, formerly "in chains," is now an "American musical composition." In fact, it is America's most "original invention." When Whiteman states that "it is the only *original* idea we have produced" his use of the collective "we" eclipses the African American contribution. Whiteman's statement reveals a desire to rehabilitate the image of Anglo-American culture in Europe by suppressing the contributions of blacks.

Whiteman's attitude was understandable. Downplaying the black element was a prerequisite for jazz's diffusion in America. For jazz to be integrated and absorbed into the mainstream, jazz had to be deracialized. This was best expressed by *Current Opinion* in September 1924 in an article entitled "Jazz Comes to Stay," which asserted that jazz's triumph in America was related to jazz's passing as Anglo-American: "Jazz music—an American contribution to the arts, is as thoroughly and typically American as the Monroe Doctrine, the Fourth of July or baseball."[34] Jazz, however, only shaped America's national identity when it lost its primitive and black aspects. The quantity of Whiteman's favorable reviews reveals the success of his program.

Henry O. Osgood, for example, claimed that *Rhapsody* "is a more important contribution to music than Stravinsky's *Rites of Spring*."[35] This comparison, which suggests an inferiority complex among American classical musicians, claims that America achieved its first significant breakthrough with symphonic jazz. Osgood does not discuss other forms of jazz or its origins. Deems Taylor announced that *Rhapsody* "is genuine Jazz music." William J. Henderson called Gershwin "a free and independent creator." Even Gershwin himself seemed to agree with this view, calling jazz "an original American achievement" while failing to mention its black origins (Ewen, 54). Here, "American" does not connote African American but, rather, suggests an American blend in which blacks play a subordinate and negligible role.

Like Whiteman, Gershwin certainly knew the original, black face of jazz. David Ewen describes an encounter Gershwin had with the "shouting Gullahs" of South Carolina, whose sound was "terrifying in its primitive intensity," and writes that Gershwin admitted that their rhythm was an important source of inspiration for his compositions (Ewen, 154). Ewen claims that "Gershwin has influenced the direction of modern music more than any other single composer" and that "Gershwin proved that jazz was a speech worthy of the respect of every serious musician," but he never expounds on the link between serious jazz and those "shouting Gullahs."

These examples reveal the logic of downplaying the contribution of African

Americans to the making of jazz. While this is obviously a continuing theme in the discourse of primitivist modernism, there are certain differences between the structure of denial in the context of art and in the context of music. Before jazz had gained national acceptance, most reviews focused on its cultural roots. Once jazz became an integral element of American popular modernism, its black side was hardly ever mentioned. Only in whiteface—as commercialized "sweet" or "symphonic" jazz—did the music make its way into the heart of popular culture; in return, white jazz musicians were elevated to the ranks of nobility: Irving Berlin was called "King of Ragtime," Paul Whiteman was crowned "King of Jazz," and Benny Goodman held sway as the "King of Swing."

The music that diffused through the American social fabric had little to do with the music played on the streets of New Orleans or with the music presented on February 12, 1924, at the Roseland when Louis Armstrong played with the Fletcher Henderson Band. Duke Ellington, Count Basie, and Louis Armstrong were never known as "King." Indeed, it is likely that they claimed their titles of nobility in reaction to Whiteman's coronation, a title many African Americans deeply resented. There were even many white critics who expressed their dissatisfaction with symphonic jazz. Virgil Thompson, the famous American music critic and composer, for example, asserted that "the rhapsody is at best a piece of aesthetic snobbery." In his *Vanity Fair* article, "The Cult of Jazz," he complained that "the worship of jazz is just another form of highbrowism."[36] Three months later, Thompson published another article in *Vanity Fair* in which he argued that Whiteman "had refined [jazz], smoothed its harshness, taught elegance to its rhythms, blended its jarring polyphonies into an ensemble of mellow harmonic unity. . . . He has suppressed what was striking and original in it, and taught it the manners of Vienna."[37] Thompson's claim that jazz moved too close to Vienna and should be more like the jazz played in New Orleans echoes Edmund Wilson's 1926 repudiation of Whiteman's jazz as "a little dry, a little deliberate, a little lacking in lyric ecstasy."[38] Wilson rejected Whiteman's "mechanical and unsatisfactory" style as pseudo-jazz, anticipating by sixty years Schuller's radical assessment of Whiteman's style as an aberration: "It was not jazz—of course—or only intermittently so" (Schuller, 192).

Ernest Newman dismissed the entire approach to creating "straight music" as such. He declared in March 1927 in the *New York Times Magazine* that "the further jazz is 'developed' and the more musical talent there is in the composer who 'develops' it, the less like jazz will it be. But I should not call such a process 'development'; I should call it the abandonment of all that makes jazz jazz."[39] What makes jazz jazz is its black rhythmic element, Newman implies. His critique of the notion of "development" signifies on Whiteman's title "The Progress of Jazz." Newman implies that the earlier crude jazz was not inferior to the refined version and challenges the very opposition of "jungle music" on the one hand and "symphonic jazz" on the other. Although he did not write about individual black musicians, an image painted by Miguel Covarrubias that accompanied Newman's full-page article "The

Jazz Orchestra in Full Blast" shows a group of black jazz musicians playing in abandon.

Samuel Chotznoff had made this argument explicit in his essay "Brief History of Jazz," published in 1923 in *Vanity Fair*: "But this music needs no apology. Created—and recently again stimulated—by the musical talent of the negro, it constitutes the musical contribution of this country. . . . The negro genius has been chiefly responsible for whatever development America can boast."[40] This passage is remarkable, but its message was forgotten after the breakthrough of symphonic jazz. As opposed to Whiteman's appraisal of jazz as "the only original idea we have produced," Chotzinoff gives credit to "the musical talent of the negro" as the source of the national innovation.

Leopold Stokowski, the famous and well-respected American composer and director, also emphasized that African Americans played a fermenting role in the making of jazz. Moreover, in his statement, quoted in *The New Negro* (1925), he identified jazz with the throbbing swiftness of modern life:

> [Jazz] is an expression of the times, of the breathless, energetic, superactive times in which we are living, it is useless to fight against it. . . . America's contribution to the music of the past will have the same revivifying effect as the injection of new, and in the larger sense, vulgar blood into dying aristocracy. . . . The Negro musicians of America are playing a great part in this change. . . . They are not hampered by conventions or traditions, and with their new ideas, their constant experiment, they are causing new blood to flow in the veins of music. The jazz players make their instruments do entirely new things, things finished musicians are taught to avoid. They are pathfinders into new realms.[41]

The peculiar wording—that the Negroes "are causing new blood to flow in the veins of music"—is an adequate description of the process of appropriating and modifying black musical expressions. This racial "injection" has, indeed, "revivified" American music and has put it at the forefront of modern music globally. Stokowski's comment—that jazz was an "injection" of "vulgar blood" into a "dying aristocracy"—draws on the rejuvenation metaphor to argue that black influences invigorated both an obsolete musical tradition and a moribund popular culture. Stokowski suggests, then, that jazz is more than a musical phenomenon: it is the epitome of modernity, an expression of a "breathless, energetic, superactive time." This common view, that syncopated music suits the urban lifestyle, enormously aided the acceptance of jazz. If jazz expresses the "throbbing beat" of the modern city, and not the "Congo tom-tom," as earlier commentators asserted, then it is inextricably and irresistibly related to modern America.[42] In Stokowski's reevaluation, jazz was no longer a threat to civilization. Rather, it was an expression of the modern world.

Since most Anglo-American musicians were still entrenched in the European tradition, it makes sense that African Americans, being less "hampered by conventions or traditions," were the most likely agents of this "revivifying effect." As such, African American musicians were not just symbols of rebellion; rather, they were "pathfinders into new realms." The rhythms of jazz suited the quick pace of the Machine Age and its newly emerging socioeconomic order. Stokowski's tribute to African American musicians resists both the stereotypical image of the natural and the trope of libidinal regression. Advocating black music as the epitome of a new age, Stokowski suggests that blackness is a progressive and utterly modern force. Stokowski implicitly advocates that black Americans are role models from which white Americans can learn about modernity. If "we" emulate "them," he seems to say, "we" will elevate our own musical tradition. As a composer, Stokowski is primarily interested in the formal aspects of black music. But his choice of words indicates that he believes blacks exert a much broader impact on American culture. Stokowski implies that blacks were crucial in the broader transition from premodern to modern culture.

The African American critic and journalist Joel A. Rogers makes explicit the black role in this transition in his essay "Jazz at Home." Picking up on the metaphor of "revivification," Rogers claims that the injection of black cultural expression has brought about a shift in the overall sociocultural paradigm: "Jazz is rejuvenation, a recharging of the batteries of civilization with primitive vigor."[43] Jazz's energizing effect, its "primitive vigor," Rogers argues, spurred the shift from the genteel tradition to the modern. If this is true, as I believe it is, we should think of the "affinity of the modern and the primitive," as Rubin put it, as extremely productive and invigorating.

Ironically, one reason that the traditionalists rejected jazz had to do with the fact that it came to symbolize the hyperproductive modern world—an era that was to refer to itself as the Jazz Age. Intuitively identifying jazz with the fast pace, hedonism, and sexual liberation of the Roaring Twenties, such commentators as the Reverend Dr. A. W. Beaven denounced jazz as a "combination of nervousness, lawlessness, primitive and savage animalism and lasciviousness."[44] The anti-jazz fanatics manipulated the antagonism between civilization and savagery to preserve the ideological foundation of their age. Their objections to jazz—even when couched in moral, religious, or pseudoscientific language—were weapons in a cultural war to stop the emergence of the modern world. The debate about jazz was often, in other words, not about jazz per se, but about the emergence of the Jazz Age and the official status of the Negro and Negro culture.

The debate was touched also by the steady rise of mass production and consumerism. Many people were less concerned with preserving the old culture than with ushering in the new efficiently. In the era of the assembly line, the ethos of asceticism was outdated because the emerging consumer society relied on people's spending money on mass-produced goods (as well as on the rapidly growing entertainment industry). At least part of the anti-jazz faction must have associated the new way of life with what they considered blacks to be: shiftless, idle, and lascivious. The survival of civilization, they felt, depended on the ability of Euro-Americans to be immune to illogical "savage" art forms. They feared that if the barriers between primitive peoples and rational, Western culture were breached, the ideological foundation that upheld the Protestant work ethic would crumble. The conservative response can be understood in the context of postwar hysteria. America's assumption that Western civilization was superior to savage barbarism was deeply undermined, and its faith in the Christian ethic, which had remained virtually unchallenged during the nineteenth century, deteriorated.

The jazz debate was, in other words, an overdetermined discourse because jazz came to symbolize both the primitive past and the emergence of new socioeconomic, artistic, political, and cultural systems, and of a new power elite. The crusade against jazz was a symbolic assault on that new elite and its values. Or, to put it differently, it was designed as a symbolic bulwark to stop the decline of one cultural elite and its replacement by another. The ongoing transformation, which had started before World War I and which fully manifested itself in the 1920s, saw the newly rich claim economic and cultural power. The upper-middle classes became the driving force of a socioeconomic system whose survival depended upon mass consumption.

With the emergence of mass production, the number of affordable consumer goods increased and advertisement became important for securing a demand for mass-produced goods. Appliances such as washers, refrigerators, gramophones, telephones, and Kodak cameras became common items in most American households. By 1929, Americans owned 23 million cars. The emergence of Fordism—a system of accumulation that depended on the intricate balance of mass production and consumption—triggered drastic sociocultural transformations. After World War I, the United States assumed a leading role in the world. It met increasing demands on the international market and exported to Europe; its trade and industry expanded, while stock markets boomed.

It is commonly accepted that America underwent powerful economic and cultural changes. Neo-Marxist critics, such as Joachim Hirsch and Roland Roth, have analyzed the interdependency of the emergence of a Fordist socioeconomic regime and fundamental cultural shifts. *The Making of the Modern* by Terry Smith illustrates this brilliantly, utilizing the Ford plant as a key for explaining the course of modernity in America. But little has been written about the role blacks played in this process.

Frederick Lewis Allen's *Only Yesterday* shares similar flaws.[45] His "informal history of the 1920s," published in 1931, was an early and illustrative account of the cultural history of the Roaring Twenties. America underwent "a revolution of morals and manners," Allen asserts. His book demonstrates that the tumultuous decade witnessed countless fads, such as crossword puzzles and dance marathons, as well as the emergence of a youth culture and a new concept of womanhood. Allen, who does not talk about African Americans at all, mentions jazz only once, when he quotes a certain William Bolitho's calling the music "endlessly sorrowful yet endlessly unsentimental with no past, no memory, no future, no hope," which Allen identifies as the "*Zeitgeist* of the Post-war Age" (Allen, 11).

Curiously, Allen fails to refer to F. Scott Fitzgerald's essay "Echoes of the Jazz Age," published by *Scribner's Magazine* in 1931. In this famous article, Fitzgerald defines jazz: "The word jazz in its progress toward respectability has meant first sex, then dancing, then music. It is associated with a state of nervous stimulation, not unlike that of big cities behind the lines of a war."[46] Identifying jazz with modernity, sex, dancing, and music, Fitzgerald does not relate it to African Americans. In fact, the only time he mentions them is the obscure statement, "For a while bootleg Negro records with their phallic euphemisms made everything suggestive, and simultaneously came a wave of erotic plays" (Fitzgerald, 18). He ends his essay asserting that people drank a lot, that girls wore short skirts, and that "people you did not want to know said 'Yes, we have no bananas,' and it seemed only a question of a few years before the older people would step aside and let the world be run by those who saw the things as they were" (Fitzgerald, 22). Why does Fitzgerald ignore the impact African Americans had on the Jazz Age?

Perhaps it was because he was more captivated by those girls with the short skirts. No doubt, the self-assertive, rebellious, sexually liberated flapper with her bobbed hair was the epitome of the new age. Because of her boyish appearance and her tendency to drink and smoke, she undermined traditional gender roles. But while the flappers rejected older ideas of civility and gentility, they were not a marginalized subculture. In fact, modern women—who did most of the shopping and who were the primary readers of magazines—became the focus of marketing attention. The Jazz Age, in other words, was also the Women's Era (to borrow an older phrase the Black Club Women used for their publication in the 1890s). What was at stake in the jazz controversy was, in other words, not just the question of musical preference but also the fear of abandoning cultural hegemony and passing it on to the new—female and jazz-listening—generation.

Fitzgerald humorously alludes to the prerequisite for America's becoming a jazz-listening nation: the invention of phonographs and radios. In the early 1920s the record industry boomed, selling more than 100 million disks. In 1920, Victor Phonograph Company, the company that signed Whiteman, had a business worth $50 million a year. Whiteman, who released his first record in October 1920 and followed it with one or two records a month, had sold tens of thousands of records by the spring of 1921 (DeLong, 43). National distribution increased his popularity. As his records proliferated, Whiteman contributed to this rise of the cultural industry, a business that spread nationally during the 1920s and that today exerts enormous influence globally.

Whiteman, as we know, was only able to reach this mass audience by expelling any overt references to black rhythms from his compositions. In fact, his entire career had been purposefully designed to that end by his record company. According to George Morrison, the African American violist and graduate of the New England Conservatory, a recording by a black blues singer precipitated Whiteman's first record deal. In an interview with Gunther Schuller, Morrison remembered that Perry Bradford, a black composer and music store owner, came to his hotel room and suggested that Morrison's orchestra record a song with a black woman named Mamie Smith. Morrison agreed. He even spent $150 to buy a new outfit for this woman, whom he had never met before. With delight, Morrison recalled that Mamie Smith paid him back after they made the recording with General Phonograph Company. Morrison described the outcome:

> That was my last dealing with them [Bradford and Smith]. But I was responsible for her to get started.
>
> Naturally I had to tell Mr. King [executive at Victor company] I couldn't record for him. So he said, "Well, Morrison, do you know of a band out west — a good jazz band?" I said, "Yes, I know of someone; he and I studied together, practiced together; he's a white boy and his daddy's in the music department in a school out in Denver. He's a pretty good musician; his name is Paul Whiteman." . . . So he signed Paul Whiteman up and brought him back to New York and gave *him* one hundred thousand dollars. He told him, "Go and get the best there is, we've got to outsell Columbia." (Schuller, 367)

This statement refers to two crucial moments in the history of the recording industry: the almost simultaneous "discovery" of Paul Whiteman and the origin of records marketed to blacks. LeRoi Jones asserts that on February 14, 1920, the day Mamie Smith recorded "That Thing Called Love," America "ushered in the era of race records" (Jones, 99). Indeed, Smith's record, which was issued on the OKeh label (OKeh 4113) marked the beginning of a development unforeseeable at the time. Since the sales of the record were unexpectedly high, General Phonograph invited Mamie Smith to return to the recording studio. In August 1920, she cut Perry Bradford's "Crazy Blues" (OKeh 4116), which was released in November. According to Schuller, it sold "75,000 copies within the first month and over a million in the first year" (Schuller, 226).

When the record companies realized the tremendous demand among African Americans for records made by African American musicians, a new market was born. Initially, these discs exclusively targeted black consumers, and they were advertised in the black press as "colored records." In 1922, the designation "race records" became common usage, and by the end of 1922 they were available in all northern cities. They were issued in series with separate numbers (e.g., OKeh 8000 or Paramount 12000); they appeared as separate listings in the general record catalogs. Although set off from the mainstream, race records constituted a niche in the emerging cultural industry.

In 1922, Mamie Smith alone recorded nineteen OKeh race records, a fifth of their annual output. By the end of that year, there were approximately 100 race records on the market. Among the 200 new race records that were issued in 1923, Bessie Smith's "Down Hearted Blues" was the most popular. It sold 780,000 copies that year alone. The market was booming and competitive. Apart from the three major companies — General Phonograph, Paramount, and Columbia — there were also Victor, Vocalion, and a smaller company known as Pace Phonograph.

Pace, which issued its records on the Black Swan label, differed from the other companies because it was run by African Americans; as its president, Harry H. Pace, emphasized in the *Chicago Defender* in 1923, "All stock-holders are Colored, all artists are Colored, all employees are Colored. [It is the] Only company using Racial Artists in recording high class song records. This company made the only Grand Opera Records ever made by Negroes."[47] Among the first dozen Black Swan records were "numbers of a higher standard," as well as such popular singles as Ethel Waters's "Brown Baby"/"Ain't Gonna Marry" and "Memphis Man"/"Midnight Blues." Pace criticized American racism: "The race that is naturally musical [the black race] . . . has never been given a chance."[48] He took action to change this by representing "our best singers and high class musicians [who] have had no recognition from large white companies who furnish all the records that are supplied."[49] Pace's company tried to fulfill two tasks: to vindicate the status of the Negro while thriving economically. Unfortunately, while the company was successful in 1922, Pace had financial problems by the following year and was forced to sell his shares to Paramount in 1924.

"The Paramount Co.," *Talking Machine World* announced in April 1924, "recently closed arrangements whereby it purchased the business of the Black Swan Phonograph Co., New York, manufacturers of records by colored artists."[50] This was the end of the first all-black record company. Apparently, the executives at Black Swan felt confident that Paramount would follow their policy of releasing records by high-class black musicians. The buyout meant that Paramount padded its catalog with several hundred Black Swan records, and it meant that the field was left to white companies to compete for the black public. In spite of this "merger," Paramount was still second to OKeh, which remained the strongest force in the race record market.

The third major company, Columbia Records, which had initiated its race record series 14000D in late 1922, arranged a recording with Bessie Smith after she had been turned down by Black Swan and OKeh. On February 15, 1923, Bessie Smith recorded the single "Down Hearted Blues," backed with "Gulf Coast Blues." It sold 750,000 copies in the first six months according to Schuller, though Edward Brooks claims that the single sold only 250,000 copies.[51] Even for her later recordings (Bessie Smith made more than 150 recordings for Columbia Records), Smith got only $125 to $200 per usable side and never received royalties. That is to say, in spite of the fact that Bessie Smith sold about 6 million copies by 1929, she only grossed about $40,000.[52] Compared to other race record artists, Bessie Smith's income was enormous. Indeed, "Bessie had become the highest paid black entertainer in the country and had been proclaimed the Empress of the Blues," as Chris Albertson put it.[53] But compared to what Josephine Baker earned in Europe, Smith received very little. Compared to what Paul Whiteman received, it was petty cash, and it was virtually nothing at all compared to the profit Columbia Records made from her records. Marshall Stearns, the jazz critic, went so far as to suggest that "Bessie Smith's records kept the early Columbia Record Company from bankruptcy. For the first half of the twenties, record sales were off about 85 per cent, due perhaps to the fast-growing popularity of radio" (Stearns, 168).

The already competitive record market had become increasingly competitive because of the availability of radios. There was also a tremendous increase in radio stations: in 1920, KDKA in Pittsburgh was the only broadcasting station, but by the fall of 1926, there were more than 700.[54] The number of radio listeners was 13 million in 1929, but listenership soared to 30.5 million by 1935 (Jost, 75). This boom led to the decline of the record company industry as a whole. Overall sales had peaked in 1921 at $100 million. The sales of race records, on the other hand, increased exponentially. In the years from 1926 to 1929, ten new race records were released every week. Columbia, for example, pressed 11,000 copies of each record in 1927 before slowing its production to 5,000 copies each in 1929. Paramount doubled its production of race records from 1926 to 1927.

During this period (1926–1929), 500 race records were released annually, amounting to an annual sale of about 5 or 6 million copies.[55] In fact, to extend the repertoire of race records, the major companies organized scouting trips to the South to discover and record new artists. OKeh had been recruiting blues singers this way since 1923, and in 1927 Columbia began to do the same. In 1928, Victor Talking Machine Company, which had just initiated its V38500 race record series, became another competitor. Within two weeks, Victor's field recording crew managed to record thirty titles by unknown black blues singers and jazz musicians. Later, they also recorded white country blues musicians.

In the race among the giants of the record industry, Columbia became increasingly competitive. It bought out OKeh in 1926 and formed the OKey Phonograph Corporation.[56] Victor, a pioneer in the record industry since the recording of "The Original Dixie Land Jazz Band" in 1917, had never been among the leading forces in the race record market. In late 1925, when new technology allowed Victor to introduce electrical recording, its sales numbers increased. There was a strong demand for records of superior quality. In 1926 and 1927, Victor Company proudly announced that its sales grossed $47 million and that the "sales curve is still going up."[57] But in 1929, Victor Talking Machine Company was forced to merge with the Radio Corporation of America in order to survive the Crash.

The stock market crash drastically affected the record market; it reached an all-time low of 6 million discs sold in 1932, 98 million fewer than in 1927. The number of race records fell to a low of 150 titles annually, not so drastic a drop compared to the industry overall. After the low point in 1933–1934, the race record industry picked up again around 1937, reaching a peak of annual production of about 450 titles. But it never regained the earlier level of sales when female blues singers had dominated the field.

Apparently, the audience for race records was primarily black. The fact that race records were mostly advertised in the *Chicago Defender* suggests that there was purchasing power in the black community. Since race records were sold at record stores, bars, barber shops, and drug stores or by street vendors in the black part of town, white consumers had little access to them. One record-store owner in Chicago, for example, remembered that "colored people would form a line twice around the block when the latest record of Bessie or Ma or Clara or Mamie come in . . . sometimes these records they was bootlegged, sold in the alley for four of five dollars a piece . . . nobody never asked for Paul Whiteman; I doubt if they ever knew about him."[58]

Black commentators were outspoken in celebrating the blues as an authentically black cultural production. Richard Wright's definition of the salient characteristics of the blues is illustrative:

> The burden of woe and melancholy is dialectically redeemed through sheer force of sensuality, into an almost exultant affirmation of life, of love, of sex, of movement, of hope. No matter how repressive was the American environment, the Negro never lost faith in or doubted his deeply endemic capacity to live. All blues are a lusty, lyrical realism charged with taut sensibility.[59]

This manifesto for the sensibility and "sheer force of sensuality" preserved in the blues appears to be a manifestation of a kind of black primitivism. If blues constituted an "exultant affirmation of life, of love, of sex, of movement, of hope," it was a symbolic device—a weapon—that helped its listeners to ward off repression and find a positive identity in the midst of hardship.

Langston Hughes's comment on Bessie Smith's popularity is also telling; he writes in *Black Magic*: "Bessie Smith became a top-drawer attraction—but only among Negroes in Negro theaters. . . . she was too basic for the general public—even in the Twenties when primitivism in Negro art was a fad."[60] Why would Bessie Smith not appeal to the white audience that yearned for the primitive and the exotic? Was her blend of rural and urban blues, sung mostly in the pentatonic mode, too radical for the American mainstream? Her disregard for European melodic concepts must have upset those who preferred Whiteman's symphonic jazz. Or maybe they were shocked by her vocal attack (shouting the blues without a microphone). Bessie Smith's style (her vocal glissandi, her moaning and drawn-out syllables), though it followed the standard twelve-bar blues pattern, was unique. Her vernacular lyrics were sometimes charged with sexual allusions. "Respectable" people might easily be offended by lines such as "Nobody in Town Can Bake a Sweet Jelly-Roll Like Mine," or by her song, "You've Been a Good Old Wagon," which is about an aging lover who has "done broke down."

But race records were not exclusively consumed by blacks. In fact, white consumers could also buy these records. Sears, Roebuck & Company's Chicago mail order catalog, for example, offered thirty-three "selections by Negro artists" (Foreman, 179). Another record store proprietor in Chicago remembered that

> Negroes were the first to buy [race] records but soon white boys and girls came, and listened by the hour. The store was like an outpost on a mysterious, perhaps dangerous, frontier. Among those who came often, staying long, was Carl Sandburg. White musicians, music students, came to listen. (James Lincoln Collier, 13)

Given the racial tensions in this country, the sheer act of buying records in a black record store was something of a subversive act because those Anglo-Americans who ventured into the forbidden territory of race records violated the culture of Jim Crow laws. At a time when blacks were generally not allowed in white homes—other than as domestics, of course—a race record was something of a harbinger for integration.

Black jazz was everywhere by the mid-1920s; its dissemination on race records played a significant role in the expansion of the music. During the 1920s, black jazz was dispersed through many channels: on sheet music, piano rolls, and race records and in musical shows and clubs. Jazz was broadcast on the radio or featured in movies, such as *St. Louis Blues* (1929), with music by Bessie Smith and Louis Armstrong. Jazz—white as well as black—was an integral and pivotal part of the culture industry, starting with the musical *Shuffle Along.*

Shuffle Along was designed as a revue by Negroes for Negro audiences. It was the first black show on Broadway, and it ran for months. Premiering May 22, 1921, its scores were written by Eubie Blake and Noble Sissle; their song "I'm Just Wild about Harry" became a big hit. The plot was based on vaudeville sketches written by Aubrey Lyles and Flournoy Miller, who also starred —in blackface. Two of the show's chorus girls were Florence Mills and a young Josephine Baker. Among the famous artists who appeared were Paul Robeson and William Grant Still, who played the oboe.

Shuffle Along was pivotal; its fermenting effect launched a genre of Broadway shows produced, organized, and performed by blacks. *Liza* (1922) and *Runnin' Wild* (1923) brought the "Charleston" to Broadway. Sissle and Blake's next show, *Chocolate Dandies* (1924), was a musical comedy with blackface routines that also played on Broadway. *Lucky Sambo* (1925) gained popularity with white audiences at the Columbia Theatre. *My Magnolia* (1926) played at the Mansfield Theatre, and *Bottomland* (1927) appeared at the Princess Theatre, another midtown establishment. *Keep Shuffling* (1928), which featured music written by the stride pianist James P. Johnson and by Fats Waller, played at Daly's Theatre. The musical revue *Hot Chocolates* (1929), to which Andy Razaf contributed lyrics and Fats Waller the music, and in which Louis Armstrong performed "Ain't Misbehavin'," ran for 216 performances at the Hudson Theatre on Broadway. The list of all-black musical shows following *Shuffle Along* includes at least forty names. The ferment also caused many white companies to produce shows about blacks. Bruce Kellner lists 342 titles under the heading "Plays, by, about, or featuring Afro-Americans, 1917–1935."[61]

The quantity, however, says little about the quality of these shows. Many seem to have been operating in the minstrel tradition with black actors performing in blackface. Their burlesque humor suggests that these shows tried to entertain white audiences by reaffirming racist stereotypes. That most chorus girls were light-skinned indicates this bias as well. Nevertheless, a significant number of African American actors, singers, and songwriters managed to break into the ranks of white, mainstream entertainment; their presence and popularity could no longer be ignored. Job opportunities opened up for black entertainers who had been forced to work for the Theatrical Owners and Bookers Association (TOBA), which paid low wages and was, as the acronym's popular rendition put it, "Tough on Black Asses."

Breaking into the stronghold of Broadway constituted an important step for black performers and was a harbinger of integration. Historically, it was a further step in undoing a racist legacy that had started when white minstrel performers began to profit by mocking African Americans. For now, African Americans were to make a profit by making white audiences laugh. Since blacks were the actors and performers, they were players and not just props. For the first time, perhaps, they were able as a group to assume agency on the stage.

James Weldon Johnson noticed this in *Black Manhattan* (1930) when he commented on the Negro performer's ability to "make for himself a definite place on the legitimate stage of New York, the theatrical capital of the world." Johnson, who had suggested in 1922 that the solution to the race problem was to be found in the field of literature and poetry, seemed to have changed his mind. In 1930, he prophesied that blacks' "remedy lies in the development of Negro playwrights."[62] The extraordinary success of black revues no doubt persuaded him to reconsider his former strategy of racial uplift and to include popular art forms, such as musical comedies.

It is difficult to ascertain how many Anglo-Americans saw a "Negro" revue. Given that some of the 342 shows ran for 200 performances, we can assume that the number is quite high. But what consequences did this interracial encounter have? One consequence was certainly that Anglo-Americans developed a keen interest in black entertainment. The initial breakthrough on Broadway contributed to a new practice: those white New Yorkers who were not satisfied with watching Broadway musicals began to venture into Harlem to see black entertainment firsthand. Very quickly, a new fad for Negro entertainment ignited; the 1920s became the decade "When Harlem Was in Vogue," as Langston Hughes put it.

The Cotton Club was one of the most popular places for white New Yorkers who wanted to listen to black music and be entertained by blacks without having to share a table or the dance floor with them. The club's all-white policy and the extravagant cover charge of $2.50 made the club nonthreatening to these night tourists. The white club owner, Owney Madden, was a criminal who had been imprisoned for manslaughter; he supervised the club's opening in the fall of 1923 from his prison cell. Walter Brooks, the former director of *Shuffle Along* worked as his front man. The waiters, bartenders, and performers were African Americans mostly wearing black suits. The large horseshoe-shaped room, which had a seating capacity of 700 guests, was decorated with artificial palm trees, bongo drums, and geometric African designs.

This stylized, primitivist interior drew countless devotees. The primitive was what they yearned for, and this is what the Cotton Club offered in the form of its interior design, its music, and its floor shows. "The Cotton Club allowed the timid and well-heeled," Steve Watson recently remarked with a tone of sarcasm, "to cautiously dip their stylishly shod feet into the roaring waters of primitive Uptown."[63] Marshall Stearns remembers a floor show at the Cotton Club where a "light-skinned and magnificently muscled Negro burst through a papier-mâché jungle on the dance floor. . . . [He] rescued the blonde [white goddess] and they did an erotic dance. In the background, Bubber Miley, Tricky Sam Nanton, and other members of the Ellington band growled, wheezed, and snorted obscenely" (Stearns, 183–184).

In December 1927, Duke Ellington's band had become the house band. Realizing that the audience yearned for primitive exoticism, Ellington's band gave them what they wanted most; his music played a crucial role in this simulation of the jungle of forbidden sexuality. When Stearns describes Ellington's band's growling, wheezing, and snorting obscenely, he is referring to a famous effect included in compositions such as "Jungle Jamboree," "Jungle Blues," "Jungle Nights in Harlem," and "Echoes of the Jungle." This growling effect, produced with a plunger, and its evocation of "African" sounds—or what people took to be the sounds of Africa—enchanted the audience immersed in the Cotton Club's jungle life.

The Cotton Club was the most renowned among white thrill seekers, but there were many other white-only clubs that the slummers liked to visit, such as the Nest Club, Barrons, the Spider Web, the Saratoga Club, Ward's Swanee, the Catagona, the Bamboo Inn, the Jungle, the Immerman's Club, the Club Deluxe, and the Lenox Club. Apart from the whites-only clubs, there were also many mixed clubs, of which the Savoy Ballroom was the most famous. Covering the entire block on Lenox Avenue between 140th and 141st Streets, it had space for 4,000 dancers and was known as "The Home of Happy Feet." There were two bands each night that alternated; the music never stopped, and the Lindy Hop contests continued incessantly. Most black entertainers had at least one appearance there, including Louis Armstrong, Cab Calloway, King Oliver, Chick Webb, and Duke Ellington. The nights lived up to the promise made in a pamphlet distributed at the club's opening: "You will be bombarded with a barrage of the most electrifying spasms of entertainment ever assembled under one roof."[64] The spasms of entertainment were the hot rhythms for which the Savoy became legendary.

David Levering Lewis argues in *When Harlem Was in Vogue* that the Savoy became the seedbed of jazz and that "Fletcher Henderson's Rainbow Orchestra symbolized purely and simply, the debut of jazz as a product for national consumption" (David Levering Lewis, 173). Until the end of the 1920s, the national, black jazz sound was the swinging syncopation of Henderson's orchestra, with the Cotton Club orchestra of Duke Ellington (smoother and somewhat "whiter") placing a close second. Many Savoy sessions were broadcast over the radio. Lewis claims that these sessions "were to American popular music what Dearborn was to transportation" (David Levering Lewis, 173). Broadcasting Fletcher Henderson's band meant that popular jazz was no longer the exclusive domain of white musicians. This act of reclaiming jazz was an important symbolic act in the broader dynamic of cross-cultural exchange.

The fermenting effect of live jazz had been inconceivable when the first night spots had opened, but now, at one NAACP ball, there were "10,000 well dressed, orderly, and apparently cultured Americans who crowded the boxes and balconies," George Schuyler noticed (David Levering Lewis, 106). If we

realize that about 3,000 other people were dancing at the Savoy that same
night, and if we include the number of visitors that partied at all the other
clubs and rent parties in Harlem, we can understand readily Langston Hughes's
observation that "thousands of whites came to Harlem night after night."
Stating that Harlem had turned into an amusement center for white guests,
Hughes complains that Anglo-Americans were given "the best ringside tables
to sit and stare at the Negro customers—like amusing animals in a zoo."[65]
Why did "Nordics," to use a popular term at the time for whites, venture into
the unknown territory? Did they think of Harlem as a kind of black Disney-
land, or as a place where they could immerse themselves in Nubian bliss?

Several articles contributed to this image of Harlem as an amusement center, spurring the primitivist pilgrimage. *Variety*, for example, informed its
readers that

> Harlem has attained pre-eminence in the past few years as an amusement
> center. Its night life now surpasses that of Broadway itself. From midnight
> until after dawn it is a seething cauldron of Nubian mirth and hilarity.
> Never has it been more popular. One sees as many limousines from Park and
> Fifth Avenue parked outside its sizzling cafes, "speaks," night clubs, and
> spiritual seances as in any other high-grade white locale in the country.[66]

To think of Harlem as an "amusement center" where "limousines from Park
and Fifth Avenue" lined up seems absurd from today's perspective. But during the 1920s, upper- and middle-class whites seeking a "seething cauldron
of Nubian mirth and hilarity" took part in this nightly intracity migration.

On March 1, 1925, the *New York Times* published an article by Mary Ross,
"Harlem a Race Capital. Community of 175,000, Now Largely in Negroes'
Hand, Has Become a Cultural Center." The article begins with a powerful
image:

> Black fingers whipping furiously over the white keys, beating out cascades
> of jazz; black bodies swaying rhythmically as their owners blow or beat or
> pluck the grotesque instruments of the band; on the dancing floor throngs,
> black and white, gliding, halting, swinging back madly in time to the
> music—this is the Harlem of the cabarets, jazz capital of the world. Down-
> town specialists who have wearied of the tricks of Broadway come north-
> ward to this new center of pleasure. In some of the fifteen cabarets black
> and white eat together, dance together in the rich abandon of the race which
> evolved that first jazz classic, the Memphis Blues; which refined the cake-
> walk into the fantastic fling of the "Charleston."[67]

Drawing upon virtually the entire gamut of primitivist tropes—vitality, gaiety, rhythm, movement, color, and laughter—this article is the virtual primal
scene of primitivism in the American press. Ross describes the scene as a
hellish inversion of the labor of slavery: "black fingers whipping furiously
over the white keys." Her discussion of Harlem gravitates to the body: "black
and white bodies gliding, halting, swinging back madly." Moreover, Ross insinuates that whites experience "the rich abandon" of the black race only
through cultural and sexual miscegenation.

But Ross also opposes the conventional view that Harlem is the home only of the politically and economically disenfranchised; she claims that "Harlem is not a ghetto or a quarter or a slum. It is an American city." She presents Harlem as an economically, intellectually, and artistically self-sustaining "race capital." Months before the publication of the manifesto of the New Negro movement, she wrote: "Harlem is the setting for the new negro art, built on race consciousness, influenced by the America of which it is one element." This act of symbolic annexation—claiming that Harlem was a prosperous and integral part of New York—is striking, particularly if we consider that white residents had fled when the first blacks moved into this neighborhood. The president of the Property Owner's Protective Association had objected strongly to blacks moving into the area on the grounds that they would lower real estate prices. Ross's declaration that black Harlem had something to offer and that it was an integral part of America marks a turning point in the general attitude toward both blacks and Harlem. Did this primitivist account of Harlem's night life that promised rejuvenation for weary white people contribute to a revision of the public image of Harlem?

If so, then the new image was one that did not acknowledge the achievements of the New Negro movement but saw Harlem for what white New Yorkers wanted it to be. By the end of the decade, one could read in the *New York Herald Tribune* that "the attitude of the average white New Yorker to Harlem is one of tolerant amusement. He thinks of it as a region of prosperous night clubs; of happy-go-lucky Negroes dancing all night to jazz music."[68] This devastating account of the Harlem Renaissance suggests that white Americans did not think of Harlem as a center for arts and letters, as black intelligentsia so ardently wished, but rather as the home of "happy-go-lucky Negroes." White Americans reinscribed blacks into the old Sambo image updated to the context of a modern leisure society. Their view of the carefree black ignored Harlem's "talented tenth," as well as its dreadful social realities.

By 1929, most black inhabitants of Harlem suffered from the severest economic hardships; the unemployment rate was about 50 percent, and Harlem rents were 20 percent higher than the rest of New York. According to Adam Clayton Powell, Jr., "one-half is not working, the other half is existing on the crumbs," and "ten thousand of the Harlem citizenry" were "living in cellars and dark, damp, cold dungeons."[69] Those who had apartments took in boarders, so that overcrowded apartments were as much a part of Harlem's reality as ill-equipped classrooms, juvenile delinquency, drug addiction, and a remarkably high infant mortality rate. (Harlem's infant mortality rate in 1928 was twice as high as that of the rest of New York.)

These facts were reported in the *New York Times*, where one article informed its readers of Harlem's high mortality rate and told them that the tuberculosis death rate was four times as high as that among the white population.[70] Another article, in the *New York Herald Tribune,* described Harlem as "the poorest, the unhealthiest, the unhappiest and the most crowded single large section of New York City."[71] It is astonishing that the average New Yorker was persistent in embracing the image of a happy-go-lucky Negro.

And it is surprising that the slummers were able to enjoy themselves know-ing about these conditions. The popular press's discourse of primitivism por-trayed Harlem's night life in a way that consigned its daily reality to oblivion.

The historian Gilbert Osofsky argues in *Harlem: The Making of a Ghetto* that the "American racial consciousness refused to recognize any but the suppos-edly joyous side of Negro culture" and that "American society voluntarily blinded itself to the harsh realities of Negro existence."[72] According to Osofsky, white Americans blinded themselves to the bleak socioeconomic realities of blacks because they were unwilling to take action against economic and polit-ical injustice. Apart from the unwillingness to make political changes, there is another reason they preferred to think of Harlem as an amusement center, ignoring the fact that it was a slum. To account for this structure of collective denial, it is necessary to explore further the symbolic dimension of jazz in the sociocultural context of the 1920s.

The Fordist mode of production provided the middle class with sufficient resources—that is, with time and money—which they could spend on af-fordable consumer goods and leisure activities. Desperate to make up for a hard day's work, people longed for excitement and "revivification," as they commonly put it. An entertainment and consumer industry came into exis-tence that catered to the needs of the middle class. This system relied, how-ever, on a lavish attitude. In fact, the advertisement agents tried to lure the consumer into buying instead of saving. To secure a perpetual demand for consumer goods, the consumer society had to rid itself of a Puritan value sys-tem that cherished a rigid morality and was hostile to wasting money on at-taining pleasure. The survival of consumer culture depended on replacing the Protestant ethos that valued hard work, frugality, and self-denial (at least in part of the population).[73] To transcend the old attitude of self-restraint and to attain the modern, hedonistic self-realization, many white New Yorkers discovered the image of the happy-go-lucky-Negro.

The uninhibited, carefree Negro was, curiously, a hidden role model for white New Yorkers in their attempts to reinvent themselves. Constructing a black alter ego was a means by which to free themselves from Puritan atti-tudes and a preliminary step in taking on a modern identity. At a time when Jim Crow laws prevailed, thousands transgressed the color line and discov-ered Harlem as the space where they could best experiment with the new lifestyle of self-abandonment. The primitivist setting at the Cotton Club cre-ated an ambience that allowed its guests to feel irreverent. In "jungle alley," slummers encountered what they were desperately seeking, something that deviated from the concept of "civilization," as the preceding generation had defined it, and that deviated from the rigid morality most slummers had in-ternalized. Harlem provided a space—a heterotopia where anything seemed to be accepted and everything seemed exciting.

No wonder, then, that so many Americans sought out the extraordinary, the ultimate—the lion's roar from the jungle—the black tumult. A midnight em-brace of the black primitive other, this symbolic rendezvous between black and white, the primitive and the modern, proved to be an effective weapon in

Figure 3.1   Reginald Marsh. *Tuesday Night at the Savoy Ballroom*. (1930). Courtesy of the Rose Museum, Brandeis University, Waltham, Mass.; Gift of the Honorable William Benton, New York.

the struggle to overcome internalized patterns of repression and self-restraint. This symbolic affiliation with the black other was one way of distinguishing oneself from the preceding generation, as well as attaining a new and modern self. Harlem's clubs were to the slummers what those "dusty manikins" were to Picasso—the site of exorcism.

A *New York Times* article entitled "Jazz for the Nerves" suggests that jazz had such healing powers.[74] According to Dr. Armour, "jazz music, lively parties, week-ends in town" helped to alleviate mental discomfort and a sense of unease that an increasing number of people suffered from. Diagnosing these nervous disorders as the symptoms of monotony and routine, the doctor recommended a "riotous evening of gaiety." His prescription echoes Joel A. Rogers's description of jazz as "a safety valve for modern machine-ridden and convention-bound society" and, thus, helpful to "release all the suppressed emotions" (Locke, *The New Negro*, 217). Comparing jazz with "a blowing off of the lid," Rogers suggests that it allowed for a loosening of the Id.

While most whites remained voyeurs staring at Negroes from a safe distance, others yearned for closer contact. For them, only the thrill of miscegenation was sufficiently invigorating. Reginald Marsh's painting *Tuesday Night at the Savoy Ballroom* (1930), represents this setting (figure 3.1). In the foreground, we see thirteen dancers, while in the background there are four white guests sitting at a table. One of the four African American dancers, a tall, sturdy, grinning black man, is at the center. A gray-haired woman wearing flashy red lipstick is following his lead. A black couple on the left-hand side of the painting seems to be enjoying the bump and grind of a syncopated tune. An opening between these two dancing couples allows us to gaze at the table in the background. Two people are kissing while a man sitting behind them screams. A white woman, sitting in front of the couple right next to the dance floor, rests her head on the table; she is either depressed or drunk, maybe both.

If we shift our gaze to the right-hand side of the painting, we see a group of four white people—two female and two male—standing together closely. They seem to enjoy the body contact and are laughing hysterically. On the far right-hand side, we see another black man. His mouth is open, as if he is laughing. Around his shoulder is the arm of a white woman, who pulls him closer. *Tuesday Night at the Savoy Ballroom* illustrates what the *New York Times* wrote about "the jazz capital of the world": "on the dancing floor throngs, black and white, gliding, halting, swinging back madly in time to the music." One wonders, however, if such a night at the "Home of the Happy Feet" is what Dr. Armour meant when he recommended a "riotous evening of gaiety." Here, the joyous world of pure amusement and Dionysian bliss seems infused with fear and anxiety. The painting reveals the primal side of the unconscious, usually concealed by the veneer of decency. Here, the encounter between black and white people is depicted as the encounter with the darker side of the souls of white folks.

In contrast to Guy C. McElroy, who argues that Marsh's caricature only expresses the hysteria over race mixing, I do not think that this painting is about xenophobia. Rather, it explores what can happen to white people when racial miscegenation occurs.[75] Marsh's caricature lays bare the darker side of American primitivism in popular culture. In a twist to the hypothesis that the modern self fashioned itself through a symbolic embrace with the other of color, this painting suggests that interracial encounters might also bring out undesired sides of one's psyche. *Tuesday Night at the Savoy Ballroom* is about the unleashing of the primitive.

This doubleness, or relation between the other within and the cultural other, is a crucial part of the dynamic of popular primitivism. It ignores, however, the black response to the white appropriation of black culture. So far, we have explored instances of the dynamic of cross-cultural exchange: the race records and, more specifically, the black comedy revues that integrated Broadway, triggering this vogue for black entertainment, and the nightly migration to Harlem that was part of this larger movement and seems close kin to the French *vogue nègre*. But the major difference between the cult of primitivism in popular American culture and European primitivist modernism is its obviously paradoxical nature in America. The group that had tremendous symbolic prominence was socially marginalized and partially disenfranchised. Blacks were present and absent within American culture at the same time. This is the inherent contradiction of daring to approach blacks at night while avoiding close contact with them during the day, symbolized by laws mandating segregation even in the bedroom.

How did blacks respond to this outrageous discrepancy? What did they think of jazz and the white people who loved it so much? The black cultural elite was very often hostile to jazz. Ironically, their objection to the music coincided with that of the white conservatives who thought of jazz as a vice. David Levering Lewis argues that "upper-crust Afro-Americans still mostly recoiled in disgust from music as vulgarly explosive as the outlaw speakeasies and cathouses that spawned it" (David Levering Lewis, 173). If that was the case, they must have loathed scenes such as that represented in *Tuesday Night at the Savoy Ballroom*.

Alain Locke had realized the importance of jazz as early as 1925 when he decided to include J. A. Rogers's primitivist essay "Jazz at Home" in *The New Negro*. Nine years later, he published an article entitled "Toward a Critique of Negro Music" (later extended into a book, *The Negro and His Music*) in *Opportunity*. In the article, Locke calls for "good jazz," by which he means a kind of jazz that would get rid of "shoddy superficiality and its repetitious vulgar gymnastics" (Locke, Toward a Critique of Negro Music, 330). Locke does not clarify, however, what he means by its implied opposite: bad jazz. The jazz style he calls for, which he refers to as "jazz classic" or "classical jazz," should be played by academically trained musicians who try to preserve the Negro folk idiom. Their compositions should combine, Locke argues, jazz and symphonic music. Locke does not discuss the "symphonic jazz" genre of white musicians, but implicit in his challenge is that black people should produce a comparable figure.

Locke believed that only two musicians were capable of doing so: William Grant Still and Duke Ellington. Still, the famous African American composer, was academically trained and widely acknowledged as one of the most distinguished musicians. But, to Locke, Ellington was "the pioneer of super-jazz and the person most likely to create the classical jazz." Without expounding on Duke Ellington's style, Locke refers to the jazz critic Robert Goffin, who praised Ellington for rationalizing jazz. Then he quotes R. D. Darell, who saw Ellington's major achievement as creating a balance between rhythm and harmony. Ellington is one of the few musicians who is able to combine musical elements as "logical parts" so they form a grand whole, Darell declares.

Locke discusses other "promising developments in Negro music": the Negro choir of Hall Johnson and *Kykunkor*, an African dance opera. In assessing the importance of *Kykunkor*, Locke makes a striking statement: "[*Kykunkor*] has given us our first glimpse of the African tradition in a healthy pagan form with primitive cleanliness and vitality instead of the usual degenerate exoticism and fake primitivism to which we have been accustomed."[76] Here, he distinguishes degenerate "fake primitivism" from a primitivism that is healthy, pagan, clean, and vital. Locke does not reject primitivism as such, but instead dismisses the white version as degenerate and calls for an authentic—that is, black—primitivism to emerge in the field of music.

In *The Negro and His Music*, Locke is more specific about this primitivist musical expression in which "the art music and the folk-music must be fused in a vital but superior product."[77] This synthesis will be the musical branch of black primitivist modernism, a counterpart to the black fine arts Locke called for in "The Legacy of Our Ancestral Arts." In fact, Locke's musical argument is an almost direct transposition of the argument he made about art, but he does not refer this time to the European primitivists' discovery of the beauty of black art. Locke's choice of words is in itself primitivist: "Someone had to devise a technique for harnessing this shooting geyser, taming this wild well" (Locke, *The Negro and His Music*, 100). He hoped that by taming the wild rhythms, and by refining the crude aspects of folk music without sacrificing its vitality, a new variant of black primitivist-modernist aesthetics would emerge.

Locke is annoyed by the fact that white musicians outdid Negro musicians in the marketplace. Disdainfully, he writes: "listening to the originators, [white musicians] finally became masters of jazz, not only rivaling their Negro competitors musically but rising more and more to commercial dominance of the new industry" (Locke, *The Negro and His Music* 82). Again, Locke urges the young African American artists to compete with their white counterparts by reclaiming "their" music. Black musicians should reappropriate their musical idiom, master it, and become commercially successful. Although it was to take a few more years until black jazz musicians would dominate the field, Locke was prophetic in calling for a black primitivist modernism in music.

How did the general black press comment on jazz? Surprisingly, there are only very few articles published in *Crisis* and *Opportunity*, for example, that discuss jazz at all. The *Chicago Defender* ran a column, "The Musical Bunch," by Dave Peyton.[78] Peyton focuses on symphonic musicians and does not discuss jazz musicians or call for a combination of the two. A front-page article, "Hayes Modestly Receives Medal," published in the *Amsterdam News,* is another example of this tendency to report on serious musicians.[79] The photograph accompanying the article shows the conductor of the New York Symphony Orchestra, Walter Damrosch, bestowing Roland Hayes, the Negro tenor, with a Springarn Medal. It is unlikely that a jazz musician would have received that honor and equally unlikely that a jazz musician would have made the front page.

Apart from the fact that many African Americans objected to its vulgar side or did not think that the right kind of jazz yet existed, there is another reason why jazz was not seen as a respectable expression of black arts. An editorial in *Opportunity* observed a "mad vogue of certain Negro creations": "First it was music, then African art, then jazz, and now it is the Charleston dance." The editorial maintains that this "purely Negro dance" is not a "vulgar or a sensuous dance." White people of all ages and classes loved to dance to the "fierce, irregular rhythm," because they felt that this music "rejuvenates," as one devotee of the Charleston craze put it.[80] The article suggests that African Americans were reluctant to acknowledge jazz and jazz dance because of the very fact that it was in vogue among white people.

The best commentary on this Negro resistance to the white fad is Rudolph Fisher's "The Caucasian Storms Harlem," published in *American Mercury* in 1927. Fisher complains about "the Nordic invasion" that had caused him literally to be bumped off the dance floor and had turned his favorite clubs white. He remembers a group of "'fays' [who] would huddle and grin and think they were having a wild time. Slumming." Insinuating that "fays" had no business flooding Harlem clubs, Fisher talks about "this sudden, contagious interest in everything Negro" with a condescending tone. He writes, "Granted that white people have long enjoyed the Negro entertainment as a diversion, is it not something different, something more, when they bodily throw themselves into Negro entertainment in cabarets? Now Negroes go to their own cabarets to see how white people act."[81] Watching white people "camel and fish-tail and turkey" and "skate and buzzard and mess-around," Fisher admits with a sense of envy: "they do them all better than I." The language suggests that Fisher is on safari, or at a zoo. Fisher sees himself as a distant observer, "a traveler from the North . . . watching an African tribe-dance."

Making himself into a northern explorer who is looking at white people performing wild dances is an interesting inversion—one that calls to mind Renoir's movie, *Charleston*. Fisher, like the African scientist in that movie, feels tempted to join the wild dance, yearning for something he thinks the cultural other has. Fisher mentions white people's listening to the music coming from the Negro quarters and Stanley's being fascinated by African drums; he concludes that this interest is a "basic human response, the effect of which, once admitted, will extend beyond cabarets." He wonders, "Maybe these Nordics at last have tuned in on our wavelength. Maybe they are at last learning to speak our language." This final sentence seems to be a reconsideration of this fad. Here, Fisher interprets the "interest in the Negro" as a universal phenomenon in which one group is naturally curious about another. Perhaps jazz can be a language for communication across racial boundaries.

Black jazz's success in Europe seems to indicate that to some extent this was true. Black jazz musicians, starting with Lieutenant James Reese Europe and his regimental band, regularly played in front of British, French, German, and Belgian audiences. The blasting tunes of this marching band—and the regimental drums played by Bill "Bojangles" Robinson—celebrated America's military victory. This was the beachhead in the jazz conquest of Europe. After James Reese Europe's band and the 1,300 black soldiers returned to Harlem in February 1919, many other jazz bands and black revues went overseas.

According to Björn Englund, however, the show that really introduced black jazz to Europe was *Chocolate Kiddies*. This black troupe left for Germany in June 1925 and played in July at Hamburg's Thalia Theater.[82] Most of the songs had been written by Duke Ellington, though Sam Wooding and his eleven-piece orchestra were hired to play the tour. The band assumed an unusually prominent role in the show; the second act was billed as a "Symphonic jazz concert by Sam Wooding Orchestra at the Club Alabama in New York." Wooding's band played in their signature style, a black version of "symphonic jazz." The third act included three songs by Ellington, the last of which, "Jig Walk," became the hit of the show.[83] To many Europeans, "Jig Walk" was the epitome of the jazz spirit. The song was copied by a dozen European and American orchestras. This boom of black revues preceded the more serious performance of Louis Armstrong in 1932, when he played at the Palladium in London and was received by the Prince of Wales. The following year, Duke Ellington's fourteen-piece band also performed in England, exporting hot jazz to respectable concert stages.

The impact of black jazz was tremendous. Not only did "le jazz hot" become a sizzling commodity in Europe, but there were also serious attempts by European classical musicians and directors to introduce jazz to European symphonic orchestras. The director of the conservatory in Frankfurt went so far as to assert that "the teaching of jazz is not only the right but the duty of every up-to-date musical institution." He made the remarkable claim that "an infusion of negro blood can do no harm. It will help to develop a wholesome sense of rhythm, which after all constitutes the life element of music."[84] Instead of downplaying the black element, as had happened in America, many Europeans amplified the black element while still commenting on jazz favorably.

While the *New York Times* commented on the extraordinary success of jazz abroad with apprehension—"American jazz in its triumphant sweep through Europe has seriously threatened the supremacy of the Viennese brand of opera"[85]—articles such as "The Jazz Band and Negro Music," originally published in the German magazine *Der Querschnitt*, stressed the music's black origins and celebrated jazz's triumph. The writer, Darius Milhaud, writes of jazz's success: "There is no doubt that the origin of jazz music is to be sought among the Negroes. Primitive African qualities have kept their place deep in the nature of the American Negro and it is here that we find the origin of the tremendous rhythmic force as well as the expressive melodies born of inspiration which oppressed races alone can produce."[86] Colonizers, Milhaud argues, are unable to create a music so rhythmic and expressive.

Another example of this lauding of African rhythmic forces is an article originally published in a popular monthly magazine in Berlin. The article, "The Triumph of the Jungle," was written by one "Jaap Kool"—obviously a riff on "hot jazz." Talking about the origin of the jazz band, Kool claims that the word *jass* goes back to a black drummer named Jack Washington, who played a rhythm so fierce that whenever it was his turn to play percussion solos, the crowd would cry in delight, "Jack! Jack!" From their frantic cry, Kool asserts, "the odd name 'jazz' is derived. But what the Negro played had an inspired frenzy in it—had, as the French would say, *le feu sacré*, a fire that soon blazed up and swept across the whole world."[87]

According to Kool's myth, the sacred fire is what ignited jazz musicians and listeners. As absurd as this story is, the notion that jazz was related to frenzy was widely spread. In fact, it was a common theme in European primitivism. One of the first Europeans to write a scholarly account of jazz was the Belgian critic Robert Goffin. He was quite up-front about the reason behind his fondness for black jazz: "I know of no white musician who is able to forget himself, to create his own atmosphere, and to whip himself up into a state of complete frenzy."[88] Goffin, who apparently thought that attaining "a state of complete frenzy" was quite an achievement, fails to explain why blacks had this capacity to whip themselves up into what Goffin thought was a desirable state.

This association of jazz with ecstasy or frenzy is a stereotype that re-emerges in several other early critical accounts of jazz. The second important European jazz critic was Hugues Panassié, author of *The Real Jazz*. In his book, originally published in French, he writes that "jazz, like all other primitive music, is a music which is perpetually in motion, a living music."[89] Attributing motion to jazz is key to this discourse that praises jazz for its "non-logical," "spontaneous" qualities. What appear to be terms of praise in fact reduce playing jazz to a purely kinetic, noncerebral, or nonrational activity. The jazz critic Ted Giola recently commented on the prominence of such derogatory attitudes lingering in much of jazz criticism. At the core of the "primitivist myth" is a view of a "jazz musician as the inarticulate and unsophisticated practitioner of an art which he himself scarcely understands."[90] While Giola notices that the primitivist myth is just another version of racism, he fails to distinguish the key difference between the two: the racist believes himself superior, whereas the primitivist believes—or pretends to believe—in the superiority of the other. It is the latter version that is most common in European primitivism, as the passages quoted above indicate.

Neil Leonard claims that the primitivism of European musical criticism quickened the acceptance of jazz in America (Leonard, 70). The opposition between the civilized European and the wild Negro—so crucial to the anti-jazz camp—was undermined when European professors of music acknowledged the superior quality of jazz's syncopated rhythms. The fact that jazz became popular in Europe increased its symbolic value in America. Furthermore, Americans eventually realized that by adapting this musical expression as "their" national tune, America had something to contribute to global culture. Exporting jazz, America, perhaps for the first time, made an impact on European culture. This process reversed centuries of transcultural relations. Jazz was a predecessor or vanguard for many other American cultural artifacts that would soon make a triumphant sweep through European popular culture.

In "The Revolution in Musical Taste," Martin Cooper analyzes the dynamic between a shifting of aesthetic values and a reversal of the transatlantic cultural exchange. He maintains that "the fashion for American Negro rhythms and tone combinations was in fact the symptom of a profound shifting of aesthetic values."[91] This fashion was not just a symptom. Jazz, I argue, played a founding role in this transformation. Although the *vogue nègre* did not directly cause a revolution in manners and styles, it was a constitutive factor in the shift; the cultural exchange between the Old and the New World was no longer unidirectional. The pivotal achievement of jazz lies in this twofold accomplishment of simultaneously revitalizing the musical idiom and reversing the direction of Euro-American cultural exchange. Jazz, predicated on a break with the Anglo-American music tradition, constituted a new beginning. It is the moment when American culture asserted its "own" complex identity and when Europe began to take an unprecedented interest in American culture. Jazz's symbolism was so prominent that by 1935 the Nazis feared it, declaring it degenerate and forbidding its broadcast by radio. Jazz's history—from being ousted as savage by "respectable Americans" to its triumph in Europe and its dismissal by a regime that was to display unprecedented barbarism—underscores the ironic and curious transformation of the musical version of primitivist modernism.

4

THE BLACK BODY

The Negroes are conquering Paris. They are conquering Berlin. They have already filled the whole continent with their howls, with their laughter. . . . The Revue Nègre, which is rousing the tired public in the Théâtre des Champs-Elysées to thrills and madness as otherwise only a boxing match can do is symbolic.

Negroes dance with their senses. (While Europeans can only dance with their minds.) . . . Their revue is an unmitigated challenge to moral Europe. There are eight beautiful girls whose figures conjure up a stylized purity, reminiscent of deer and Greek youths. And at their head, the star, Josephine Baker. . . . But the leading role belongs to Negro blood. Its drops are slowly over Europe, a long-since dried-up land that can scarcely breathe. Is that perhaps the cloud that looks so black on the horizon but whose fearsome downpours are capable of so white a shine? . . . The Negro question is pressing for our entire civilization. It runs like this: Do the Negroes need us? Or are we not sooner in need of them?

—Ivan Goll (January 15, 1926)

October 1925. December 1927. In two years, Joséphine [sic] Baker has become a celebrity and conquered the old Europe with the "Charleston" spirit! . . . Nothing will characterize our epoch to future historians more than the fast rise to glory of this little girl who came to realize with ingenuity the new art the young generation has waited for.[1]

—Paris Midi (January 29, 1928)

Early in her career, Josephine Baker was only one of a number of popular, black female performers in New York; her peers were Florence Mills and Ethel Waters. With Mills she had danced as a blackfaced chorus girl in Noble Sissle and Eubie Blake's *Shuffle Along;* with Waters she had performed at the Plantation Club in Manhattan. While all three performers were popular in the city, it was Baker who was to embark on an unparalleled career that would last fifty years and make her a celebrity around the world. It was a remarkable rise from humble origins: Baker, in her early teens, had worked in vaudeville shows; touring with the blues singer Clara Smith, she had performed mostly burlesque numbers.

In 1925, when Baker was working at the Plantation Club, she was discovered by Caroline Dudley, who was recruiting performers for an all-black show in Paris. Dudley was originally from Chicago, but she had lived in Paris (next door to Gertrude Stein) and had been convinced that Parisians would give unprecedented support to a black revue. Dudley made Baker the astonishing offer of $1,000 per month.[2] This was a remarkable amount of money compared to the $9 a week Baker had earned when she first started working in 1919.

October 2, 1925, was opening night for *La Revue Nègre* at the Théâtre des Champs-Elysées. In the first act, Josephine Baker crawled onto the stage on all fours. Then, bent over, she scatted: "Boodle am, Boodle am Boodle am now. Skoodle am, Skoodle am Skoodle am now. . . ." It was light entertainment. In the final act, "Charleston Cabaret," Baker was carried to the stage on the shoulders of a muscular black man, Joe Alex. Both were scantily dressed, their bodies adorned with pearls and feathers. She lay across Alex's back, bent backwards, head down, feet up, and her bare breasts exposed to the audience. As Baker started to dance, a pink feather between her thighs began to bounce. Her steps grew progressively wilder. The seemingly uncontrolled, spontaneous, and fierce movements captivated her audience; it went wild immediately. At the end of *la danse sauvage*, when Baker and Alex walked off the stage, they received a hysterical standing ovation. Overnight, nineteen-year-old Josephine became a megastar.

The Parisian audience fell in love with this sultry young woman from St. Louis. Many returned to see the show five or six times. Due to the show's extraordinary success, *La Revue Nègre* played ten weeks at the Théâtre des Champs-Elysées, most nights to sold out crowds. Since the theater had been booked by Anna Pavlova with her Ballet Russe and the Symphonic Orchestra, *La Revue Nègre* had to move to the Théâtre de l'Étoile. The fact that a massive crowd followed *La Revue Nègre,* and that the great Pavlova lost much of her audience, is an indicator of the significant shift in public taste.

This collective infatuation with Josephine Baker was at the center of the broader trend we know as the *vogue nègre*. The French audience and critics went so far as to gallicize her name, symbolically adopting and naturalizing her as "La Bakaire" or simply as "Joséphine." How was it possible that a nineteen-year-old girl who had previously appeared only behind blackface in burlesques was now widely celebrated as *la vedette noire*, the black star? One answer is that Baker's *danse sauvage* offered a novel blend of exoticism and eroticism that appealed to a jaded bourgeois audience yearning for excitement; a significant part of her appeal had to do simply with the color of her skin. Almost all reviews of her show made reference to her black or "African" background. Key tropes in the French press's coverage of Baker were the terms "savage," "primitive," and "jungle." One critic, Carol-Bérard, went so far as to claim that "Joséphine Baker is the synthesis of an Africa that, while losing its mystery, turns legendary."[3]

Indeed, Baker's performance catered to Europe's most exotic fantasies. She crawled on the floor, she walked on all fours, and she moved her chocolate

Figure 4.1   Walery. *Josephine Baker Dances in "La Fatou"*. (1926). Courtesy of Sammlung Bodo Niemann, Berlin.

body in tantalizing ways before reverting to one of her favorite postures: knees bent, behind extended. Then she would gyrate, criss-cross her eyes, and smile coyly at the audience. This outburst of (sexual) energy was the core of her appeal; as Jean-Claude Baker, the author of her most recent biography, points out: "Shameless, she seems to be making love to him [Joe Alex] in front of everyone" (Baker and Chase, 5). The Parisian spectators became voyeurs: Baker's black body was their object of desire. While every striptease or go-go dancer tries to attract and seduce an audience, only a few have ever been as successful as she (figure 4.1).

Josephine Baker appealed to colonialist fantasies of the exotic. Dressed in a skirt of bananas, she was all-too-easy prey for the voyeurs. Inviting the French gaze, she became their pet, or, should we say, their panther, titillating and tame—potentially dangerous. The image of Baker as an exotic animal was so prevalent that Paul Colin captured it in one of the paintings in his series *Le Tumulte Noir* (figure 4.2). Her breasts exposed and her legs and arms turned outward, Baker seems ecstatic. Her feet are not touching the ground; she seems to be flying or hovering. Her thick lips, dark skin, and seductiveness make her the epitome of the savage. Gray iron bars across the painting signify her imprisonment. The fact that Baker is caged, and thus inaccessible, increases her allure even as it makes her into something like a wild beast.

e.e. cummings's description of Baker's debut is indicative of the fascination of the exotic animal. His description of her appearance is cryptic and poetic:

Figure 4.2   Paul Colin. *Le Tumulte Noir.* Courtesy of Henry Louis Gates, Jr.

She enters through a dense electric twilight, walking backwards on hands and feet, legs and arms stiff, down a huge jungle tree—as a creature neither infrahuman nor superhuman but somehow both: a mysteriously unkillable Something, equally nonprimitive and uncivilized, or beyond time in the sense that emotion is beyond arithmetic.[4]

The jungle decor, a metaphor reinforcing her black nudity, called out to repressed Europeans to colonize, consume, and symbolically devour the black body. In cummings's view, Baker was a mysterious and uncanny being who walked a tightrope between the world of the jungle and the world of modern technology. Neither primitive nor civilized, both "infrahuman" and "superhuman," Baker represented what cummings can only call "a mysteriously un-killable Something."

Nancy Cunard, the British American heiress and the editor of *Negro*, also stressed Baker's exoticism. Writing in 1934, Cunard remembered "the wild-fire syncopation of Josephine Baker's beautiful brown electric body." Here it is the body itself that is electric. Stressing the noncivilized aspects of her performance, Cunard points to the fact that the European public

> raved over this sleek and exquisite Afro-American head, flawless torso and whirl-wind limbs speeding and stamping through the exactitudes of the fierce "hot rhythm" . . . the dancing could be compared to the purest in African motion—it was *free*, perfect and exact, it centered admirably in the spare gold banana fronds round the dynamic hips.[5]

Connecting Baker's style and the uncivilized, Cunard sees Baker's dance rhythms as combining "hot rhythm," (African American jazz) and "the purest in African motion" (African dance). In the dance that Cunard describes, a group of dark-skinned Africans play the drums underneath a jungle tree; Baker's agile body moves frenetically to their rhythm with a belt of bananas fronds around her waist. This belt became Josephine Baker's trademark in 1926 when she first employed it in the dance "Fatou" during her show, *La Folie du Jour.*

In a curious twist, many critics connected Baker to the primitive because of her resemblance to primitivist art. For the dance critic André Levinson, the "Black Venus . . . evoked all the prestige of the best Negro sculpture. The plastic sense of a race of sculptors and the vigor of the African Eros caught us in its grip."[6] Hanry-Jaunet claimed that it is "impossible to resist her charm, her gaminerie [feminine insouciance], her rhythm," and remarked also that "her body [is] always sculptural" (Abatino, 21). Janet Flanner, the American journalist who wrote a column about life in Paris for the *New Yorker,* described Josephine Baker as "an unforgettable female ebony statue."[7] Further-more, Flanner claimed that Baker's "magnificent dark body [became] a new model that to the French proved for the first time that black was beautiful." It seems as if Flanner is trying to convince her American audience as well to consider that black can be beautiful.

Two reviews are noteworthy because they reveal how confused critics were when it came to describing this exotic beauty. In November 1925, in a review for *Candide*, Pierre de Régnier wondered about her androgyny:

> Is it a man? . . . Is it a Woman? . . . The lips are painted black, the skin has a banana color, the hair already short, sticks to her head as if she were cov-ered with caviar, the voice is high-pitched, she is in a perpetual tremble. . . . Is she horrible? Is she charming? Is she black, is she white? Had she painted her hair or her skull black? Nobody knows. One has no time to find out. She came back as fast as she had gone, fast as a one-step. This is not a woman, this is not a dancer, this is something extravagant and fugitive as music it-self, you might call it the ectoplasm of all the sounds one hears. . . . This dance of a rare indecency, is the triumph of lubricity, the return to the dead of the early ages: a silent declaration of love. (Sauvage, 20–24)

The French, Régnier tells us, accepted Baker without knowing whether she was black or white, man or woman. But his doubts as to her gender are confusing. Was it not more than obvious that Baker was a woman? After all, we might assume that her femininity was the basis of her sex appeal. Without resolving the question of her identity, he makes Baker into a metaphysical principle, arguing that she represented "the fugitive," "the ectoplasm of all sounds," the "triumph of lubricity." (The German edition translates *lubricité* as *Geilheit*—"horniness.") His language is obviously overblown; *La danse sauvage* presented a "rare indecency," but the French had no reason to fear "the return to the dead of the early ages."

This fragmented and cryptic passage reflects the difficulties critics encountered when they attempted to define the conundrum of Baker's gender and color. This lack of clear writing in accounting for her popularity only enhanced Baker's mysterious aura. A review by Paul Brach, published in *Comoedia*, is even more obscure:

> Joséphine, a reed both dark and pale, who abandoned the heat of a tropical river has come to breathe on the banks of the Seine and unto our grey and tired lives; we thank you. We have been distracted by the grace of your naivety. Unconsciously and without malice, you parody our turmoil and our ravings with your voice, your gestures, and your countenance: you cover our everyday worries with a blanket of sound. Your brilliant feathers might serve as a sign of our times, just as a poet's [illegible] is a versification of the sentiments of our age. In any case, you make preparations for the inevitable emergence of romanticism during the '30's. (Abatino, 14)

Thanking her for being the saving grace of France, Brach's tone verges on deification. His reiteration of "your" and "you" imitates the structure of prayer. Brach implicitly claims that Baker is a spiritual "weapon" (of the sort Picasso mentioned) to fight any sense of fatigue and to alleviate "everyday worries." To Brach, Baker is the messiah of a dawning romanticism, but one imported from black Africa.

Reviews such as these indicate that Baker was more than Europe's "exotic animal." Her significance exceeded that of the primitive *femme fatale*. Her function was to rejuvenate and redeem, and she occupied a large space in the collective cultural imagination of mid-1920s Paris. Baker's stardom was an integral part of—as well as the latest manifestation of—the *vogue nègre*. Primitivism on stage, as embodied by *La Bakaire*, was based on a symbolic economy: the audience yearned for something lacking in modern European culture; Baker, in turn, gave them what they needed. She took off her clothes, crawled on the floor, engaged in a frenzied, apparently spontaneous gush of energy, and *staged* "the primitive." In the process, Baker managed to rewrite the collective image that Europeans had constructed of black female sexuality.

The key nineteenth-century image of the black female as sexual object was that of the "Hottentot Venus." The term originally referred to an African woman known as Sarah Bartmann (or Saartje Baartman).[8] For ten years, this woman was exhibited at street fairs and dances across France. Her physiognomy itself was considered a curio and attracted many visitors who were amused by her hair, her buttocks, and her breasts. In 1815, at the age of twenty-five, the Hottentot Venus died in Paris. After an autopsy was performed, she became an object of enormous scientific interest. Several treatises (e.g., those by Georges Cuvier in 1817, R. Verneau in 1875, and Cesare Lombroso and Guillaume Ferraro in 1893) analyzed her physiognomy. Her extended buttocks, hypertrophic labia, and large pelvis were pathologized as anatomical anomalies (Gilman, 88). It is quite likely that most Europeans at the end of the nineteenth century thought of black female sexuality as gross and degenerate.[9]

While Europeans poked fun at the Hottentot Venus—often quite literally poking at her hips and her vagina—during the nineteenth century, the twentieth century adored and almost deified Baker as the "Ebony Venus." While the Hottentot Venus had elicited amusement or disgust, this sparsely clad black woman with a string of bananas around her waist elicited enthusiastic lust. The response to Baker's black body indicates that the Victorian ethos of the nineteenth century had drastically diminished. During *les années folles*, when the French tried to supersede the moral concepts of their father's generation, when sexuality was no longer considered amoral, this display of black female sexuality on stage was a conduit through which many spectators tried to subvert received social and religious attitudes toward sexuality, curiously enough, by symbolically embracing the black other.

Baker's black body was a catalyst that awakened the "weary" European spectators from torpor. Erich Maria Remarque maintained that Baker brought "a blast of jungle air, elemental power and beauty to the weary Western civilization" (Abatino, 51). Although this sounds exaggerated, Remarque's observation that the strip-tease dancer was, curiously enough, at least seen as a means to revitalize Western civilization is on the mark. Remarque echoes a key trope of primitivist modernism: that the black cultural idiom—be it a West African sculpture, or syncopated jazz, or an evening at the Savoy—is, somehow, primarily invigorating.

The "revivifying" effect her shows had on her spectators exceeded that of sexual stimulation, as a devout testimonial, published in *Volonté* in 1929, illustrates:

> Joséphine Baker, you who represent instinctual youth and the first spring in the mechanic and hectic cities, you continue to dance your savage dances. You who symbolize youth throughout the world, you who are the basis of life . . . continue to dance to the rhythms of primitive dances. All the metropoli of the world bow to you to learn about the secret that would impede them from dying from the weight of civilization.[10]

Baker embodied youth, vigor, and unrestrained joy. Representing the opposite of stasis and pretentiousness, she was understood to provide a symbolic corrective against aging and boredom. Baker was a counterforce to the weary and anemic mechanical world that Paris felt it had become. She was the great black hope, so to speak, who would impede the process of decay—and thereby stop the metropoli "from dying from the weight of civilization."

Reviews at the time confirm a curious reversal of the discourse on the jungle as it applied to Baker. One French critic, for example, asserted that "Joséphine Baker, this gracious little exotic animal, is the one who teaches us about the brutality only certain races have. . . . Always natural, she embodies vitality and rhythm. She is a combination of harmony, savage acrobatics and gracefulness" (Abatino, 24). In a statement by a German critic who claimed that "[i]n her [Baker] survives the untamed wildness of her forebears who were transplanted from the Congo basin to the Mississippi," Baker is named the ambassador from the jungle (Baker and Chase, 127). This ambassador to the old world had come from Africa via America as an expatriate to remind industrialized European cultures of what they had lost—that is, "untamed wildness." The European audiences were willing to make *La Bakaire* into a role model for liberation—sexual liberation—as well as the liberation from their overcivilized culture.

In the preface to *Le Tumulte Noir*, a writer known as "De Rip" makes a remarkable claim about the effects of this fascination: "In fact, we adopt their costumes, we learn their dances, we blacken ourselves more . . . All Parisians demand a heliotherapy to transform their white skin into that of leather." Here, the symbolic function Baker served can no longer be cast merely in metaphors of revivification. De Rip suggests that the governing metaphor will be submissive emulation. De Rip's tribute to *"la gloire de la fameuse étoile noire"* culminates in the denotation: *"L'impératrice Joséphine Baker."* Baker was more than the latest fashion on the Parisian stage; she was conquering Paris and, following her world tour in 1929, the entire continent. She was on top of the world, though dressed in a minstrel mask of primitivist stereotypes.

Baker was aware of the contradictions of her role. In a handwritten letter, signed by her and added to the cahier of Paul Colin's sketches, she writes:

> When the rage was in New York of colored people
> Monsieur Siegfied of Ziegfied Follies said its geting darker and darker on old
>   Broadway
> Since La Revue Nagri came to Yoe Parée, I'll say its geting darker and darker
>   in Paris.
> In a little while it shall be so dark untill one shall light a match then light
>   another to see if the first is lit are not.
> As the old saying is I may be a dark horse but you will never be a black
>   mare.

Whoever would have thought that the black girl from St. Louis could win the race and attain such fame? In that sense, she is a dark horse, but by mockingly claiming "you will never be a black mare," she is telling the French that their attempts to turn their white skin the color of leather are in vain. Baker's comment on the "blackening" of Broadway and Paris has an undercurrent of condescension. The number of spelling mistakes reminds us that Baker never received a thorough education. But her struggles with literacy were no hindrance to her capacity to cater to Europe's imaginative needs.

This attitude gives us some insight into Baker's motivations. The recurring theme in critical reviews of her shows is that of rejuvenation and revivification, but it is difficult to understand how this could have been a reciprocal process. Since the French often took her to be a curio from Africa, her appearance on stage sometimes amounted to a blend of freak show and peep show; she must have felt some sense of humiliation. Why would Baker be complicit in her own objectification or, symbolically speaking, her own incarceration?

Baker herself seemed to have been aware that her stardom was predicated on her embodiment of the *primitive de luxe*, and she consciously decided to give the French what they so desperately wanted. Playing off the imagery of the jungle, she adapted the racist stereotypes by which black people had been oppressed and exploited them for her own commercial success. In her first biography, published in 1927, Baker is quoted as saying:

> In the magazines and newspapers of Berlin, they wrote that I was a figure of
>   the contemporary German expressionismus, of German primitivismus,
>   etc. . . .
> Why not?
> And what does that mean anyway: I was born in 1906, twentieth century.
> Alles für Josephine.
> Why not?[11]

Baker knew that she was being categorized as a figure of primitivism and that she was fulfilling the exotic yearnings of Europeans. She knew that she owed her success to this dubious *"primitivismus."* Although Baker had heard about primitivism in the arts — e.g., in expressionism — she did not seem to have a thorough understanding of what *primitivismus* meant and why and how she had become a part of it.

Apparently, she willingly played the role of the savage as long as she was adequately compensated. As long as she was rewarded ("Alles für Josephine." [Everything for Josephine.]), she deliberately gave the audience all they wanted: "Why not?" In return, she became a millionaire, one of the few black people who could actually afford everything she wanted. "Alles für Josephine." This is the crucial difference between European artists' appropriating African sculptures and European audiences' consuming Baker's black, nude, and sculptural body. By entertaining and energizing the spectators, Josephine Baker received an enormous amount of money and fame. With Baker, in other words, the process of reinvigoration went both ways.

This was a conscious and even calculating project; Baker could not have remained the Ebony Venus or the darling of Paris had she not worked assiduously to keep her appeal alive. Starting with her first performance of *la danse sauvage*, she shaped her artistic persona and did everything she could to control her audiences. Far from being a passive object of the voyeuristic gaze, as the Hottentot Venus had been, Baker was an exhibitionist who did everything possible to turn her spectators into voyeurs. In fact, what is most notable about Baker is that she was both the subject and the object of primitivism.

Though she had never been to Africa, she shamelessly impersonated the *primitive de luxe*, adopting all its stereotypes as part of her costume and act. Recognizing that Africa was *en vogue,* she blended what were often racist ideas about Africa with the music and dance of African American culture to create primitivism *á la Bakaire*. She improvised her movements as the "author" of her own complex public personae. Her angular dance, the iconic posture of her bent knees, and her criss-crossed eyes were choreographed hallmarks of an advanced stage personae. It was a remarkable example of self-creation, but it came at a high price; most of her audience saw only either a titillating display of flesh or the exotic metaphors she invoked. Few seem to have attributed a complexity to her motivations.

Given Baker's fame in the Old World, one might wonder what America thought of the most famous American in Paris. Surprisingly, the (white) American press chose not to report on Baker until the fall of 1927—two full years after her triumphant success in *La Revue Nègre*. The *New York Times*, which published its first article on Josephine Baker in November 1927, printed only twelve short articles on her, totaling 170 lines, between 1927 and 1930.

While the most common position was denial, several forms of racism manifested themselves in the American press. There were blatantly scornful and insulting articles, such as a *Time* article that declared, "Joséphine Baker is a St. Louis washer-woman's daughter who stepped out of a Negro burlesque show into a life of adulation and luxury in Paris during the booming 1920's. In sex appeal to jaded Europeans of the jazz-loving type a Negro wench always has a head start."[12] But direct slurs were rare. More common was a selective reporting on the disreputable sides of Baker's perception in Europe. A journalist from the *New York Times* reported that the Austrian Parliament objected to Baker's "'perverse acting' and commented mostly unfavorably upon her black body and figure."[13] Baker was "banned from dancing in Vienna," the headline reads; the fact that the Austrian Parliament spent an entire afternoon discussing Baker's appearance in Vienna is never mentioned.

The *New York Times* also reported on the decision by the City Council of London forbidding Baker to perform because her "semi-nude appearance aroused considerable public indignation" and on the Yugoslavian government's objection to her appearance. The headlines are telling: "Vienna Bars Negro Dancer," "Josephine Baker's Dances Forbidden," and "Missiles Hurled at Josephine Baker."[14] Reporting Baker's appearance in Berlin, the *New York Times* writes: "Hundreds of angry theater-goers stormed the box office tonight when they learned that neither Josephine Baker, American negro dancer from Paris, nor the American comedian Al Sherman would appear in the revue."[15] Instead of relating this rush to Baker's extraordinary popularity (she sometimes gave two shows a night to meet the demand), the article stresses that theatergoers got angry at her for not showing up, insinuating that Josephine Baker was unreliable and irresponsible.

An article in the *Boston Herald*, which includes the first photo of Baker to appear in the daily (white) American press, announced her return to America at the Boston Opera House on Christmas, 1935:

> For 10 years Josephine Baker has been the sensation of Paris. Season after season, the Parisians have continued to scream their approval of their banana girl; her caviar coif, her saxophone contortions, her colossal vitality.

They have liked having her running around their stages on all fours, der-
riere up, head down, dressed in three feathers.[16]

With a condescending undertone, the writer makes Baker "their" banana girl.
While the passage humiliates Baker, it also formulates an attack against the
French; in fact, it seems as if she is only a pretext for the petty, nationalistic
sniping. This disguised antipathy for the French reveals how racism was
often paired with American nationalism. Surprisingly, the same article presents Baker as an amicable person who dresses modestly and loves animals
and antique furniture: "Miss Baker at home is simple, cordial, sensible." The
accompanying photo shows an elegant lady holding a bouquet; the caption
reads, "A stranger returns to her native land."

How did the black American press report on her? The first notice of Josephine Baker appeared in W. E. B. Du Bois's *Crisis* magazine on February 3, 1927
—a year and a half after her breakthrough, but nine months before the *New
York Times* first reported on her. The article proudly announces that "the colored dancer, Josephine Baker, continues to be the most popular of all the stars"
at the Folies Bergère.[17] While most reviews in the black press were equally
straightforward in their positive appraisal of Baker's success, we can also
identify a subtly different stance toward Baker.

Many articles made Baker into a role model. An article published in *Crisis*
relates Josephine's story in the rags-to-riches formula: "Josephine is truly a
Cinderella child. The poverty and struggle of her first few years have been
changed into riches and success by the wands of ambition and work."[18] Stressing that Josephine has claimed fame through her own agency, the article
concludes that she personifies the black self-made woman who is welcomed
among white people. Similarly, the *Pittsburgh Courier* praises "Jo" for her sudden fame and compares her life to that of a protagonist of a fairy tale: "Josephine Scaled the Ladder of Her Dreams More Quickly Than the Girl of the
Fairy Tale." The last sentence of the article continues this motif: "Let us follow her as she climbs the ladder to stardom."[19] These sympathetic accounts of
Baker use her as living proof that there is a black version of the American
dream.

This fairy tale was made literal when Baker married the Count Pepito de
Abatino; she became "America's first Negro countess," as the *New York World*
wrote in an article titled "Josephine Baker, of Harlem, Adds a Noble Husband
to Conquests Abroad."[20] At a time when miscegenation laws generally forbade
mixed marriages, it was remarkable that a black woman became the wife of a
white man, not to mention a man of nobility. The marriage generated considerable controversy.[21] During the months of June and July, eight articles published in the black press dealt with Baker's claim to nobility. The public debate over this event stirred the black imagination to such an extent that an
editor of the *Amsterdam News* protested that "too much 'to-do' is being made
over this sort of thing."[22]

Even Joel A. Rogers, a contributor to Alain Locke's anthology *The New
Negro,* devoted attention to the issue. In an interview with the "Countess
Pepito di Albertini," Rogers suggests that Baker's marrying into nobility is

more significant than any of her accomplishments as a performer. His intent is not to denigrate her aesthetic contributions but rather to make a political point; when he asks Baker what it was like to live in Europe, she responds that in America, black musicians "had to take a more or less inferior place simply because of color. . . . I could never think of making my home again in America after all of this."[23] Rogers's interview, then, not only introduced the readers to the only living black countess but also was a subtle but effective weapon to critique racial injustice. When he quotes Baker as saying, "Europeans are different . . . Everyone has been so kind to me," his readers learned that there was less racism in Europe than there was in America.[24]

The use of Baker as an instrument for working out racial animosity manifested itself in a heated debate between *Time* magazine and the *Chicago Defender*. When *Time* printed the claim that "in sex appeal to jaded Europeans of the jazz-loving type a Negro wench always has a head start," the *Chicago Defender* responded with an open letter to the magazine's editors. Politely, but with an undertone of sarcasm, the *Chicago Defender* commented: "We are rather inclined, for the sake of charity, to believe that *TIME* unfortunately selected a member of its staff whose idea of journalistic decency finds fit and proper association in the gutter . . . the vile word 'wench' is not the language of cultured gentlemen."

Roi Otley, a columnist for *Amsterdam News,* claimed that many blacks did not like Baker and reported them as saying: "She has no business trying to be white." Otley felt that this attitude was pernicious; he advised his readers to "rally to the side of this courageous Negro woman. We should make *her* insults *our* insults."[25] But the fact that he had to remind blacks to make Baker's insults theirs indicates that they did not think of her as a member of the black community. This symbolic expatriation was based on the assumption that Baker had betrayed her people—that she had turned her back on them.

The indictment that Baker's successful integration into Parisian society had caused a lack of racial solidarity was also made in an essay by Nancy Cunard. In her contribution to *Negro*, Cunard puts together comments French critics made about Baker:

> The Ebony Venus—the banana dancer—let us gaze at this extraordinary example of rhythmic life—is it a youth, is it a girl? . . . But she has worked hard to please us [the French]—this cannibal beauty with her fetish face— She is anyway too exquisite for a Negress—she seems to whiten as we gaze at her—By far the best possible example of the perfecting of the black race by its intellectual contact with European civilization—What a difference between the little savage of the early days with her delirious, grotesque dances and the toned-down, refined *artiste* transformed by Paris. . . . Civilization has done its work—Josephine is from now on assimilated by the western world. . . . "Josephine est blanche . . . (Josephine is white)!" (Cunard, *Negro*, 329)

The self-satisfied triumph of Western civilization's assimilation of the primitive obviously annoys Cunard, who argues for an "authenticity" of Africans and African Americans. Cunard scolds the "dreary gang of French critics" for their lack of taste and for their self-righteousness in claiming that Baker was proof blacks would become more civilized in close contact with Europeans. Their desire to make Josephine Baker "a whitened, gallicized actress" reveals the prejudice of French nationalism and racism, which, Cunard argues, was equal to—if not worse than—that of the Anglo-Saxon countries. Cunard concludes that France is not the "un-prejudiced heaven for the black man that so many Negroes in America think."

Cunard's assessment is based on a premise that "hot rhythms" represent "pure" African motion and that "the wild-fire syncopation of Josephine Baker's beautiful brown electric body when she first appeared in Paris in 1925" was an "authentic" black expression. Her critique is of a style that Baker adopted after 1930, which was more refined and "civilized" than *la danse sauvage*; the French called it "pure art." To Cunard, however, this stylistic shift was a sign of surrender, indicating the triumph of bourgeois French national taste masquerading under the guise of "civilization."

Cunard's lampooning of the French critics is a dismissal of Josephine's artistic transformation. Admiring "the whirlwind limbs speeding and stamping through the exactitudes of the fierce 'hot rhythm,'" she expresses her disregard for Baker's dismissal of primitivism from her post-1930 performances. Baker's distancing herself from the tradition of European primitivism was, to Cunard, a betrayal of her race. Cunard disapproves of Baker's "diamond paraphernalia"; she prefers the "spare gold banana fronds round the dynamic hips." Scolding Baker for allowing the French to feel triumphant, Cunard ignores the fact that Baker declared independence from European fantasies of who and what a black woman is and, doing so, displayed her own agency. Her indignation over the change of Baker's public persona is itself a racist attitude disguised as love for the primitive.

The source of the debate is this. In 1929, Baker had decided to change her persona. After studying French and taking lessons to improve her dancing and singing, the untutored strip-tease dancer became a sophisticated performer who sang mostly in French. Baker abandoned the banana belt, and the song "J'ai deux amors"—which was about her loving two countries, America and France—became her new trademark. Baker renounced the role of the primitive *femme fatale*, appeared in glamorous gowns, wore diamonds, and became a "lady." The primitive seductress, in other words, had transformed herself into a prima donna through "art." After Baker changed her performance style, many French critics referred to her as an *artiste*. One contemporary reviewer maintained: "She is not just a dancer, or just a singer with a beautiful voice. She belongs now to that great race of artists with overwhelming personalities that the public takes to their hearts."[26]

In her column for the *New Yorker*, "Letters from Paris," Janet Flanner commented on this change: "At the Casino, beautifully costumed, staged, chorused, in a fair way to becoming what I called an artiste, she is far from that unknown chorus girl, selected by Michel Covarrubias, who a few summers ago made her Paris debut carried in upside down, à poil, and doing the split" (Flanner, 73). Quite literally, Baker no longer appeared upside-down, or on the

the floor; rather, she presented herself in the most erect posture. While she was still performing in music halls and not in the *l'opera* like classical ballet performers, Baker had moved closer in style to dancers such as Isadora Duncan, the acknowledged queen of modern dance, or to the dancers in Diaghilev's Russian Ballet.

Baker had also ventured into other forms of artistic expression. In September 1926, she had released her first record, produced for the Odeon label. Eventually (by the time of her double-album, "Josephine A Bobino," in 1975), she would record more than 230 songs for Odeon, Columbia, Pacific, and RCA. Baker also became a film actress, though still utilizing her primitivist persona. She starred in *La Sirène des Tropiques* (1934), for which Luis Buñuel was an assistant director. Baker plays an island girl who wants to teach Europeans a new dance. In *ZouZou* (1934), she plays the role of a black girl in love with her white stepbrother, acted by Jean Gabin.

Princesse Tam Tam (1935) is probably Baker's most interesting film. Here, Baker plays a barefooted, easygoing African princess who becomes the muse for a French novelist with writer's block. She triggers his imagination and inspires him to write a novel that turns out to be a bestseller in France. To express his gratitude, the novelist introduces her to Parisian high society, where she is welcomed as an African queen. Dressed in elegant costumes, she becomes very popular among the French elite. The plot is a metaphor for Baker's own story; it echoes the revivification trope underlying the dynamic of primitivism.

Baker's ability to entice her audiences, as well as her ability to work with different media—film, music, dance—was at the core of her later success. Her versatility calls to mind contemporary artists such as Madonna or Whitney Houston. Kariamu Welsh Asante goes so far as to suggest that Baker was a harbinger of performance art:

> Josephine Baker was the first and greatest Black dancer to emerge in the genre now called performance art. She epitomized through dance what freedom of expression and artistic expression really meant for generations of artists worldwide. Baker was one of the few artists in the world who were acclaimed and awarded for being themselves. Her genius resided in her conception of music, dance, and comedy. . . . Not merely an entertainer, Baker was in every sense of the word an artist, and it was as an artist that she made her mark on the world.[27]

Although it is questionable whether or not Baker was actually "being herself" on stage, it is safe to argue that she was "not merely an entertainer." In fact, our argument is precisely that her persona was a conscious production and that, as such, it was prototypically modernist.

In which way can Baker be taken as an expression of—or even a creator of—the modernist aesthetic? There are many facets to this question. We might mention that her performances attracted many modernist artists, including Ernest Hemingway, Le Corbusier, Jean Cocteau, Adolf Loos, Alexander Calder, Gertrude Stein, Paul Morand, Scott Fitzgerald, Henry Miller, Man

Ray, and André Gide. To Le Corbusier, Loos, and Calder, Baker was even a source of inspiration. But obviously, asserting an affinity between known modernists and Baker does not make her a modern artist.

Among the critics who have argued for Baker as an integral part of modernism is Michele Wallace. In her article "Modernism, Postmodernism and the Problem of the Visual in Afro-American Culture" (in a collection of essays entitled *Black Popular Culture*), Wallace calls attention to the fact that most discussions of modernism fail to refer to Baker at all. Wallace accounts for this neglect by positioning Baker as the "Afro-American 'other' of Euro-American Modernism" (Wallace, 45). But Wallace fails to specify Baker's role in relation to modernism; it remains unclear if Baker represents the other in terms of race or gender, as a representative of popular culture, or as a different type of avant-gardism.

Given Baker's omnipresence in the French culture industry, it seems inadequate simply to maintain that she was the other. Although Baker was a cultural outsider and member of a socially marginalized group, her role in the context of the French entertainment industry was never peripheral. Baker, though an expatriate like so many other American artists, did not just live in Paris; her art performances had a sustaining, shaping effect on French popular culture. But popularity is not the same thing as modernism.

The biographer Phyllis Rose approaches our question when she claims that "the black revue came to symbolize postwar modernism—the new, Cubist sensibility which savored angles and fragments rather than curvilinear forms, juxtaposition rather than fluidity as a principle of coherence, frenetic energy rather than graceful lyricism."[28] But saying that the revue symbolized modernism does not necessarily mean that Baker herself created a modernist expression. Nor does it suffice to claim that Baker's dance style should be considered modern just because it was angular and fragmented.

What is safe to say is that Baker's performance, particularly in her early career, included mostly improvised dance numbers; she, perhaps unknowingly, transgressed the conventions of choreographed dance. She boldly deviated from the conventions of ballroom dancing and standard dance choreography. Prior to 1930, Baker had not taken dancing lessons and her *danse sauvage* seems to have been, for the most part, her own invention. Baker created dance movements as she went along, apparently on the spot. She "made it new," as Pound admonished the modern artist to do.

Mindy Aloff, the senior dance critic of *Dance* magazine, went so far as to argue that Baker "created one of the great dance effects of the 20th century."[29] What made her dancing so sensational was, to Aloff, Baker's ability to move different parts of her body to different rhythms. She writes: "Everything moved for the spotlight: eyes, tongue, cheeks inflated with air, shoulders, upper back, pelvis, elbows and hands, knees and ankles, and all of them in delicious syncopation."[30] Aloff, then, credits Baker with having added syncopation to dance and suggests that, in doing so, Baker revolutionized the genre.

This revolution of physical expression was recognized by some of Baker's contemporaries. In the late 1920s, Max Reinhardt, the director of the Deutsches Theater, described Baker's preeminent quality as an "expressive control of the whole body, the spontaneity of motion, the rhythm, the bright emotional color" (Rose, 85). In this respect, Baker has to be understood as the counterpart to the widely acknowledged modern dancer Isadora Duncan. In his pioneering study, *The Dance* (1929), W. A. Roberts asserts that the United States made two contributions to dance: one was Isadora Duncan, because she "liberated costumes and the use of the body"; the other was Negro-American jazz dancing, in which "the entire body is employed as a medium of expression."[31]

No one has expressed this relationship so succinctly as Phyllis Rose: "Isadora Duncan had refreshed European culture bringing it the spirit of an Americanized Greece. Jo Baker would refresh it by bringing the spirit of an Americanized Africa" (Rose, 18). This staging of an Americanized Africa "refreshed"—again, Rose draws on the metaphor of rejuvenation—European popular culture at a time precisely when even the American-classical style of Isadora Duncan had become outdated. Baker represented an Americanized, pseudo-African alternative aesthetics to a derivative neoclassicism.

Baker also bridged two traditions in dance. In the New York City of the 1920s, the dance critic Elizabeth Kendall maintains, there existed a considerable gap between musical comedy and art-dance. While musical comedies were assumed silly and lighthearted, art-dance was "heavy lyricism, perfume, and drama." Though Kendall accords the bridging of this gap to Martha Graham, we know that this also happened when Josephine Baker combined lighthearted rhythmic play with black lyricism and serious dance.[32] Or, looking at it in a diachronical way, Baker reinvented her artistic style from a comic minstrel self to the primitivist self epitomized in the *danse sauvage*, and then, finally, to her artistic performance mode.

It is difficult to assess the significance of this fact. If we remember, however, that at the beginning of this century, the concept of art was based on the strict separation of high and low culture, we might grasp the broader implications. The high arts—enshrined at the National Gallery or put on stage at the Staatsoper—were worlds apart from plays performed in dialect or musical comedies. Baker's blend of eroticism and exoticism not only appealed to audiences across class lines but also constituted an unprecedented crossover between high and low culture.

Baker was not just another "African object." She was primitivist modernism in blackface and on two legs. What is crucial to Baker's particular version of primitivist-modernism is that it is dynamic, dialectical, and ultimately self-referential. In the previous examples we have examined, the act of cultural appropriation was a one-way process in which, initially, a white person made use of a black expression. What is unique about Josephine Baker is that she was both "the primitive" and "the modernist." Baker was both the object and the subject of primitivist modernism.

Due to her artistic guile, Baker managed to capitalize on playing the role of the primitive. Instead of walking into a museum to be inspired by African art, as Picasso had done, Baker turned her body into a museum and invited the audience to enter it. Putting on a black mask, she became a cultural impersonator who subverted the received order of Western dance conventions and pioneered a performance art. Baker, then, created an artistic expression we might call popular modernism. It is not surprising that Pablo Picasso himself felt an affinity for Baker; he is reported as saying that "she is the Nefertiti of now," a modern goddess—the icon of the twenties.[33]

What might be surprising, however, is that Baker once commented on Picasso. In a self-mocking tone, she camouflages her critique and says:

> I am so old-fashioned, so stupid maybe because I think that when one looks at a painting one has to be able to see right away what it is supposed to mean. It used to be like that. But today! Take the other day, a rich woman, a bourgeois lady showed me with ostentatious enthusiasm a very small painting. She had paid an extraordinary amount, eh oh! et ah! . . . [She asked me] whether I thought that it was great. It was by him, you know, Pinarzo, or what is his name, the one everybody talks about?
>
> "Picasso?" [the interviewer asks]
>
> Right, Picasso, and it was nothing but a few lines. They weren't even straight. You know, I find that terrible! Now, you could certainly say that I talk about things I don't understand. Well let me respond to you then in telling you a fairy tale by Andersen: "Once upon a time there was a king who had a closet full of clothes, one more luxurious than the next . . . ."[34]

Of course, she knew who Picasso was. In fact, according to her adopted son, Jean-Claude Baker, she and Picasso had an affair. In this passage, Baker signifies on nonrepresentational aesthetics, the genius of modernism, and the docility of his admirers. After admitting that she does not know much about art, Josephine mentions the fable "The Emperor's New Clothes" in order to scorn modernism for being all appearance without essence. Her joke seems to be that since she purposefully wore no clothes—emperor's or otherwise—she had created an art that was all essence.

Here, Baker casts herself as a critical commentator and transcends her image as an object of exoticism comparable to African sculpture. Although Baker suggests that she differs from Picasso—the mispronunciation of his name is an indicator of this distance—she still compares herself to the famous artist. We can extrapolate from her self-assertiveness that she thinks of herself as a counterforce to him. In the very act of negation—saying that she does not know anything about modern art—Baker presents herself as an opinionated person whose status is equal to Picasso's.

Baker was extremely conscious of this equality: crossing the color line had been the fundamental accomplishment of her career. Her vaudeville performances had taken place in front of all-black audiences at a time when most theaters in America were strictly segregated. *Shuffle Along* was the first major black show that played in front of white audiences, and as a chorus girl in the show Baker was among the first blacks to transgress the color line in the field of performance art.[35] Later, as the star of her own shows, Baker actively fought for integration; during the 1950s she refused to perform in front of segregated audiences.

Baker's fight against segregation in show business had a rather curious corollary. In 1931 she published a melodramatic novel, *Mon sang dans tes veines*, jointly written with Félix de la Camara and Pepito Abatino. The plot of the novel, which has never been translated into English, is based on Baker's ideas about segregation and the "one drop" rule. The protagonist is Fred Barclay, son of a wealthy chewing gum manufacturer. The novel is set in a town called Oaks, where Fred grew up with Joan, the daughter of his family's black maid. During their childhood, they had been close friends. But when Fred became an adult, he stopped associating with her and fell in with a crowd of young, successful, and racist Anglo-Americans.

The discrepancy between their arrogance and the appeal of the beautiful and humiliated Joan makes the reader sympathetic to her. Joan's naive indignation at the fact that white and black dogs eat from the same bowl, whereas black and white people in Oaks rarely share meals, is typical of obvious metaphors on which the narrative rests. One day on a walk through the woods, Joan finds a black madonna inside an abandoned church. When she learns that it is a Polish icon, Joan concludes that Europeans must be above racism because they can worship a black mother of God.

The climax of the story is tragic. Fred is run over by his own Rolls-Royce. He loses so much blood that he needs a transfusion to survive; Joan volunteers to give blood to the man she has adored all her life. During his recovery, Fred asks the doctor about the donor, but Dr. Anderson gives an evasive answer, saying that most donors are anonymous walk-ins. In a conversation with the doctor's assistant, Fred learns that his donor was a young woman; Fred assumes that his fiancée, Clarence Clifton, had given him back his life. After she tells him that this is not the case, Fred becomes even more eager to discover his donor's identity. One day in the assistant's office, Fred picks up a piece of paper that had dropped to the floor; it happens to be a listing of blood donors. Fred reads his name next to Joan's and announces with horror: "I . . . I . . . I now have black blood in my veins." The assistant tries to calm him: "Don't worry Mr. Fred it doesn't show."

Fred, however, is devastated—even mortified. The day he is released from the hospital, just after he returns to his mother's house in Oaks, he tells his fiancée in a trembling voice: "Clarence . . . you know I love you . . . but I can't marry you!" Repeating himself, "I can't marry you," Fred stutters: "Joan was the one who . . ." It is unspeakable. Clarence turns pale, her face stiff. Feeling genuine pity for him, she responds: "Poor Mr. Barclay, so you have *her* blood in your veins, you have become a black white man." The novel concludes: "In their irreducible opposition, the combination of the two words [*nègre blanc*] marked the end of their relationship; the memory of a dark shadow settled forever on an impossible happiness."[36]

It would be difficult not to read this story as a satire on American race phobia. Baker used her success to publish a novel attacking America, where inter-marriages were still illegal in most states and where blood transfusions were still legally segregated even though it had been common knowledge in the scientific community since the early 1920s, when Karl Landsteiner discovered the existence of the four types of blood, that race was an insignificant factor in the division of the blood groups. Despite this knowledge, American blood banks separated blood into separate white and black stores until the early 1950s.[37]

The novel mocks centuries-old European beliefs espoused by thinkers such as Immanuel Kant, who predicted that "in all probability, the mixing of tribes will by and by obliterate character."[38] It satirizes authors such as John Campbell, who believed that the survival of the white race depended on strictly segregating the races. Campbell's book, *Negro-Mania: Being an Examination of the Falsely Assumed Equality of the Various Races of Men* (1851), suggests that race equality actually meant the "extinction of one race [white] and the substitution of another [mixed]."[39] Alfred Schultz is another example of this type of thinking. The title of his book *Race or Mongrel* (1908) expresses succinctly the either/or mentality underlying its racist thesis. Schultz is concerned about "the danger of degeneration through crossing." Like many other writers at the turn of the century, he believed that "promiscuous crossing destroyed many of the noblest races" (Campbell, 349).

Baker's novel about a "black white man" parodies this either/or mentality at the center of the discourse of miscegenation. *Mon sang dans tes veines* signifies upon the paranoia of inter-racial intercourse and blood-mixing. With an undertone of malicious glee, Baker seems to say that Fred deserves his fate; it serves him right if he thinks of himself as a fallen man, as the dreaded *blanc nègre*. Baker mocks the idea that a person—and by extension, a culture—of mixed blood is socially dead. Since Baker uses the novel as a weapon to strike a humorous assault and revenge her race, *Mon sang dans tes veines* becomes Baker's abreaction—an exorcism text—against Jim Crowism and those who were convinced that one drop of black blood meant the end of civilization itself.

The peculiar novel is, in part, a coming to terms with the humiliation Baker experienced in her own life. In the preface to *Mon sang dans tes veines*, written by Baker alone, she makes several autobiographical references, among them: "I have known this poor Joan, whose story you will read, . . . or rather, I did not know her personally but a dozen little girls from Saint-Louis who were all black" (3). This statement is followed by a rhetorical question asking whether the fact that there were many black girls living in that quarter in St. Louis was related to the fact that it was an industrial zone. The next paragraph starts with a direct quotation that brings the moment of the past into the present; it adds a sense of immediacy: ". . . they always tell us [that] . . . the different bloods would fight against each other and could not mix . . . I [Josephine] reassured her [Joan] that by the coincidence of life, my veins carried blood of three colors. My father was white, my aunt Elvara Indian, Joan remembers well. . . ." And this is how the paragraph ends.

This manifesto for mixed ancestry, which strangely excludes her black mother, Carrie, follows a surreal lyricism that talks about Josephine's and

Joan's desire to escape an "unjust continent," to reach "a country where they would treat us like fairy tale princesses. . . . We would dance covered with diamonds, with pearls and feathers; we would sing under lights much brighter than the African sun. But Joan said that she would have preferred the beautiful country of humility" (6). It seems an obvious metaphor for Baker's own life. Once a poor black girl who desired to escape poverty and degradation, she reached the European continent. Although she danced in bright spotlights and not under the African sun, she self-consciously evoked the illusion of Africa. And for evoking a carefree, sexualized jungle-life, the French showered her with diamonds and pearls. Baker became so rich that she could afford to adorn the neck of her leopard, Chiquita, with a diamond collar worth $20,000.

The preface suggests that these precious objects are part of the symbolic economy we have previously discussed. For taking on the role of the erotic-exotic African, Josephine Baker received things she had always dreamed of. Capitalizing upon Europe's unfulfilled exotic desires, she could satisfy her own materialist fantasies and escape the fate most other girls in St. Louis had to endure. But the last sentence of the preface—"Joan said that she would have preferred the beautiful country of humility"—is disconcerting. Was Josephine Baker signifying on her own public primitivist self and the wealth it had brought to her? Or was she expressing a sense of nostalgia for what she had left behind, paying homage to the many black women who had no choice but to remain in a country that humiliated them?

To illustrate how it was possible that Baker escaped that fate, it is instructive to look closely at another image of her drawn by Paul Colin, *La Joie de Paris,* which advertised a revue that opened in December 1932 at the Casino de Paris (figure 4.3). Colin's image is an illustration of the first-act finale, "Soul of Jazz," in which Baker is accompanied by twenty-two young black musicians, known as "The Baker Boys." Colin's minimalist image depicts only three figures: one black, one green, one red. They occupy the center of the piece and are surrounded by musical notes and drawings of musical instruments. The simple and geometric image resonates with the animated spirit of jazz.

Colin captures the dancing figures in motion; one feels the tension of movement not completed. The black body in front—the only dancer with facial expressions—is contrasted with and complemented by the flatness of the two other figures. The angularity of the body shapes—the rear-ends as well as the arms set at sharp angles—express a sense of artifice. The reduced and ideographic mode of representation, particularly evident in the green and red figures, makes it a perfect example of minimalist, nonmimetic art characteristic of what Robert Goldwater called "intellectual primitivism." It seems that Colin here was inspired by Picasso. But the difference between this image and *Les Demoiselles d'Avignon* is vast. Picasso's image is static and gloomy; Colin's poster is more abstract, energetic, and light-spirited.

The black figure is dynamic and fluid. Easily recognizable as *La Bakaire*, it is statuesque and vibrant and brings to mind Baker's rhythmic virtuosity.

Figure 4.3　Paul Colin. *La Joie de Paris*. (1932). Courtesy of D.A.G.P., Paris, and D.A.C.S., London. (Reprinted in Bryan Hammond and Patrick O'Connor. *Josephine Baker*. Boston: Bulfinch Press, 1988, 116.)

It echoes Cunard's description of her sleek and flawless torso as an expression of the "purest in African motion." But it also echoes a description Colette made of Baker as "the most beautiful panther, [and] the most charming woman" (Abatino, 51). Indeed, in this particular image, Baker is represented as an animal embodying sensual power in motion.

Colin's style is based on an aesthetic inspired by Africa, but his image also reflects Baker's agency. The smiling black figure that so resembles Baker is holding a baton in her right hand; we get the sense that she is the conductor of her own unrestrained and spontaneous performance. Colin's poster sug-

gests that Baker has consciously choreographed her movements in a calcu-
lated effort to make her audience forget the technical side of her art—the
training, her burlesque past, the demands of staging such a revue—in order
to convey a sense of spontaneous African "authenticity."

Sensing the symbolic demand for the "authentic," Baker became an impersonator of the "primitive," as if she intuitively grasped in the 1920s what Walter Benjamin would express a decade later: that in an age of mass reproduction, art loses its aura. A mass-reproduced work of art, such as a photograph
or a poster, cannot convey a sense of uniqueness; the awe-inspiring aura between the object and the spectator is lost, as is any sense of authenticity.[40] It
was this deficit to which Baker's live performances purposefully responded.
Baker embodied the *élan vital*, a bursting vivacity that was associated more
with premodern and non-Western worlds than with early twentieth-century
Europe. Nevertheless, it was precisely the popular, modernist European
world—it tensions, its contradictions, its ironies—that she embodied in
blackface.

THE BLACK BOOK

It is an insult to the great Caucasian race, the father of all the arts and sciences, to compare it to that black and kinky race which lived in a state of black and ignorant savagery until the white race seized it and lifted it to its present position.[1]

—Ray Stannard Baker (1908)

The African with his love of color, warmth, rhythm and the whole sensuous life, might, if emotionally liberated, do interesting things to a "Nordic" stock, so bustling and busy, so preoccupied with "doing things" in the external world, as almost to forget, sometimes, that it has any senses. And it would be one of fate's quaint but no means impossible revenges if the Negro's real contribution to American life should be in the field of art.[2]

—*New York Herald Tribune,*
reprinted in *Opportunity*
(June 1925)

In the fall of 1925, the philosopher Alain Leroy Locke published *The New Negro: An Interpretation*, a collection he had edited with the intent of providing a forum for the younger generation of black writers so that they could be heard in both black and white America. This chorus of raucous voices, with Locke as maestro, was the first anthology of black art to reach a large white and black audience. Its texts—a colorful kaleidoscope of genres, including poetry, short fiction, portrait painting, decorative arts, and critical essays on art and society—aimed to revolutionize the image of the Negro in the American imagination. *The New Negro* was the birth certificate of a new type of Negro, one who was culturally articulate, self-assertive, and proud of his heritage. In the final sentence of the foreword, Locke claims that the book is an offering that embodies "ripening forces as culled from the first fruits of the Negro Renaissance." Announcing that Negroes had entered their "cultural adolescence" and were beginning their "approach to maturity,"

Locke points to a "racial awakening on a national and perhaps even a world scale."

Locke's choice of metaphors suggests that this type is still emerging, more potential than fully realized; indeed, the anthology was meant to function as a blueprint, a manual for how to become the New Negro. A prerequisite for raising this New Negro was to discard the stereotype of the docile, illiterate Negro and replace it with a collective "public, Negro, self," as Carter G. Woodson put it: the energetic, entrepreneurial, and artistically poised Negro. *The New Negro* tried to function as a catalyst in this process; it intended to reinvent the image of the old Negro by carefully crafting a counterimage to white stereotypes. This symbolic reconstruction of the race's image meant, as Henry Louis Gates, Jr. has so deftly demonstrated, that the (negated) white text remained the New Negro's ultimate referent.[3]

The strategy of refashioning the public image of the old Negro necessitated grappling with the centuries-old indictment that the descendants of Africans were incapable of producing art. The book's very existence was meant to be proof that Negroes were a race of artists and intellectuals; it set out to strike a symbolic blow against the long history of racism, refuting bigots such as Ray Stannard Baker, who felt that the Caucasian race was the "father of all the arts and sciences." *The New Negro* intended to demonstrate that the black race was not living in "ignorant savagery"; on the contrary, it was in the midst of a Renaissance and experiencing a "dramatic flowering of a new race-spirit," as Locke announced in the foreword.

Ironically, the attempt to prove Negro artistry to the American public caused Locke to turn toward Europe; he refers to the renowned European art critic, Roger Fry, who had claimed that ancient African sculptures were "greater" than anything Europe had produced in the Middle Ages. His reevaluation of what most people had considered "fetishes" as "masterpieces of art" made Locke optimistic about the future of American Negro art. Locke surmised that what had happened to African sculptures in European art criticism might also happen to Negro art in America. If Europeans could discover beauty in historically benighted African art, then America might also discover the beauty of a "new" Negro art, the first cousin of *l'art nègre*.

Locke inferred that if the New Negroes connected themselves to this ancient artistic tradition, they would see themselves as descendants of a race of African sculptors rather than merely of slaves. This view of themselves would have a germinating effect on the flowering of the race spirit. Locke's vision of an African American Renaissance that would sweep away the old racist iconography of "Sambo," "Uncle Tom," "Aunt Jane," and "George" was inspired by the European appreciation of African art, particularly the cubism Locke had studied at Oxford, in Berlin, and at the Collège de France in Paris between 1907 and 1912. Locke's encounter with his cultural others—European and African art—led to his constructing a strategy that would allow whites to see Negroes as a race of artists, a process that would ultimately change the attitude of the Anglo-American toward the Negro.

If we take a close look at the structure of the book, we notice an unmediated gap between part I, "The Negro Renaissance," and part II, "The New Negro in the New World." The first section (to which Locke contributed four essays, including "The New Negro" and "The Legacy of the Ancestral Arts") is devoted to aesthetics. Works of fiction and poetry by younger Negroes, such as Langston Hughes, Zora Neale Hurston, Claude McKay, and Jean Toomer, take up more than 100 of the 267 pages that make up part I. This part of the anthology basically calls for a black modernist aesthetic.

The second part, however, is concerned with social and political questions; black sociologists, journalists, and historians dominate. It begins with an article by Paul Kellogg, the editor of *Survey Graphic,* in which he refers to the *Survey Graphic* issue of March 1925 called *Harlem: Mecca of the New Negro.* The last essay of this section is W. E. B. Du Bois's "The Negro Mind Reaches Out." While the most frequently used keywords of this section are "progressive" and "modern," the keyword in the anthology's first section is "primitive," used in any of three ways: as a synonym for ancient African art (in romantic references to the mythical motherland); as a synonym for the vital and vigorous (as in J. A. Rogers's description of the invigorating jazz spirit we discussed in chapter 3), or as a synonym for the natural and spiritual (as in Albert Barnes's essay on the nature of Negro art).

The trope of black vigor as the saving grace of an otherwise fallen civilization runs throughout *The New Negro.* It echoes W. E. B. Du Bois's seminal article "The Conversation of Races," in which he declares that the black spirit is the necessary counterpart to the Teutonic race. Du Bois had announced in 1897:

> At that point, we are Negroes, members of a vast historic race that from the very dawn of creation has slept, but half awakening in the dark forests of its African fatherland. We are the first fruits of this new nation, the harbinger of that black tomorrow which is yet destined to soften the whiteness of the Teutonic today. We are that people whose subtle sense of song has given America its only music, its only American fairy tales, its only touch of pathos and humor amid its mad money-getting plutocracy.[4]

"To soften the whiteness of the Teutonic" is the Negroes' self-acclaimed mission in America, but Du Bois suggests that to realize this goal in the future it is necessary to remember and conserve the racial legacy of the "African fatherland."

Albert C. Barnes's essay, "Negro Art and America," which follows Locke's essay, "The New Negro," works within this same paradigm. Barnes declares:

> It [Negro art] is sound art because it comes from a primitive nature upon which a white man's education has never been harnessed. . . . The outstanding characteristics are his tremendous emotional endowment, his luxuriant and free imagination and a truly great power of individual expression. . . . Through the compelling powers of his poetry and music the American Negro is revealing to the rest of the world the essential oneness of all human beings. (Locke, *New Negro,* 19, 23)

Barnes idealizes Negro art because it is closer to nature, praising "the American Negro" for his spiritual and emotional endowment. Then, he claims that the overly educated and materialistic white American, who is inferior to the Negro in these respects, needs the more spontaneous black cultural alter ego to complement his culture, to compensate for a lack of emotion.[5]

The white American, moreover, should learn from his black brother a sense of collectivism, what Barnes calls "the essential oneness of all human beings." Barnes muses: "what our prosaic civilization needs most is precisely the poetry which the average Negro actually lives." He also claims that in addition to poetry, Negroes' lives contain passion, beauty, rhythm, emotions, lyricism, color, and joy—the word *joy* is mentioned six times in his short article. Barnes calls upon his people to discard their racist apprehensions; Anglo-Americans should acknowledge Negro art and appreciate the Negro because he can teach them to bring joy and poetry into their lives: "it is incredible that we should not offer the consideration which we have consistently denied to [the Negro]" (Locke, *New Negro*, 25).

Ironically, "the Negro" whom Barnes celebrates as the epitome of the life-force is premodern and nonrational—the opposite of the modern and intellectual "New Negro" that Locke envisioned. In equating "the Negro" with "joy," Barnes falls prey to the racist tendency so characteristic of the discourse of romantic primitivism. This primitivist adulation is a general theme throughout part I of Locke's anthology. The crucial role this strategy plays is revealed clearly if we compare the March 1925 *Harlem: Mecca of the New Negro* issue of *Survey Graphic* (the forerunner to *The New Negro*) to the actual anthology. In the *Survey Graphic* issue, Locke promised, "we may dramatically glimpse the New Negro," but he did not prophesy the coming of a "Negro Renaissance," as he would in the heading for the first part of the book.[6]

The New Negro was, for the most part, a reprint of the *Survey Graphic* issue, which had sold an astonishing 42,000 copies. Among the few additional articles was Locke's essay "The Legacy of the Ancestral Arts," in which he expressed his philosophy of racial uplift. Observing that African art had a fertilizing effect on European art, he lists a number of European artists whose works were inspired by African art: Matisse, Picasso, Derain, Modigliani, Utrillo, Pechstein, Stern, Marc, Archipenko, Epstein, Lipchitz, Lembruch, Zadkine, Faggi. Locke also extends his thesis to French poetry ("Apollinaire, Reverdy, Salmon, Fargue") and to modern music ("Berard, Satie, Poulenc, Auric, Honegger"), revealing the hidden agenda of his anthology—an attempt to synthesize a unified theory of the germinal role of the African presence in European modernism.

As we have seen, his goal for such a theory was to import what he calls a "galvanizing influence." But the attempt to put European primitivist modernism to his own ends blinded him to the contradictory claims of his argument.[7] For example, when Locke mentions that Europeans and black Americans are equally removed from African art, he is obviously contradicting his claim of an essential, blood relation between African art and African Americans: "this art can scarcely have less influence upon the blood descendants, bound to it by a sense of direct cultural kinship, than upon those who inherit by tradition only" (Locke, *New Negro*, 256). Locke seems to want to have it both ways: the Negro claim to the power of primitivist modernism will be both purely formal ("equally removed") and based on birthright. He asks: "If the forefathers could so adroitly master these mediums, why not we?" (Locke, *New Negro*, 256).

After constructing a kinship, however distant, between Negro artists in Africa and America, Locke claims that African art might have a "galvanizing" effect on African American art. Once this occurs, "then the Negro may well become what some have predicted, the artist of American life" (Locke, *New Negro*, 258). According to Locke's vision, a connection between African art and the American Negro "folk temperament" would generate a new offspring —a black primitivist modernism. Locke is very explicit about his tactic, declaring, "The work of these European artists should even now be the inspiration and guide-posts of a younger school of American Negro artists." Once the New Negro artists started to experiment with African styles, they would come into their own; like a black phoenix ascending out of the ashes of slavery, a modern black art would emerge.

Locke's conception of a black modernism owes a fundamental debt to European primitivist-modernism: he encouraged the New Negro artist to reconnect with "his forefathers" because he had learned a lesson from his cultural alter ego. Locke's plea was not in vain; in fact, as we have seen, Loïs Mailou Jones took his advice to heart in defending her right to African art as a source of inspiration. Jones's works are now exhibited at the National Gallery in Washington, D.C., and Bill Clinton came to her studio on Martha's Vineyard in 1992 to look at her art; Locke's strategy was fairly successful. It is partly as a result of Locke's work that contemporary African American artists (e.g., Jacob Lawrence, Jean Basquiat, Roman Bearden) are now widely acknowledged.

On the other hand, Locke's assumption that massive social change would inevitably follow the creation of a black modernism was overly optimistic. In general, the idealistic notion that high culture could be the agent of social change is at the heart of *The New Negro*.[8] This bias, that "cultural recognition" is gained by proving a race's "worth" artistically, was inspired by European primitivist modernism. Here, Locke is echoing statements that Paul Guillaume made in an article entitled "The Triumph of Ancient Negro Art." Guillaume accredits a "life-giving art . . . born in tropical jungles" for having "bequeathed modern times" and prophesizes that "the Negro cause will henceforth be an accepted thing."[9]

The article, published in *Opportunity* magazine, reports Guillaume as saying at the opening of an exhibition that "the spirit of modern man—or of modern woman—needs to be nourished by the civilization of the Negro." His audience (mostly well-to-do citizens of Paris) approved his announcement with wild applause. Locke hoped that similar sentiments would prevail in America. But his attempt to transfer a European fad to America, so fundamental to the New Negro, failed to take into account significant cultural differences. Locke should have foreseen the problems involved in his project to solve the race problem in America by using a cure lifted from the French imagination. And he should have addressed the cleavage between the first half of the anthology, which focuses on the notion of "the primitive," and the second half, which seeks to define the notion of "the modern."

James Weldon Johnson's essay, "Harlem: The Culture Capital," is symptomatic of the ideology perpetuated in the anthology's second part, entitled "The New Negro in a New World." The underlying assumption here is that the main task of the New Negro is to modernize black America, specifically Harlem. Johnson presents Harlem as a healthy and stable community—a nation within a nation—replete with Negro-owned shops, restaurants, theaters, dance clubs, libraries, and schools. Stressing the rise of a black middle class, Johnson focuses on the economic achievements of black Americans. These achievements demand, Johnson implies, that New York accept Harlem as an integral part of the metropolis. Hoping that New Yorkers will one day appreciate black Americans, Johnson declares that the "Negro loves New York and is proud of it" and asserts, "The rapidity with which Negroes become good New Yorkers is one of the marvels to observe."[10] Instead of explaining what a "good New Yorker" might be, Johnson suggests that once Negroes were integrated and once they had demonstrated their civility, discrimination would end.

In his essay "The Negro's Americanism," the famous anthropologist Melville J. Herskovits observes that black New Yorkers are already very much like white New Yorkers. He argues that Harlem "was a community just like any other American community. The same pattern, only a different shade!" (Locke, *New Negro*, 353). Thoroughly assimilated, the Negro has lost his distinct cultural traits and leads a typically American life, or, as Herskovits claims, "Of the African culture, not a trace." This concise assertion is astonishing, first because it contradicts the assumption of cultural difference that the anthology's first section so systematically constructs, and second, because Herskovits's later work would be pivotal in establishing a link between African and African American cultures. His conviction that Harlem is a "typically American community" and his rejection of the Negro's cultural uniqueness derives from a wish to convince white Americans that the Negro could be assimilated easily into the American way of life.

On the same tack, the black sociologist E. Franklin Frazier argues that the black middle class in Durham, North Carolina, has developed typically American, bourgeois values. Frazier attempts to demonstrate that African Americans can achieve socioeconomic progress just like the rest of America. He makes a plea for what we might think of as capitalistic uniformity:

> These younger [Negro] men are truly modern business men. They have adopted the technique of modern business and are saturated with the psychology of the capitalist class. They work hard, not because of necessity, but to expand their businesses and invade new fields. They have the same outlook on life as the middle class everywhere. They support the same theories of government and morality. They have little sympathy with waste of time. Their pleasures are the pleasures of the tired business man who does not know how to enjoy life. (Locke, *New Negro*, 338)

Stating the similarities between the white and the black middle class, Frazier privileges class over race. In claiming that neither the white nor the black businessman knows how to enjoy life, Frazier dismisses claims that Barnes and Rogers made about the Negro's innate sense of joy. Frazier even replaces the trope of the culturally refined and sensuous "modern" Negro with that of the economically ambitious modern black man. Once black America has produced its Henry Ford, or a class of black entrepreneurs, and once the majority of the black community has become prosperous consumers, argues Frazier, the problem of the twentieth century, the problem of the color line, will dissolve.

The hero of Frazier's concept, the modern Negro businessman, is a close cousin to Locke's hero, the black bohemian. Locke's New Negro is closer to Baudelaire and Picasso, say, than to Henry Ford or Rockefeller; we can imagine him subsidized by Frazier's businessman. Next to these two avatars of the New Negro, there is a third; she is dignified, elegant, and race-conscious. In Elsie Johnson McDougald's essay, we catch a dramatic glimpse of the New Negro Woman:

> She is courageously standing erect, developing within herself the moral strength to rise above and conquer false attitudes. She is maintaining her natural beauty and charm and improving her mind and opportunity. She is measuring up to the needs of her family, community and race, and radiating a hope throughout the land. (Locke, *New Negro*, 382)

According to this image, the New Negro woman cares about her personal well-being as well as that of her family, community, and race. While McDougald maintains that "race" is key to the New Negro woman, she takes "class" into account by distinguishing among four types, according to their social status. This feminized presentation of the New Negro differs from the image of the primitivist modernist artist just as it differs from the image of the efficient businessman. But it symbolizes the promise of a charming, morally concerned, and caring individual who is proud to be a member of the race.

This vision is not reflected anywhere else in the two sections of the book. It is unlike the Fordist identity expressed in the anthology's second section because its understanding of progress suborns technology and economics to personal morality. It is unlike the ideology at work in the first part, since it does not share that section's atavistic primitivism—as expressed in the title "The Negro Digs Up His Past" or in Arthur A. Schomburg's opening statement: "The American Negro must remake his past in order to make his future." The construct of the New Negro woman combines progress with ethics, whereas the New Negro of part I combines aesthetics with ethics.

Whereas the first section stresses cultural difference (contrasting Nordic sterility with Negro rhythm) to show that Negro Americans have something unique to contribute to American civilization, the second section stresses cultural sameness. Focusing on the social and economic achievements of black Americans, the second section tries to prove that blacks are just as "modern" as European immigrants. These two claims, of cultural uniqueness and of cultural sameness, are the two unreconciled—and paradoxical—strivings at the heart of *The New Negro*. Since this rift is located at the ideological and programmatic foundation of the Harlem Renaissance, it could only weaken the political effectiveness of the movement's blueprint, this anthology.

Among the most striking features of this fissured book are the bold illustrations by the German artist Winold Reiss. The fourteen realistic portraits of leading members of the New Negro movement are an important but rarely discussed aspect of *The New Negro*. The reason for this neglect is simple: only the first edition of *The New Negro* features these color illustrations. Later editions have only reprinted Reiss's decorations and Aaron Douglas's designs, which are in black and white and therefore less expensive to reproduce. Of the eleven portraits of prominent and distinguished figures of the Harlem Renaissance included in the 1925 edition, seven are contributors to *The New Negro*. We will take a close look at two.

Facing page 6 of the volume is a representation of the editor (figure 5.1). Alain Locke is sitting upright, his head slightly bent, his gaze melancholic but determined. His lips are bright red and match the color of the ring he is wearing on the middle finger of his left hand. The raised blue veins of that hand are remarkable; they call attention to his mulatto status. The way he holds a metal clip expresses a sense of fortitude. The natural fierceness of his eyes is ameliorated by the softness of refinement, which gives the image an impression of warmth.

Due to Reiss's technique of leaving the clothes and the background white and empty, Locke's brown complexion and his facial expressions are the most striking features of the portrait. His coat is sketched with a few lines—obviously not a realistic representation of any sports jacket he would wear. Reiss deliberately refrains from an accurate depiction of Locke's clothes in order to focus on his head, coffee-colored skin, and hands. This synthesis of minimalism and naturalism brings out the racial and the individual traits of the model while ignoring such incidentals as clothing or setting. The combination of the representational and the abstract, characteristic of all of Reiss's portraits of black intellectuals, creates a visual tension and makes the portrait appear larger than life.

The intensity that the technique creates is also pronounced in Reiss's portrait of James Weldon Johnson (figure 5.2). The contrast between the naturalistic black face against a white outfit and background focuses on the racial features in a man whose negroid features might otherwise be indistinct. The effect would be barely visible in a black-and-white reproduction since the image depends on the radiant brown of his skin. But what is easily recognizable, in any reproduction, is that his expression is a combination of melancholy and pride. He appears stern and serious; there is vigor in his expression. The bald forehead and the determined gaze focused on the distance enhance our impression of this person as a thinker of aristocratic authority. The image arrests the viewer's attention; the spectator looks at Johnson, but the attempt to establish eye contact and to fix the visual text are thwarted. It

Figure 5.1   Winold Reiss. *Alain Locke.* (1925). Courtesy of
the National Portrait Gallery, Smithsonian Institution; Gift
of Laurence A. Fleischman and Howard Garfinkle with a
matching grant from the National Endowment for the Arts.

is difficult for the viewer to come to terms with the awkward tension between
ostentatious absence and striking presence.

As a whole, the eleven portraits of the leaders of the Harlem Renaissance
bespeak a silent but powerful presence. Their images do not casually adorn
the volume—they are meant to demonstrate the beauty and intelligence
of Negroes. The images are a counterattack against stereotypes; they attempt
to visualize what is called for throughout the book, the emergence of a class
of noble and artistic New Negroes. The display of these eleven respectable
New Negroes is a visual hagiography. Given the significance of these images,
it might seem surprising that Locke chose an artist who was not a Negro
himself. Locke's curious choice seems to have been influenced by his desire

Figure 5.2 Winold Reiss. *James Weldon Johnson.* (1925). Courtesy of the National Portrait Gallery, Smithsonian Institution; Gift of Laurence A. Fleischman and Howard Garfinkle with a matcing grant from the National Endowment for the Arts.

to find an artist who would fully realize the Negro's potential to be the subject of modernism. In other words, these portraits seem to reconcile the fault between parts I and II of the anthology; here, Negroes are both black and modern.

Winold Reiss was born September 16, 1886, in Karlsruhe, Germany. He attended the Academy of Fine Arts in Munich (1911–1913), where he became familiar with Fauvism, German Expressionism, and the Blaue Reiter. According to Jeffrey C. Stewart, who organized an exhibition on Reiss at the National Portrait Gallery in 1989, Reiss had visited an exhibition of Pablo Picasso's

African-inspired works in Munich in 1913. In October 1913, by the time Reiss emigrated to America, he had already been exposed to more modern art than most American artists. Unlike his Anglo-American colleagues, Reiss was very much influenced by the primitivist style, as his interior designs for the restaurant of the Hotel Alamac, "The Congo Room," demonstrate. But it was the interior of the Crillon Restaurant (1919), done in a nonprimitivist modern decorative style, that earned him his reputation as one of America's foremost modern interior designers. Reiss was a cofounder of the Society of Modern Art (1914), and he illustrated the first issue of *The Modern Art Collector* (1915). His work was exhibited at international shows along with the works of Pablo Picasso, Henri Matisse, Stuart Davis, and Joseph Stella.

Winold Reiss was an idiosyncratic modernist. His first exhibition, held at the Anderson Galleries in New York (December 1922–January 1923), included thirty-eight realistic representations of people from many backgrounds. As opposed to the trend toward abstract modernism, Reiss had decided to paint portraits, particularly of indigenous peoples. He went on several trips to find models: in 1919, he traveled to Montana to paint Blackfoot Indians; in 1920, he went to Mexico to paint the descendants of the Aztecs; in 1922, he returned to his native country to paint people from the Black Forest and Bavarians from Oberammergau. During these three trips, he completed 150 portraits, a collection of a wide range of racial types.

Reiss's fascination for cultures that preserved their traditions stemmed in part from his childhood reading of Karl May's "Wild West" novels. The two main characters, Winnetou, the noble Indian, and Old Shatterhand, a German cowboy, formed a union that left an indelible imprint on several generations of young Germans. This was the seedbed for Reiss's romanticism and he, like many other Germans of the time, esteemed non-Westerners for being closer to nature and to spiritual forces than Europeans were. Reiss's primitivism differs from Picasso's because his passion is rarely formalistic. Instead of appropriating "primitive" artifacts to forge a new style, Reiss made "primitive" people the subject of his work. Curiously, despite his interest in non-Caucasian models and his presence in the United States since 1913, Reiss only began to use black people as subjects in 1924.

That year, after Reiss had illustrated a *Survey Graphic* issue on Mexicans, his editor, Paul U. Kellogg, introduced him to Locke, hoping that the two would collaborate on the Harlem issue. Locke agreed and gave Reiss access to prominent black leaders. By the end of the year, Reiss wrote to Locke, informing him that he had drawn Mr. Roland Hayes, Mr. Jackman, Mrs. McDougald, and Mr. Morgan, and that he was looking forward to painting Mr. Robeson. The portrait of Roland Hayes, framed by a primitivist-expressionist design, became the cover for the March *Survey Graphic* issue.

It is likely that Kellogg urged Locke to use Reiss as illustrator, but the choice of a German immigrant to take up the critical task of portraying the elite of the black intelligentsia for *The New Negro* was an unlikely move. Locke could have commissioned James Van Der Zee, the prominent Negro photographer known for his flattering portraits of the black upper class. Sensitive to public perception, Locke explained his decision:

> The work of Winold Reiss, fellow-countryman of Slevogt and von Reuckterschnell, which has supplied the main illustrative material for this volume has been deliberately conceived and executed as a path-breaking guide and encouragement to this new foray of the younger Negro artists. In idiom, technical treatment and objective social angle, it is a bold iconoclastic break with the current traditions that have grown up about the Negro subject in American art. It is not meant to dictate a style to the younger Negro artist, but to point the lesson that contemporary European art has already learned— that any vital artistic expression of the Negro theme and subject in art must break through the stereotypes to a new style, a distinct fresh technique, and some sort of characteristic idiom. (Locke, *New Negro*, 266–267)

More than serving an ornamental function, Reiss's portraits are meant to teach young black artists not only to make Negroes the subject matter of their work, but to paint them in a new, iconoclastic style. Since Anglo-American artists often had treated the Negro subject in a stereotyped and demeaning fashion, young black artists should orient themselves toward Europe. Suggesting that many European artists had already learned the lesson that black is beautiful, Locke maintains that Reiss is a good example of a fresh, distinctive, modernist style of representation, one that brings out the beauty and dignity in the faces of the black subjects. Reiss's ability to capture the character of an individual, as well as his ability to convey the beauty of a race, made him worthy of the role of the illustrator for *The New Negro*.

Locke called Reiss a "folklorist of the brush and palette, seeking always the folk character back of the individual, the psychology behind the physiognomy" (Locke, *New Negro*, 419). Locke aspired to an effect similar to that of Reiss's "Exhibition of Recent Portraits of Representative Negroes." It had been held at the 135th Street branch of the New York Public Library and had attracted hundreds of visitors. Kellogg mentions the exhibit in his own contribution to *The New Negro*:

> Mr. Reiss's pastels were shown that month in the Harlem Public Library, and at the instigation of Mrs. McDougald, hundreds of Negro school children passed before them. There they saw plain people depicted, such as they knew on the street, and, also, poets, philosophers, teachers and leaders, who are the spearheads of a racial revival; forerunners, whose work might be passed on to them, men and women treated with dignity and beauty and potency altogether new. Images they could carry with them through their lives. Their pioneers! (Locke, *New Negro*, 277)

Ironically, these "pioneers" became visible to Harlem's public through images painted by a German. Even if we agree with Kellogg that the Harlem Renaissance was about the Negro "finding himself anew in his own eyes," we have to add that these school children found "dignity and beauty and potency" in their own people through the vision of a German.

Reiss played a catalyst's role in the promotion of a cultural elite and the development of the New Negro movement; his impact manifested itself in this exhibit, in his images in *The New Negro,* and indirectly in Locke's call for black artists to imitate Reiss. Loïs Mailou Jones mentioned to me that she went through a "Reiss period." Aaron Douglas paid homage to his mentor, Winold Reiss, for revealing to him the beauty of black art. At a decisive and early point in his career, Douglas profited enormously from his German American teacher. The spelling of Douglas's own contribution to *The New Negro,* entitled "African Phantasie: Awakening," pays homage to this German source, either consciously or unconsciously.

Reiss played a pivotal role within the Harlem Renaissance, not only for individual artists, but more broadly as a shaper of its visual culture; as Jeffrey C. Stewart points out:

> Reiss's influence extended on the entire design aesthetic of the Harlem Renaissance, with adaptations of his style appearing on the covers of small literary magazines, civic club meeting brochures, and literary contest announcements. The reason for this extraordinary enthusiasm was that Reiss's work shared the romantic idea articulated by Alain Locke in *The New Negro* that the Harlem Renaissance was an aesthetic revival of American forms. . . . Reiss found in the folk the inspiration for a more holistic, spiritual engagement with the world through art. He was an artist who fused the twin aspects of early twentieth-century modernism—the effort to break away from Western nineteenth-century tradition and, through primitivism, to reconnect with alternative (folk) traditions that exemplified a more integrative role for art in everyday life.[11]

Although European primitivism was not about reconnecting with an alternative folk tradition but rather about redesigning the received artistic tradition, Reiss's primitivism was unique in giving special attention to the people of all races. His work resonates with, as Stewart put it, "the idealistic notion that art can transform the world, by showing the beauty and dignity that exists in all people." In the case of his representations of black people, it was an idealism with political implications.

Locke's choice of Reiss to create the portraits for *The New Negro* is indicative of Locke's basic approach to the aesthetics of racial politics. Locke frequently collaborated with white Americans to finance "the flowering of the race spirit," as he called it. He established a system of white patronage with Carl Van Vechten and Charlotte Osgood Mason at its center.[12] Van Vechten and Mason were both exponents of primitivism; however, they represented two different visions. Van Vechten admired joyous Harlem's night life and the liberated spirit of exoticism. In his bestseller, *Nigger Heaven*, he presents Harlem as an exotic world in which African Americans love gin, dancing, and sex more than anything else. Mason, on the other hand, despised the vulgar and materialistic. She felt it her mission to preserve the spirituality she attributed to primitive people.

In 1927, after listening to Locke lecture on African art, Mason shifted her interest toward supporting African American artists. Locke functioned as a mediator between the needy black artists and this "Godmother," as her protégés called Mason. In 1927 she granted Langston Hughes a monthly stipend of $150 and paid Zora Neale Hurston about $200 a month for collecting folk material in the South. Locke coordinated these arrangements. Rumor had it that Mason spend approximately $75,000 in the cause of promoting African American art. While she was generous, Mason made sure she got what she paid for. In her arrangement with Hurston, Mason retained publication rights for the folklore material that Hurston had collected.

Mason demanded that her protégés resemble the image she had of them—that is to say, she wanted them to be like "real" primitive people. Mason once called Locke "a golden star in the Firmament of Primitive People." Hurston was smart enough to comply with Mason's expectations, but did so self-consciously. She once called Mason "the guard-mother who sits in the twelfth heaven and shapes the destinies of the primitives" (Watson, 147, 148). The reason that Locke put up with Mason, who referred to him as her "precious Brown Boy," is obvious—without her donations many black artists would not have had the leisure to produce art. While numerous commentators have been sharply critical on the issue of white patronage, Jeffrey C. Stewart has recently argued that the black artists had no choice but to turn to white patrons since the few black patrons at the time still believed in nineteenth-century values and were unwilling to support experimental art.[13]

Obviously, the dependence was precarious. This tendency toward the aesthetic, Du Bois had warned in another context, might "turn the renaissance into decadence."[14] By placing so much faith in the social power of art, Locke had perhaps ignored a more pragmatic approach. The stock market crash in 1929 halted the New Negro movement. White patrons drastically curtailed their donations, and many black artists relied on the WPA for subsidies; in the 1930s, the New Negro movement was never as vital as it had been.

On February 15, 1934, nine years after the publication of *The New Negro*, a new anthology appeared; it was called *Negro* and had been edited by Nancy Cunard, the daughter of a British aristocrat. The anthology is so large that, far from being "an already-read" text, like most racist or primitivist stereotyped accounts, the anthology has rarely been read from beginning to end at all. If we think of Alain Locke as the midwife of the New Negro (as Langston Hughes did), then we might think of Nancy Cunard as an undertaker presiding over the New Negro's funeral. Her anthology has a signifying relation to Locke's: her title counters Locke's romantic neologism, "New Negro," with the solitary cry, "Negro." Cunard critiques Locke's manifesto of primitivist modernism with a blueprint for a black, social-realist primitivism.

The symbolic enormity of this anthology is as large as its 900 pages. It includes works by European avant-garde artists (including an essay by Ezra Pound and several translations by Samuel Beckett), white American artists (e.g., William Carlos Williams and Theodore Dreiser), and many renowned New Negro artists (e.g., Langston Hughes and Zora Neale Hurston). Among its 150 contributors—of both races—were artists, social scientists, historians, anthropologists, musicologists, and political activists. The cultural backgrounds of the contributors as well as the issues addressed in the anthology range from Europe to America, from Africa and the West Indies to South America.

The anthology includes fiction, musical scores, historical material, folk knowledge, scientific accounts, and political pamphlets. *Negro* is a treasure trove of documentary material, much of which had been unpublished: hundreds of photos of African art and portraits of Negroes, words and transcriptions to songs, listings of celebrities and stars, press clippings, and even African proverbs. The book includes valuable historical information, including Arthur A. Schomburg's essay "Racial Integrity," on black scholars and intellectuals, and Raymond Michelet's "African Empires and Civilization," in which he sketches the history of the Sudanese civilization from the third century to the twentieth.

Given its pivotal role for the black intelligentsia worldwide, it might seem strange that *Negro* was edited by an aristocratic British woman. The book was the product both of a lifelong fascination and of a love affair with a black man. In 1931—five years after she had fallen in love with a black jazz musician and three years after she had moved to Paris—Cunard embarked on the ambitious project of compiling this monument to black cultures. She sent out a call for contributions to an anthology she was tentatively calling "Color." Why she later abandoned the working title is unclear, but in this letter, Cunard writes:

> The new book on COLOR here described comprises what is Negro and descendant from Negro. It will be published in 1932 or 1933, as soon as enough material has been collected.
>
> It will be entirely documentary, exclusive of romance or fiction.
>
> There will be at least four separate sections:
> 1. The contemporary Negro in America, S. America, West Indies, Europe. . . .
> 2. Musical section African. Ethnographical.
> 3. Reproductions of African Art
> 4. Political and sociological . . . accounts of lynchings, persecution and race prejudice. I want outspoken criticism, comment and comparison from the Negro on the present-day civilizations of Europe, America, South America, the West Indies, African colonies. . . .[15]

Cunard received what she asked for; the final version, published only a year later than intended, is very close to this plan. A chapter on poetry and a chapter on Negro celebrities were added to the final version. Also, the final version is marked by communist leanings more pronounced than one would have assumed from reading her call for contributors.

The anthology had two main agendas: first, to valorize "the race" by demonstrating—by reproducing African art or printing poems by African Americans—the beauty of black art and, second, to attack contemporary racist practices such as "lynchings, persecution and race prejudice." The anthology's twin intentions—to demonstrate the genius of blackness as well as the cruelty of whiteness—is made obvious in the foreword to the 1934 edition, which Cunard begins as follows:

It was necessary to make this book—and I think in this manner, an Anthology of some 150 voices of both races—for the recording of the struggles and achievements, the persecutions and revolts against them, or the Negro peoples. . . . There are certain sections of the Negro bourgeoisie which hold that justice will come to them from some eventual liberality in the white man. But the more vital of the Negro race have realized that it is Communism alone which throws down the barriers of race as finally as it wipes out class distinctions. The Communist world-order is the solution of the race problem for the Negro. James Ford, Negro worker and intellectual, was nominated by the Communist Party as candidate for Vice-President of U.S.A. in 1932.[16]

Cunard's anthology signifies on the black bourgeoisie, generally, and specifically on Alain Locke for his belief in the liberality of white patrons such as Mason. Arguing that "it is communism alone which throws down the barriers of race as finally as it wipes out class distinctions," Cunard mocks strategies of racial uplift that assert black modernism as the solution to the race problem.

Although Cunard writes in her foreword that "it is high time a separate book were made to do justice to a people so utterly rich in natural grace and beauty, a people who have produced the diverse genius of the spirituals and blues, the superb Negro choirs of America, the syncopation and tap-dancing," her primary concern is with politics. She declares simply: "The Communist world-order is the solution of the race problem for the Negro." According to her conviction, the anthology's main task is to raise class and racial consciousness and to show that the one cannot come about without the other. The oppressed (black) race and the exploited (white) class must unite against the ruling class. In her desire to bring down white capitalism and erect a communist world order, Cunard's project seems diametrically opposed to Locke's intentions. Locke and his fellow New Negro compatriots did not hate capitalism per se—they hated racism.

While Locke thought that social change would come about through establishing a sophisticated and distinctly "black" aesthetic, Cunard's materialistic outlook calls for structural economic and political changes. While Locke's strategy aimed at launching the New Negro into mainstream American modernism on the back of an inverted primitivism, *Negro* launches an attack on Main Street America. While Locke wanted the New Negro to become a well-respected citizen of the United States, Cunard has little respect for America, on Main Street or otherwise. She believes that "in Russia alone is the Negro a free man, a 100 per cent equal." While Locke's heroes are the artist and the entrepreneur, Cunard's hero is the "Negro worker and [communist] intellectual." *Negro*, obviously in its very title, intends to challenge and critique *The New Negro*. While Locke's interest in Africa is mediated through Europe and is only a symbolic strategy, Cunard, herself a European, claims to have a genuine interest in African people; she selects "The White Man Is Killing Africa" as the last contribution to her anthology.

But these two anthologies, marked by such different concerns, have at least one aspect in common: both are informed, wittingly or unwittingly, by a primitivist discourse. Whereas *The New Negro* attempted to bring about a black modernism through the appropriation of European primitivist modernism, *Negro*—although implicitly criticizing Locke's strategy—never manages to escape the primitivism it sought to critique. These two foundational anthologies, which mark the beginning and the end of the Harlem Renaissance, are both suffused with primitivism.

We have already talked about the twoness of *The New Negro,* whose unresolved primitivist and modern sides make it a Janus-faced book. Cunard's book, which fronts as a manifesto of a black socialist-realism, is, however, also infused with several facets of black primitivism. Six variants of primitivist discourse manifest themselves in *Negro*: white romanticism, mulattoism, black primitivism, the cultural critique of "Nordicism," the cultural critique of "Negrotarianism," and the performative effect of cross-cultural projections. We will discuss each of these in turn.

White romanticism: The best example in *Negro* of the overly celebratory assertions on the nature of black people is an essay by the famous Marxist literary critic V. F. Calverton, "The Growth of Negro Literature." Here, he maintains that the art of the Negro "springs from the people, an artless art, and in that sense it is the most genuine art of the world." It is an art that does not require training or technique, for it comes "naturally." Calverton's bias is clear:

> The Negro has retained unquestionably in his art a certain primitivism that is wonderfully refreshing in contrast to the stilted affectations of the more cultured styles and conceptions. We come closer to life with these primitivisms, feel beauty in its more genuine and intimate and less artificial and cerebral forms. (Cunard, *Negro*, 103)

Distinguishing the anemic, "stilted," overly sophisticated white art from the "refreshing," more genuine black art, is only to echo Rogers's article on jazz or Barnes's essay that expressed admiration for an art that "comes from a primitive nature upon which a white man's education has never been harnessed." Calverton inadvertently disparages those he intends to praise, a fundamental component of primitivist-romanticist discourse.

What is so interesting—and almost touching—about Calverton's essay is that he attempts to rescue this discourse of primitivism:

> These primitivisms of the Negro are a singular evolution of our American environment. In describing them as primitive, we do not mean that they are savage in origin, or that the instincts of savagery linger in them, but that they are untutored in form and unsophisticated in content, and in these aspects are more primitive than civilised in character. The art of primitive peoples is often the very opposite in spirit to that of the African Negro. (Cunard, *Negro*, 103)

Arguing that Africans are not primitive in the sense of being uncivilized, Calverton frees the term from its derogatory connotations, inverts the common hierarchy, and goes on to claim that due to its "untutored" and "unsophisticated" form, Negro art is superior to traditional—that is, white—art.

The superior form of Negro art, as he sees it, is, jazz:

In jazz this vital and overwhelming exuberance of the American Negro reaches its apex in physical dynamics. If the origin of jazz is not entirely Negroid—that its fundamental form is derivative of Negro rhythms no longer can be disputed—its development of attitude and expression in America has certainly been chiefly advanced by the Negro. While the spirituals represent the religious escape of the Negro, the jazz rhythms vivify his mundane abandon. Today this mundane abandon has become a universal craving on the part of youth in Europe as well as in America. Since the war, the dance has become a mania. It is a mad, delirious dance of man and woman who have had to seize upon something as a vicarious outlet for their crazed emotions. (Cunard, *Negro*, 103, 104)

Like Stokowski, Rogers, and so many others, Calverton describes jazz with the familiar metaphors of "revivification" and "abandon." To him, jazz is rebellion, spontaneity, vitality; it is the music with which the young identify. Jazz echoes the fast pace of modernity. The "primitive," as Calverton sees it, is neither ancient nor African but utterly modern. And "the modern" is quintessentially Negro because "the riotous rhythms that constitute jazz are but an active translation of the impulsive extravagance of his life."

Arguing that the Negro's innate life-force is a riotous rhythm that suits the modern pace, Calverton makes two extraordinary suggestions to back his claim:

Whether a difference in the calcium factor in bone structure or conjunction accounting for an exceptional muscular resiliency, or a difference in terms of an entirely environmental disparity, be used to explain the Negro's superior response to jazz, his supremacy in this departure in music remains uncontested.[17]

Even comically to suggest that such an uncontested superiority could have to do with "the calcium factor in bone structure" and "exceptional muscular resiliency," is to posit a biological basis for the Negro's musical capacities. Calverton might just as well have related the Negro's musical capacity to a jazz chromosome. Such essentialist arguments are representative of the misunderstanding and condescension underlying much of primitivist-romanticist veneration.

Mulattoism: George Antheil's contribution, "The Negro on the Spiral or a Method of Negro Music," discerns "the aesthetics of the Congo" at the core of most contemporary music: "This note [of the Congo] has erroneously been called 'American,' but this note is black." For good measure, he adds, "rhythmically it comes from the groins, the hips, and the sexual organs." The superior rhythmic sense of the Negro, he maintains, has suffused throughout most modern European music. Since Wagner, "music had two gigantic blood infusions; first Slavic, and, in recent times, the Negroid. . . . Like wildfire the Negro patch spread everywhere in Europe" (Cunard, *Negro*, 346, 348).

Antheil points out that the younger generation of composers has embraced "mulattoism." His explanation of why Dvořák, Stravinsky, and many other composers and musicians have turned to black music verges on romanticism:

"Weak, miserable, and anaemic, we need the stalwart shoulders of a younger race to hold the cart awhile till we had gotten the wheel back on. But first acquaintance with this charming and beautiful creature, the Negro, made us love him at first sight; we could not resist him" (Cunard, *Negro*, 350). While Antheil's reverence is self-deprecating, it also draws on the common metaphor of rejuvenation. A sense of weakness and weariness and a loathing of stasis have made the Europeans desperate for an antidote, even a black one. Out of despair, Antheil turns to blacks, hoping that a union with the other of color will revivify European culture. His plea brings to mind a short story that Langston Hughes published the same year as *Negro*'s publication. "Rejuvenation through Joy" is a satire about a spiritual retreat center in which a handsome, athletic, black, male lecturer teaches wealthy but spiritually needy white people how to attain joy.

Antheil attributes healing power to blacks; to make his point about the significance of Europe's cultural alter ego, he creates a compelling image:

> The black man (the exact opposite color of ourselves!) has appeared to us suddenly like a true phenomenon. Like a photograph of ourselves he is the sole negative from which a positive may be drawn! Holding this negative up to the sun we see in essence that which so many eyes and ears have been trying to demonstrate on canvas, paper, and stone. (Cunard, *Negro*, 351)

This account helps to explain the *vogue nègre* because it argues that black and white are mutually constitutive: that we cannot see ourselves if we ignore our cultural other. To get an accurate rendition, we need to develop the negative first. Only by looking at the (black) negative, could white people see themselves accurately. In the collapse after the First World War, blackness was a mirror in which to see something new in the white world; this new likeness was a mulatto image.

Black primitivism: The urge to validate African American folk expressions is most pronounced in Zora Neale Hurston's anthropological essay, "Characteristics of Negro Expression." Hurston discusses aesthetic, linguistic, and cultural patterns unique to African Americans. Her characterization is based on the assumption that the aesthetic taste of blacks differs fundamentally from that of Anglo-Americans. To Hurston, the innate desire to adorn and the love for asymmetry is "typically Negro." With an equally determined tone, she writes, "Negro dancing is dynamic." Hurston also claims that the art of mimicry "is better developed in the Negro than in other racial groups." Hurston bases these characterizations on forms of expression that are part of the daily lives of Negroes: prayer, dancing, interior decoration, lovemaking, and fighting. Certainly, she avoids conventional definitions of high art when she writes: "Likewise love-making is a biological necessity the world over and an art among Negroes" (Cunard, *Negro*, 44). She argues that Negroes are unique in introducing art into life. Aesthetics is not relegated to the museum or the stage; it unfolds everywhere—in the jook as well as the bedroom.

Hurston's essay is a primitivistic paean to the race. In her typology, the Negro appears hedonistic, sensuous, and carefree; her account draws on the familiar tropes of primitivist discourse. Hurston also embraces the idea of black authenticity, arguing, for example, that only blacks can truly sing the spirituals. Even among the many blacks who perform for white audiences, Hurston finds only a handful of "the real Negro school." The real Negro is the one who does not try to please his [white] audience.

In a section of the essay entitled "Originality," Hurston confronts the common view that "the Negro is lacking in originality." She argues in favor of an innate artistry:

> So if we look at it squarely, the Negro is a very original being. While he lives and moves in the midst of a white civilization, everything that he touches is re-interpreted for his own use. . . . Everyone is familiar with the Negro's modification of the white's musical instruments, so that his interpretation has been adopted by the white man himself and then re-interpreted. In so many words, Paul Whiteman is giving an imitation of a Negro orchestra making use of white-invented musical instruments in a Negro way. Thus has arisen a new art in the civilized world, and thus has our so-called civilization come. The exchange and re-exchange of ideas between groups. (Cunard, *Negro*, 43)

Hurston lays the foundations of what we might think of as a cross-cultural dialectic, arguing that Negroes imitate and appropriate expressions of their cultural other, while white people, such as Whiteman, reappropriate black expressions. Interracial exchange and re-exchange, Hurston argues, is essential to bringing about—or rather transforming—civilization. And this exchange and re-exchange is, Hurston points out, one of the most salient characteristics of twentieth-century art.

"Characteristics of Negro Expression" is not only an adulation of black folk expressions in the guise of anthropology, it is also one of the first explicit commentaries on the *sine qua non* of primitivist modernism, cultural exchange. The remark quoted above indicates that people were not unaware of primitivist modernism and that interracial exchanges in the arts were not dismissed in an ethos of political correctness. Instead of condemning Whiteman for appropriating Negro expressions, Hurston declares in a matter-of-fact tone that cross-cultural appropriations have a catalytic effect on creating new art forms—black or white. Surprisingly, this essay sets out to discuss cultural differences but discovers a commonality, the tendency to imitate and reinterpret expressions derived from cultures not one's own.

Black cultural critique of Nordicism: Many of the essays in *Negro* strike a blow against colonialism or racism; Arthur A. Schomburg's critique is particularly strong. He states, "The whole of Africa has suffered ignominiously at the hands of European nations for inexcusable reasons" (Cunard, *Negro*, 605). Other black writers point out that Europeans fabricated the image of the barbarous Negro to justify their own barbarous acts of exploitation and destruction.

While several essays assert the cruelty of Europeans, others affirm the superiority of black cultures. George Schuyler, for example, feels that "the Africans have shown themselves most superior to what we flatteringly call modern civilization" (Cunard, *Negro*, 786). Schuyler accuses the "Caucasian civilization" of being unable to provide security and happiness, citing unemployment, insufficient and expensive insurance, disintegrated families, and a lack of collectivism as factors that have made the lives of Caucasians miserable. When these structures are imposed on African civilizations, it only disrupts their well-functioning society; the "forces of civilization," Schuyler concludes, have "remolded humanity to their sorry pattern" (Cunard, *Negro*, 788).

Rather than demonstrate how civilized Negroes are—as Locke's anthology tried to do—Cunard's anthology seeks to reveal that colonialism, lynching, racism, and fascism are testimonies to the inadequacy and brutality of the white capitalist system. Cunard's own article, "Scottsboro—and other Scottsboros," is representative of this strategy; it exposes the legalized racism behind that trial and ends with an assault on white America for the mistreatment of the defendants. For Cunard, the white bourgeoisie has no right to any sense of supremacy, moral or otherwise, over Negroes. She argues that, in fact, the Negro is less destructive and, in many ways, superior to the Caucasian.

This reversal is often concomitant with an over-appraisal of blacks. In "Harlem Reviewed," Cunard enthusiastically states her case:

> But it is the zest the Negroes put in, and the enjoyment they get out of things that causes one more envy in the ofay. Notice how many of the whites are unreal in America; they are *dim*. But the Negro is very real; he is there. And the ofays know it. That's why they come to Harlem—out of curiosity and jealousy and don't-know-why. The desire to get close to another race has often nothing honest about it; for where the ofays flock, to these night-clubs, for instance . . . the coloured clientele is no longer admitted.[18]

When Cunard argues that "the Negro is very real," she casts him in the terms of what Ann Douglas defined as "terrible honesty," a characteristically modern ethos. But Cunard's ostensibly primitivist discourse relies once again on the common trope of zest and joy. She reverses the existing racist hierarchy and constructs one where blacks are on top and "ofays" play the role of the underdog, maintaining the model of a binary opposition. Cunard accuses those who transgress the color line to "get close to another race" of mere curiosity, jealousy, and dishonesty; her argument makes a plea to keep Nordics out of Harlem—all Nordics but herself.

Cunard's accusation calls to mind Langston Hughes's objecting to whites being given the best tables to stare at Negroes, as well as Rudolph Fisher's account of "Caucasians Storming Harlem."[19] She uses the black vernacular—"ofay," Pig Latin for foe—to set herself apart from her own race and assume moral superiority over other white visitors to Harlem. She takes umbrage at Carl Van Vechten's depiction of Harlem as one big nightclub where people indulge in alcohol, cocaine, and sex. Dismissing his novel as a "cheap lithograph," she accuses Van Vechten of being one of many "profiteers in coloured 'stock.'" Cunard implies that her concern for blacks is political and, therefore, genuine.

Cultural Critique of Negrotarianism: There is a flip side to this discourse of scolding Nordics—sometimes it implies a class-chiding of Negroes. Cunard's essay, "Harlem Reviewed," is an example of a discourse that criticizes blacks for lacking sufficient race or class consciousness. Cunard attacks the "snobbery" of the "Negro blue-bloods" and chides the Harlem Renaissance writers for being "race-conscious in the wrong way"; she justifies her verdict by stating that their art possessed "a bourgeois ideology with no horizon, no philosophical link with life" (Cunard, *Negro*, 73). Of the largest movement of blacks in the 1920s, Marcus Garvey's nationalism, she says: "But it is all hot air. It is not organized in any direction or built on anything solid."

Her indictment that "the Negro race in America has no worse enemy than its own press" downplays the problem of the color line and accuses black journalism of lacking class-consciousness. When she states that *"The Harlem Liberator* is the only honest Negro paper in the States," she is merely embracing the organ of her own brand of leftwing politics. Self-righteously, Cunard laments, "The American Negroes—this is a generalization with hardly any exceptions—are utterly uninterested in, callous to what Africa is, and to what it was. Many of them are fiercely 'racial,' as and when it applies to the States, but concerning their forefathers they have not even curiosity." (Cunard, *Negro*, 69). Here, Cunard scolds African Americans for their indifference to Africa, and, indirectly, suggests that Locke's call to bond with the African forefathers remained unheard.

Throughout her essay, arrogance is accompanied by ignorance. Her comment about the history of Harlem—"Harlem was more or less 'left' to the coloured people"—reveals an ideological blindness to the role black entrepreneurs played in the transformation of Harlem from a community of European immigrants to a black community. She ignores the crucial role of a black real estate agent, Philip A. Payton, in that process. Acknowledging the fact that Payton, who was both wealthy and black, was largely responsible for turning Harlem into a black community would have subverted the binary opposition of poor, oppressed blacks versus rich whites underlying Cunard's foreword.

All too often, Cunard is guilty of a strange twist on racism herself. We remember her criticism of Josephine Baker's stylistic shift away from the primitive to a more self-consciously "artistic" aesthetic. Cunard's accusation that Baker had "sold-out" implied that Baker was complicitous with the class enemy and thus (also) a traitor to the race. For Cunard to prefer the primitivist Baker to the modernist incarnation is her right, of course. But to define Baker's primitivist-African self as her "authentic" self is a sign of cultural arrogance. Rebuking Baker for lacking race consciousness and denouncing the black cultural elite as reactionary "negrotarians," Cunard tries to appear more Negro than the Negroes themselves. Her alleged solidarity with the black race is consistently undermined by her primitivist and communist orthodoxy; in the end, Cunard's is an antiracist racism.

The performative effect of cross-cultural projections: This variant of primitivist discourse intends to transform one's own culture. Often this attempt is circular—discovering in the other what one finds desirable in oneself. Raymond Michelet's "African Empires and Civilizations" illustrates this strategy.

He praises the "harmony and wisdom the Negro constitutions attained" and quotes Delafosse's statement that "the Negroes' instinctive desire [is] to uphold the interests of the collective unit" in order to valorize the traditional African concept of collective ownership (Cunard, *Negro*, 601). Michelet constructs an opposition between African collectivism and American individualism, suggesting that Western cultures should emulate the African moral sensibility.

In his essay on Bambara sculpture, Carl Kjersmeier explores the concept of African collectivism in the arts. What he finds is that, despite a resemblance to the socialist concept of community, in the arts there is no dogmatic pressure to conform (Cunard, *Negro*, 683). His study of Bambara art and West African customs demonstrates that each individual artist creates his own style and is free to modify the tradition. He asserts that the desire for artistic independence is powerful even in traditional African culture.

Melville Herskovits's contribution to *Negro*, "The Best Friend in Dahomey," continues this trend of cultural envy. Herskovits is struck by the concept of friendship in Dahomey since it differs so much from the "casual give-and-take relationships of our own culture." In Dahomean culture, there exists an institutionalized form of friendship in which a self-appointed *Honton Daho* (a best friend, always of the same sex) "can always be counted on to help in time of need"—for example, when one's father or mother dies. Herskovits describes the caring support that this best friend provides in very positive terms. His description stresses the absence of a comparable sense of formalized loyalty and obligation in American culture.

In all of these examples, what seem to be merely descriptions of exotic social practices are actually challenges to the reader to establish something similar in his culture. These critiques by counterexample are a means to an end. Here, statements about the other—be it the attribution of "joy" or "spirituality"—are projections through which European and American cultures try to invigorate themselves. This line of argument is a subtle twist on the old trope of revivification; its assertions of black cultural superiority are meant to introduce new, rejuvenating models to western cultures.

These six types of primitivist discourse clearly reveal that *Negro* is a manifestation of, rather than a critique of, primitivism. That a primitivist subtext is woven through the fabric of *Negro* should not be surprising: Cunard had felt primitivism's call for many years. She remembered vividly that:

> About six years old, my thoughts began to be drawn towards Africa . . . [I dreamed of] "The Dark Continent"—with Africans dancing and drumming around me, and I one of them, though still white, knowing, mysteriously enough, how to dance in their own manner. Everything was full of movement in these dreams; it was that which enabled me to escape in the end, going further, even further! And all of it was a mixture of apprehension that sometimes turned into joy, and even rapture.[20]

The course from here to the publication of *Negro* is almost linear; her "kinship" to Africans was a self-fulfilling prophecy. Her desire to "go native" stemmed from her aspiration to throw off the shackles of the static, bourgeois life she was living as a child. In her dream world, Cunard could escape her dull life, become "one of them," and "dance in their manner." Cunard, of course, could never become black. But she could publish *Negro*, in which she advocated an ideology that sought to refute the bourgeois ideology which her parents embodied.

Cunard's class consciousness and primitivist bias are the two unreconciled strivings of *Negro*. The anthology's twin attempt to create a black communist manifesto while romanticizing rhythm, joy, vigor, spirituality, and emotionality is a "contradiction of double aims," to use Du Bois's phrase. *Negro* combines aims that were (according to other socialist thinkers, such as Georg Lukács) mutually exclusive. Dismissing the fascination with African art as an expression of an imperialist bourgeois ideology, Lukács declared contemptuously: "any swank who collects stained glass or Negro sculpture, and snob who celebrates insanity as the emancipation of mankind from the fetters of the mechanistic mind, could claim to be a champion of popular art."[21]

Equating kitsch, African art, and avant-garde art, he rejects these forms as pseudo-popular art. The "snobs" and "swanks" who collect and aestheticize the primitive promote a decadent, elitist, and solipsistic "artiness." "True" popular art, as Lukács sees it, grows "out of a life and history of a people." Its subject matter is the life of common people, and it is an art that is part of the common cause of the proletariat. As an advocate of Western European proletarianism, Lukács objected to the bourgeois interest in primitive art, promoting instead a socialist-realist aesthetics. Lukács would have objected to Cunard's attempt to advance the communist cause through a primitivist ideology; to Lukács, primitivist communism was a contradiction in terms.

Nancy Cunard's revolt against racism—and the white establishment condoning it—was a rebellion against her family and the silver-spoon society in which she had grown up. Her mother, Maud Burke, the wife of Sir Bache Cunard (the founder of the Cunard steamship line), represented to Nancy Cunard the worst of both the racist ideology and the capitalist bourgeois establishment. This already problematic relationship came to a head when Nancy chose a black jazz pianist from Washington, D.C., Henry Crowder, as her lover. She had seen Crowder play in Venice and had fallen in love with Crowder's "charm, beauty, and elegance"; in 1928, he moved into Nancy's apartment in Paris. Crowder helped with her newly established Hours Books Press; over the next two years they printed sixteen books by preeminent avant-garde writers. One of these books, *Henry Music,* was a collection of music by Crowder and poems by Samuel Beckett and other writers (Ford, xv).

Cunard's childhood fascination with black Africa now shifted to black America. She read voraciously and most likely had read *The New Negro* well before she and Crowder traveled to Harlem in the summer of 1931. Accompanied by Crowder, she did not feel like a tourist but rather like an insider in a world she had only known in dreams. But soon the reality of Jim Crowism put a damper on Cunard's enthusiasm. "Ofay and spade can't go together here, without there being, perhaps, an incident," Crowder warned her when she suggested that they go for a walk on Broadway (Ford, xviii). As an interracial couple in the 1930s, they were a sensation, which Cunard did not mind. As the partner of a black man, her daily life was an act of transgression and, in that sense, exciting. Her interracial liaison set her apart from other whites and enraged her mother, who decided to disinherit her daughter.

Instead of keeping her mother's disapproval a family affair, Nancy Cunard confronted her in print.[22] In a pamphlet titled *Black Man and White Ladyship*, Nancy Cunard claims that her mother disowned her not because of the race problem, "No, with you it is the other old trouble—class." She casts her mother as a bourgeois reactionary, "[although] the British Museum seems to guarantee that African art is art, her Ladyship or her like do not change their mind about Negroes." This jibe is based on her mother's dismissal as "slave bangles" the African ivory bracelets covering Cunard's lower arms from wrist to elbow —Cunard was armored with ivory; wherever she went, people could hear her before they could see her (Ford, 106).

This observation about the valorization of African art and the persistently dismissive attitude of white society is also an attack on Locke's strategy of race uplift. Cunard's experience had taught her an important lesson: proving the Negro is artistic does not guarantee that (white) people will redefine their old image of the Negro; to the old regime of Maud Cunard, the Negro will always remain a nigger. Although it was generally accepted that African art and African American music were forms of high art, the Negro was still not "received," either socially or politically. The vision that aesthetics could be the *via regia* to racial uplift, as Locke hoped, is, according to Cunard's account of her mother's racist attitude, wishful thinking. Even British intellectuals, like her close friend, the writer George Moore, who dismissed out of hand the idea that he was prejudiced, admitted that he had no desire to meet an intelligent Indian or Negro. Moore had boldly declared that "I do not think I should get on with a black man or a brown man." Such responses by friends and relatives convinced Cunard that the concept of "the New Negro" was ineffectual, and she set out to give birth to *Negro*.

Only with Cunard's own money and concerted effort did *Negro* come to life. For over three years, Cunard went to great expense to pursue her mission; she spent long hours editing the vast material and approximately £1,500 of her own money just to have it published. (She also lost a considerable amount of money by being disinherited.) The overtly political text had, in other words, very personal motivations. Not only was it a direct reaction to her mother, it also could have never existed but for the liaison with Crowder.

Her dubious, mixed motivations and her conflicting agendas should not devalue the ambitious project. *Negro* was well received among the black intelligentsia. Langston Hughes, for example characterized Cunard as a genuine humanitarian. In his essay, "Nancy: A Pina in Memoriam. If one could break it in her honor," he writes:

> But she had an infinite capacity to love peasants and children and great but simple causes across the board and a grace in giving that was itself gratitude. . . . She did not like bigots or brilliant bores or academicians who wore their honors, or scholars who wore their doctorates, like dog tags. (Ford, 1)

Echoing the key tropes—soul, life, love—of romantic primitivist discourse, Hughes expressed his respect for this white woman who was "full of life and love." Hughes appreciated her unpretentiousness and uses his praise of her to put down scholars who wear their doctorates "like dog tags," a humorous suggestion that academic degrees are useful only for identifying the dead.

William Plomer, an African-born novelist, claimed that Cunard's Negrophilism "was passionately serious, and its influence augmented other influences already at work. And ultimately [this was] of great political importance in the world" (Ford, 126). Likewise, Lawrence Gellert claimed that Cunard's aim was to attain "the full equality of the race" and pledged that her anthology stood as "a monument, a legacy and landmark to the race." In a review published in the *Amsterdam News* on April 7, 1934, Henry Lee Moon praised the book for being more than an anthology: "It is an encyclopedia of Negro life in the Americas, in Africa and in Europe."[23] And in the *New Republic*, he wrote that "it is a valuable contribution to world literature of the black race."[24] These favorable critiques of *Negro* suggest that even its self-serving personal agenda did not impinge on the book's efficacy as a weapon in the fight for the liberation of black peoples.

But not all blacks were impressed. Not surprisingly, among those who did not approve of *Negro* was Alain Locke. In his annual review of works published in 1934, Locke dismissed *Negro* as being full of "hot rhetoric, clanging emotion." Nevertheless, Locke did give the volume some credit:

> There is much of unique informational and critical value in these eight hundred pages which document both the wrongs and the achievements of the black man and capitalizes for the first time adequately the race problem as a world problem. But the capital "P" is for propaganda, not for poetry, and the book hurls a shell, bomb and shrapnel at the citadel of Nordicism.[25]

Locke dismissed the new anthology's haughty attack on Nordicism as merely a reflection of the zeitgeist, which he describes as "the eleventh hour of capitalism and the eleventh hour of Nordicism." Curiously, he calls the book a "bomb" attempting to destroy Nordicism. Locke, of course, did not approve of this radicalism; he always tried to work within the protective confines of the "citadel." Still, Locke rejected the propaganda of *Negro* not so much because it would upset those by whom he wanted to be accepted, but because he thought it bad art.

Locke discussed other literary productions that year with the same sense of concern. Langston Hughes's *The Ways of White Folks* (1934) was a similar example of this revolutionary new school of Negro fiction. Antibourgeois and genuinely proletarian, it strikes a "militant assault on the citadel of Nordicism" and it reflects "the decline of a whole ideology," by which Locke meant the ideology he had promoted in *The New Negro*. Locke himself had admitted that *The New Negro* "is radical on race matters, conservative on others"; he was opposed to changing the basic social structure. Rather, Locke hoped that his New Negro would become an integral part of it.

Negro, Locke realized in 1934, signified a radical change in ideological positioning within the black and interracial community. It was the foundational text for this *new* New Negro, a being who is radical in politics as well as in racial concerns. This rebellious Negro would break away from one set of white patrons, as Langston Hughes broke from his patron Mrs. Mason, and would join another—the Communist Party—as Cunard advised all Negroes to do. By 1934, Locke's strategy had become outdated; modernism would give way to social realism. And social realism would become the preeminent black aesthetic in the 1930s, culminating in 1940 with the classic of American naturalism, Richard Wright's *Native Son*, the first black Book-of-the-Month Club selection.

In 1936, Cunard traveled to Russia to pursue her cause. That year, Locke published yet another book on aesthetics, *Negro Art: Past and Present*, in which he makes the extraordinary claim: "In being modernistic they [black artists and, by extension, anyone] are indirectly being African."[26] Locke's attempts to eliminate the color line would still rely on primitivist modernism as his Trojan horse. But he was not willing to accept *Negro* as part of the larger project to combine modernism, primitivism, and a political struggle for equality. The trait that these two bibles of blackness framing the Harlem Renaissance do share is best expressed in a statement Du Bois had made in *The Souls of Black Folk* when he wrote about the peculiar sensation characteristic to the Negro: "this sense of looking at one's self through the eyes of others." In both anthologies, this twin glance to the [white] cultural other and to primitivism was constitutive to their making. Both *The New Negro* and *Negro* were indebted to this glance to the side.

CONCLUSION
Modernism Reconsidered

The primary concern of *Primitivist Modernism* has been for art works in which black and white cultures are mutually constitutive. To describe this cultural relation as an "affinity between the modern and the tribal"—as William Rubin, director of the MOMA exhibit, did—is a misleading gloss, not only because the term "tribal" is inaccurate, but also because "affinity" suggests that Western and non-Western art are parallel structures that can never be integrated. Instead of fearing that any closer relation might be disruptive, we should think of this relation as a vital hybrid in which white and black cultures have formed something entirely new. It is an example of what Françoise Lionnet called a "métissage"; yet structurally this hybrid is not completely equivalent to creolization because the original, culturally specific identities are no longer discernible.[1]

This book argues that the First World owes much of its symbolic cultural capital to sources found throughout the Third World. We have seen that there is no modernism without primitivism. By this I do not mean that all of modernism was informed by African art—Mondrian's and Charles Sheeler's works, for example, bear no obvious traces. Nor do I offer a monocausal account of the shaping of modernism. I suggest, however, that black cultures played a seminal role in the emergence of a new aesthetic paradigm; modernism includes the presence of the so-called primitive at its heart.

I have explored some of the ramifications of a movement that began in the first decade of this century when Pablo Picasso and his colleagues became interested in *l'art primitif* and *l'art nègre*. Those young artists discovered in black art a symbolic weapon to attack postromanticist aesthetics. The repercussions of what they accomplished are still not fully discernible. Since modernism's black antecedents were officially denied, especially during the racially troubled 1920s and 1930s, only now have we begun to comprehend Virgil Thompson's assertion that "Africa has made profound alterations in our European inheritance."[2] Only recently have scholars begun to evaluate the artistic and social implications of Alain Locke's observation that "in being modernistic, they are indirectly being African."

One consequence of our discussion of the cross-cultural interplay at the core of modernism is that we need to reconfigure our critical map to include what we have called primitivist modernism. It is finally time for the role that the primitive has played to come front and center and take its place in the accepted ranks of contributors to modernism's innovations. Critics and historians of modernism have long held that the movement developed along a number of aesthetic lines or trends. One is the highly experimental, iconoclastic avant-gardism that implicitly followed Ezra Pound's dictum to "make it new." This course, which is primarily concerned with formalistic innovation, encompasses diverse trends in painting, such as futurism or dadaism, and poetry by Pound or Stevens.

A second trend is to minimalism, the Bauhaus ethos that "less is more." This includes, for example, abstraction and precision in the visual arts but also literary techniques such as those used by Ernest Hemingway or Gertrude Stein.

A third trend is a realist aesthetic. This includes portrait paintings or social realist works in the visual arts. In literature, it manifests itself as an attempt to convey moral messages, as a psychological realism that deals with personal conflicts, or an ethnic literature that attempts to represent the life of immigrants "accurately." Moreover, it includes a politicized aesthetic that criticizes bourgeois attitudes, speaks on behalf of the proletariat, and envisions the liberation of the working class.

The ignored fourth trend, namely that of a primitivist modernist aesthetic, is composed of art works in which formal and cultural difference are interrelated. While this investigation has focused on the influx of African or African American expressions, one could also posit a study that accounted for the influence of, say, Japanese culture on the shaping of modern art. It is crucial, however, that this influence manifest itself not in terms of subject matter but rather in a fusion of forms. This trend in modernism, in which cultural difference is incorporated formally, is a harbinger of an increasingly integrated multiculturalism in the arts. While art historians (particularly scholars of cubism) might agree with this four-part model, this reconfiguration, which accounts for the seminal role black expressions have played, is certainly not commonly accepted in other art forms.

What, ultimately, will have been the effect of the African artistic influx? One way of getting at this question is to think of how this "cross-over" aesthetic distinguishes modernism from its artistic predecessors. In premodern art, say in *Jugendstil* or *art nouveau*, the European classicist tradition dominated. When a black element was introduced, as in Manet's *Olympia*, it remained marginalized literally and thematically—as the black maid in *Olympia* is shunted to the periphery. If nonwhites played a role in premodern works of art, they were only significant as objects of representation, or misrepresentation.

In modernist works, by contrast, there emerged a new way of dealing with black elements: in some, black elements were formalistically constitutive; in others, they were thematically integrated. In modernism's early phase, the Africanist presence asserted itself to the world. In modernism's more advanced phases, however, the traces of the black African catalyst were, consciously or unconsciously, effaced. While Picasso moved on to create an increasingly abstract art in the 1930s, Josephine Baker downplayed the Africanist elements in her stage performances and transformed her primitivist stage persona into that of a glamorous and dignified modern diva.

Meanwhile, cross-over aesthetics in America existed only as popular culture—as black performers playing in front of white audiences. On the level of high art, there was no equivalent in America to *Les Demoiselles* or the *revue nègre*. The American public was appalled when European modernist art was imported to New York and exhibited in the Armory Show. This collective rejection of modernism was paralleled by a national disapproval of Baker's performance in the Ziegfeld Follies in 1936. While it is a well-known fact that the American public was hesitant to accept formal artistic innovations, it is not commonly discussed that this rejection was related to an unwillingness to accept African or African American cultures and the people who made it.

The context of American racism—a racism that differed from the European version because it was sanctioned by law—has to be taken into account if we discuss any cultural difference between cross-over aesthetics in Europe and in America. During the 1920s, it was almost impossible for a black performer to become popular throughout the United States. Black musicians were forced to tour the South or play in clubs located in the black sections of metropolitan cities; they mostly played in front of all-black audiences or they recorded records for an all-black market. In both cases, the color line was initially impenetrable. When the record industry realized the profit-making potential of this business, they recorded large numbers of black musicians. Since the demand for these records was high, companies such as Columbia or Victor made a huge profit. The socially marginalized proved to be crucial for the process of consolidation of the U.S. record industry.

Listening to jazz was a sign of rebellion. Modernists used jazz as a "weapon" to oppose the old value system and to refashion their identity. It is a commonplace that the collective self-fashioning of a modern identity was predicated on a break with Victorian moral conventions and aesthetic values. However, scholars have not sufficiently addressed the fact that the negation of the received genteel code of nineteenth-century culture was sometimes concomitant with an embrace of that which their predecessors most despised —"the primitive." Whereas Picasso had used *l'art nègre* to blacken his canvas and make his images gloomy and crude, Whiteman "de-blackened" his rhythms and added harmonic elements to make his "experiment in modern music" sound more like European music than African or African American. After this act of formalistic cleansing, jazz became acceptable to a broader audience, radio stations started to broadcast jazz nationally, and, eventually, even black musicians were broadcast on national radio.

Concomitant with the white appropriation of black art was a move by blacks to reappropriate European primitivist modernism. Black intellectuals and artists of the New Negro movement relied on artistic and ideological im-

pulses derived from European cultures. The Harlem Renaissance is highly indebted to its cultural other. Since some European avant-garde artists tried to
keep the Negro element incognito, it is not surprising that Alain Locke ur-
gently sought to unveil this role and use it as a starting point to construct a
New Negro and, in the process, a "New White" as well.

If black primitivist modernism generated Locke's New Negro movement,
primitivism was also a starting point for Du Bois and helped him to initiate a
Pan-African movement. If Locke and Du Bois had not appropriated and modified Euro-American primitivism, black modernism and Negritude (the ideology of the liberation movement of postcolonial Africa) could not have assumed the forms they did. Although Europe's valorization of Africa was
generated by dubious motives, it had a fermenting effect on African cultures.
This was a crucial step toward a process in which the "primitive" would gain
cultural autonomy.

Black American artists have, in turn, parodied this practice of valorizing
and admiring the "primitive." We mentioned in the last chapter the short
story entitled "Rejuvenation through Joy," in which Langston Hughes depicts
a "high brow cult of joy—featuring the primitive." In this story, wealthy but
weary white Americans attend a retreat because they hope to be cured in an
environment that Hughes describes as "primitive modernistic." The organizer
of this "Colony of Joy" is an athletic and charismatic man named Lesche,
who gives daily lectures on how to attain joy. He teaches his audience that
"joy [is] springing from the dark rhythm of the primitive" and proposes blacks
as role models because "they [Negroes] live through motion, through movement, through music, through joy!" At the end of the story, the reader is told
that Lesche is a mulatto passing for white.

Hughes's satire mocks one of the prominent assumptions of the 1920s, a
period when Harlem was a hub of joy where New Yorkers could immerse
themselves in "Nubian mirth." Hughes's fictionalized account of the deeper
motives for slumming is a cultural critique of white people. Another such example of satire is a 1937 song entitled "Slumming on Park Avenue," in which
Ella Fitzgerald sings a captivating refrain: "Let us go to it. They do it, why
can't we do it too? Let's go slumming, let's go slumming at Park Avenue."
Fitzgerald's song calls for reversing the direction of the nightly migration; she
encourages Harlemites to join her in exploring Nordic gaiety on Park Avenue.

Another black reaction to the process of appropriation in the entertainment business was to become a prominent, if not hegemonic, force in American popular music. Duke Ellington, Ella Fitzgerald, and Louis Armstrong
were in the vanguard of reclaiming the legacy that Whiteman had tried to
make his own. They were trailblazers for Wynton Marsalis, Mary J. Blige, and
Joshua Redman. In the visual arts, we see William H. Johnson signifying on
Picasso in *Cafe* and, by extension, parodying European primitivist modernism. Another signifying gesture is Josephine Baker's walking her panther,
which she adorned with a diamond collar. Owning a wild animal of the jungle, she signified on French primitivist yearnings and the benefits she had
reaped from catering to their desires.

Between 1906 and 1938, this cross-cultural dynamic of interracial collaboration, borrowing, reappropriation, and outright parody influenced the making of European and American modernism. As a consequence, the fixed binary oppositions, which had been apparently absolute and noncontingent until the nineteenth century, started to merge or dissolve in the curious dynamism of race in European and, to a lesser degree, American art and cultural history. What had been thought of in the West as unalterable opposites began to drift into one another. The color line became more permeable, even if only symbolically or at the level of popular culture. The socioeconomic inequality between African Americans and Anglo-Americans persisted, of course; Jim Crow reality was affected by this process only slightly, if at all. Even in Cunard's socialist discourse, the primitive was still essentialized as the sensual authentic, utilized primarily as a means of ideological critique. But in spite of these structures, a dynamic interplay undermined racial divisions between black and white cultures. This cultural mixing was, by and large, a critique of binary divisions that was neither complete nor conscious but had wide-ranging effects.

In this cross-cultural interplay, we might find the seed of a method to reconsider black modernism and postmodernism. Thomas Docherty has called the exigency of postmodernism "the demand for a just relating to alterity, and for a cognition of the event of heterogeneity." According to Docherty, we are faced with two choices: "the search for a just politics, or the search for just politics."[3] To him, there is only one option: we need to find an ethical basis for an ethical demand, and therein lies "the real political burden and trajectory of the postmodern."

This investigation did not set out to discover grounds for "a just politics." But in disclosing a cross-cultural dialectic in which the socially marginalized have contributed to shaping the center of modernism, we may have taken a step toward interrelating race, modernism, and ethics. Of course, the acceptance of "the primitive" was not ethically motivated—it was at best ethnocentric, and at worst racist—and it had very little to do with a genuine concern for people of African descent or for their art. But given the social context (a racist definition of civilization that had assumed an absolute opposition between African and European cultures), cross-over aesthetics proved revolutionary in undermining this essentialist presupposition.

My assessment of primitivism differs from that of Hal Foster, who feels that primitivism is "a metonym of imperialism, which served to disavow these [imperialist] preconditions."[4] While imperialism, economic exploitation, and political oppression are responsible for primitive art's making its way to Europe in the first place, the fact that European artists used African art as a source of inspiration can hardly be dismissed as mere cultural imperialism. Foster's precondition for dismissing primitivism as an "unjust politics" is based on his equating economic and artistic practices. But equating colonizers and artists is inadequate. It was only in the sphere of the arts that a dialectical process could safely germinate. Instead of dismissing primitivism as racism, it is more instructive to consider its potential in subverting the antagonism between the races. Primitivist modernism opened a space comparable to what Homi K. Bhabha called the third space of enunciation, an ambiguous space that undermined the opposition that the colonialist enterprise was predicated upon.

On the other hand, the overly enthusiastic response to primitivism that celebrates the European appreciation of "primitive expressiveness" (as William Rubin did when he exalted: "We [Westerners] respond to them [African art objects] with our total humanity.") is equally inept. To discover in primitivism evidence of a "universal" or "trans-historical essence" is to disavow important cultural differences. Moreover, Rubin downplays the contribution black cultures have made to shaping transatlantic modernism—and it is this that is most crucial about primitivist modernism.

One hundred years ago, W. E. B. Du Bois outlined in his lecture "The Conservation of Races" (1897) a vision for the twentieth century. At the end of his talk, Du Bois emphatically articulated his convictions:

1. We believe that the Negro people, as a race, have a contribution to make to civilization and humanity, which no other race can make.
2. We believe it the duty of the Americans of Negro descent, as a body, to maintain their race identity until this mission of the Negro people is accomplished, and the ideal of human brotherhood has become a practical possibility.[5]

From today's perspective, Du Bois's statement is prophetic; the "Negro people, as a race," have indeed made such contributions to civilization, or more specifically, to modernism. The legacy of primitivist modernism has shown that the descendants of Africa have made significant contributions to the development of the arts in the Western world.

Du Bois's plea that black Americans maintain their race identity until they assume a status of equality is a rejection of (or at least a moratorium on) assimilationist tendencies. In a discussion of Du Bois's article, Anthony Appiah has argued that Du Bois's insistence on maintaining a distinct African American racial identity is part of a classic dialectic.[6] The thesis in this dialectic is, Appiah claims, the desire to minimize cultural difference, and the antithesis is Du Bois's call for accepting difference. A synthesis might be the creation of "human brotherhood." This would be a coexistence of black and white peoples in which both groups relate to one another as equals and in which cultural difference is obsolete because assumptions about racial inferiority would no longer exist. It would mean that there was little or no wage gap, that socioeconomic conditions were similar between black and white, that their level of education was equal, and that blacks and whites were equal participants in political and juridical decision-making. Of course, this is not the case at the end of the twentieth century.

A conversation of the races, to play on Du Bois's title, has long existed on the symbolic level of American culture. But even today, after the multicultural debate has resulted in restructuring the canon, the role of cultural hybridity remains obscured. Even the debates on postmodernism have not thematized the role the cultural other played during the incipient phase of modernism; the black drops added to the bucket of white modernism remain unacknowledged. Steven Connor makes an apt observation when he claims that postmodernist theory "names and correspondingly closes off the very world of cultural difference and plurality which it allegedly brings to visibility."[7]

The simultaneous avowal and denial of cultural difference has been a theme throughout this book. Indeed, we have encountered several incidents of denial. Picasso's outright negation indicated that the influences the Negroes had on him were so crucial he was unwilling to admit it. Many Americans were so bound by tradition that they were unwilling to acknowledge the artistry of black music and dismissed it as jungle music. And remember those white jazz enthusiasts who celebrated jazz as a national expression and compared it to baseball and the Fourth of July while ignoring the African American contribution.

My goal has been to shed light on a presence that has always been playing in the dark, to paraphrase Toni Morrison. It is based on a negative dialectic (in the sense that Theodor W. Adorno defined it). Adorno calls for an analysis of what is absent but present, of what is potentially existing but has not yet manifested itself.[8] A negative dialectic does not aspire to definition; it refuses even to fix meaning in order to draw conclusions. Instead of making programmatic assertions, a negative dialectic attempts to transcend the limitations of positivism by accounting for the open-endedness of the analytical process. This book has offered a combination of negative and classical dialectic, transferred to the field of cultural studies.

Ten years ago, Daniel J. Singal asserted in "Towards a Definition of American Modernism" that a "modernist embrace of natural instinct and primitivism" was the key to understanding modernism. I have focused on the formalistic "embrace" of the other of color. Given the significance of this cross-cultural embrace, one wonders if the very term "the other"—a term so fashionable in contemporary debates on multiculturalism and postmodernism—is even helpful. In fact, what we have seen is that the term quickly becomes obsolete as the "other" and the "self" are thoroughly interwoven. On the symbolic level at least, white and black cultures have been intertwined; they are mutually constitutive.

If cultural hybridity is at the core of early modernism, we might start to speculate on the effects this could have on late postmodernism. Maybe black expressions will once again yield new (white) art forms. Or perhaps the knowledge of cultural hybridity within modernism will function as a harbinger for an integrated multiculturalism in American society. Or maybe postcolonial studies will continue to explore incidents that transcend binary logic. Maybe we will come to the understanding that hybridity can not be limited to colonized cultures, that it is constitutive of white cultures as well. Even the most cursory glance at pop culture attests that this fascination with the cultural other continues America's dialectical dance of avowal and disavowal, even as it heads into the twenty-first century.

▣ NOTES

Introduction

1. Houston A. Baker, Jr., *Modernism and the Harlem Renaissance* (Chicago: University of Chicago Press, 1987).

2. Richard J. Powell, *The Blues Aesthetic: Black Culture and Modernism* (Washington, D.C.: Washington Project for the Arts, 1989).

3. Michele Wallace, "Modernism, Postmodernism and the Problem of the Visual in Afro-American Culture," in *Out There: Marginalization and Contemporary Cultures*, ed. Russell Ferguson, Martha Gever, Trinh T. Minh-ha, and Cornel West (Cambridge: MIT Press, 1992), p. 45.

4. Miles Orvell, *The Real Thing: Imitation and Authenticity in American Culture, 1880–1940* (Chapel Hill: University of North Carolina Press, 1989).

5. Terry Smith, *The Making of the Modern: Industry, Art, and Design in America* (Chicago: University of Chicago Press, 1993).

6. Jackson Lears, "Uneasy Courtship: Modern Art and Modern Advertising," *American Quarterly* 39, no. 1 (1987): 133–154, 135.

7. Frederic Jameson, "The Politics of Theory: Ideological Positions in the Postmodernism Debate," *New German Critique* 33 (Fall 1984): 63.

8. Andreas Huyssen, *After the Great Divide: Modernism, Mass Culture, Postmodernism* (Bloomington: Indiana University Press, 1986), p. 56.

9. Sidney Mintz, introduction, *The Myth of the Negro Past*, by Melville J. Herskovits (Boston: Beacon Press, [1941] 1989), p. xix.

10. Toni Morrison, *Playing in the Dark: Whiteness and the Literary Imagination* (Cambridge: Harvard University Press, 1992). The term "Africanism" here applies to the aesthetics and not as much to anthropological issues. Hence, it is used differently from the way that, for example, Joseph E. Holloway uses it in his book, *Africanisms in American Culture* (Bloomington: Indiana University Press, 1990).

Chapter 1

1. Shelley Fisher Fishkin, *Was Huck Black? Mark Twain and African-American Voices* (New York: Oxford University Press, 1993).

2. Michael North, *The Dialect of Modernism: Race, Language, and Twentieth-Century Literature* (New York: Oxford University Press, 1994).

3. Eric J. Sundquist, *To Wake the Nations: Race in the Making of American Literature* (Cambridge: Harvard University Press, 1993).

4. To prove that the Harlem Renaissance was a failure, Cruse lists several reasons. First, the black middle class failed to promote the black high arts. Owing to their elitist and genteel attitude, they also rejected black vernacular, or folk expressions. Second, the Negro artists themselves adopted middle-class values and failed to draw upon black folk expressions in their works. Third, according to Cruse, white writers assumed a dominant role in representing black life and whites assumed control in the arts, because they owned theaters, clubs, and film houses. Harold Cruse, *The Crisis of the Negro Intellectual* (New York: William Morrow, 1967).

5. Art Berman, *Preface to Modernism* (Urbana: University of Illinois Press, 1994), pp. vii, x.

6. Raymond Williams, *The Politics of Modernism: Against the New Conformists* (New York: Verso, 1989), p. 35.

7. Wolfgang Iser, *The Act of Reading: Theory of Aesthetic Response* (Baltimore: Johns Hopkins University Press, 1978), p. 108.

8. Christian Zervos, "Notes sur la sculpture contemporaire," *Cahiers d'art* 10 (1929): 465.

9. Quoted in Charles Wentick, *Modern and Primitive Art* (Oxford: Phaidon Press, 1979), p. 15.

10. Alain Locke, ed., *The New Negro* (New York: Atheneum, [1925] 1992), p. 258.

11. Julia Peterkin, quoted in "The Negro in Art: How Shall He Be Portrayed, A Symposium." *Crisis* (September 1926): 219. And two years later, the historian Hoxie Neale Fairchild extended the trope of the noble savage and applied the idealization of non-Westerners to African Americans. Discussing the Negro, Fairchild concludes that "the Noble Savage came at a time when he was needed. His virtues, though grossly misunderstood and exaggerrated, helped men to see the superficiality of those ideals of polish, worldly power, luxury, common sense and elegant learning which they had been holding before them." Hoxie Neale Fairchild, *The Noble Savage: A Study in Romantic Naturalism* (New York: Columbia University Press, 1928), p. 510.

12. For a discussion of the representation of blacks in American literature, see Seymour L. Gross and John Edward Hardy, eds., *Images of the Negro in American Literature* (Chicago: University of Chicago Press, 1966), and John R. Cooley, *Savages and Naturals: Black Portraits by White Writers in Modern American Literature* (Newark: University of Delaware Press, 1982).

13. Franz Kuna, "The Janus-faced Novel: Conrad, Musil, Kafka, Mann," in *Modernism: 1890–1930*, ed. Malcolm Bradbury and James Mc Farlane (Harmondsworth: Penguin Books, 1976), p. 446.

14. Arthur Oncken Lovejoy and George Boas, *Documentary History of Primitivism and Related Ideas* (Baltimore: Johns Hopkins University Press, 1935), p. 7.

15. Michel Leiris, "Civilization," in *Brisées: Broken Branches*, trans. Lydia Davis (San Francisco: North Point Press, [1929] 1989), p. 20.

16. Irving Howe, *The Decline of the New* (New York: Harcourt Brace Jovanovich, 1963), p. 25.

17. Lionel Trilling, *Beyond Culture: Essays on Literature and Learning* (New York: Harcourt Brace Jovanovich, 1965), p. 19.

18. Richard Ellmann and Charles Feidelson. Jr., eds., *The Modern Tradition: Backgrounds of Modern Literature* (New York: Oxford University Press, 1965).

19. Daniel Joseph Singal, "Towards a Definition of American Modernism," *American Quarterly* 39, no. 1 (1987): 21.

20. Paul Lauter et al., eds., *The Heath Anthology of American Literature* (Lexington: D.C. Heath and Company, 1990), p. 958.

21. Carl G. Jung, "Your Negroid and Indian Behavior," *Forum* 83, no. 4 (April 1930): 196.

22. See George Devereux and Edwin M. Loeb, "Antagonist Acculturation," *American Sociological Review 8*, no. 2 (April 1943): 133–147, and Stephan Palmié, "The Other Within: American Anthropology and the Study of Ethnic Minorities in the 1920's," in *Ethnic Cultures in the 1920's in North America*, ed. Wolfgang Binder (Frankfurt: Peter Lang, 1993), pp. 215–238.

Chapter 2

1. William Rubin, ed., *Primitivism in 20th Century Art: Affinity of the Tribal and the Modern,* 2 vols. (New York: Museum of Modern Art, 1984), p. 252. Rubin begins his introduction to this catalog with a very grand statement claiming that "No pivotal topic in twentieth-century art has received less serious attention than primitivism—the interest of modern artists in tribal art and culture, as revealed in their thought and work." While his definition of primitivism is too vague, I think, his observation about the neglect seems apt.

2. William Rubin in *Les Demoiselles d'Avignon.* Studies in Modern Art 3, ed. William Rubin, Hélène Seckel, and Judith Cousins (New York: Museum of Modern Art, 1995), p. 107.

3. Gelett Burgess, "The Wild Men of Paris," *The Architectural Record* 27, no. 5 (May 1910): 410. According to Burgess, Matisse owned about twenty pieces of non-Western art by 1908. If that were the case, Matisse owned the largest collection. This article was one of the earliest discussions of *Les Demoiselles d'Avignon* published in America.

4. Paul Guillaume, "African Art at the Barnes Foundation," *Opportunity* 2, no. 17 (May 1924): 140–141.

5. Jacques Lipchitz's statement was published in, "Opinions sur l'art nègre," *Action* (Paris), vol. 3 (April 1920), p. 25.

6. Judith Cousins and Hélène Seckel, "Chronology," in *Les Demoiselles d'Avignon. Studies in Modern Art 3*, ed. William Rubin, Hélène Seckel, and Judith Cousins (New York: Museum of Modern Art, 1995), pp. 197–198.

7. Françoise Gilot and Carlton Lake, *Life with Picasso* (New York: McGraw-Hill Book Company, 1964), p. 266.

8. Pierre Daix, *Picasso and the Cubist Years* (Boston: Beacon Hill Press, 1979), p. 11.

9. Danielle Boone, *Picasso* (London: Studio Editions, 1989), p. 64.

10. Helen M. Franc, *An Invitation to See* (New York: Museum of Modern Art, 1992), p. 47.

11. Apollinaire was not the only one to come up with this powerful image. Curiously enough, Salmon and Kahnweiler used similar phrases to describe the effect of Picasso's image. See Hélène Seckel, "Anthology of Early Commentary on

Les Demoiselles d' Avignon," in *Les Demoiselles d'Avignon*. Studies in Modern Art 3, p. 229.

12. See Katia Samaltanos, *Apollinaire* (Ann Arbor: UMI Research Press, 1981), pp. 3–4.

13. A. Bowness, introduction to *Post-Impressionism: Cross Currents in European Painting*, a Royal Academy of Arts Catalogue (London: Royal Academy of Arts, 1979), p. 11.

14. Franz Boas, *Primitive Art* (New York: Dover Press, 1927), p. 70.

15. Leo Stein, *Appreciation: Painting, Poetry and Prose* (New York: Crown, 1947), p. 177.

16. Guillaume quoted in Bowness, pp. 32, 33.

17. Paul Guillaume, "The Triumph of Ancient Negro Art," *Opportunity* 4, no. 41 (May 1926): 147.

18. Kirk Varnedoe argues in his book, *A Fine Disregard: What Makes Modern Art Modern*, that most first-year college students would know that black art influenced the rise of cubism. Varnedoe's assertion—"Two of the favorite stories of modern art's beginnings involve a trip to the islands, and a visit to the museum."—suggests not only that Gauguin's interest in people from the South Sea and Picasso's visit to the Trocadéro are essential to the emergence of modernism, but also that this is common knowledge. Students today, I think, are not informed about the pivotal role non-European cultures played in the formation of modernism. Moreover, to reduce the influence of African art to Picasso's visit to the ethnography museum and Gauguin's trip to Tahiti—as Varnedoe does—is to ignore the broader implications of this intercultural exchange. The discrepancy, for example, that black African art had a decisive influence in European art while "third world cultures" were of little interest politically or economically is something most students have not yet been told. Kirk Varnedoe, *A Fine Disregard: What Makes Modern Art Modern* (New York: Harry N. Abrams, 1992), p. 183.

19. Edward F. Frey, *Cubism* (New York: McGraw-Hill, 1966), p. 39.

20. Stein quoted in Manfred Smuda, *Der Gegenstand in der Bildenden Kunst und Literatur: typologische Untersuchungen zur Theorie des ästhetischen Gegenstands* (Munich: Wilhelm Fink Verlag, 1979), p. 116.

21. Astradur Eysteinsson, *The Concept of Modernism* (Ithaca: Cornell University Press, 1990), p. 49.

22. Robert Goldwater, *Primitivism in Modern Art* (1938; Cambridge: Harvard University Press, Belknap Press, 1986), p. 16.

23. Goldwater uses the term "romantic" synonymously with "harmonious."

24. Robert Goldwater encourages art historians to collaborate with anthropologists and to study the cultural context of African art. Although equally formalistic, he at least conceeds the limitations of his expertise: "Never having done field work, my contact with primitive art is through objects no longer in use and my knowledge of primitive societies is only indirect." Goldwater, *Primitivism in Modern Art*, p. 303.

25. Dore Ashton detects what she calls a "visible disjuncture in the exhibition"; that is, the show's attempt to juxtapose anthropology and art criticism results in sacrificing art to anthropology. Dore Ashton, "On an Epoch of Paradox: 'Primitivism' at the Museum of Modern Art," *Arts Magazine* 59 (November, 1984): 76–79.

James Clifford, however, feels that anthropology is given short shrift. To Clifford, "the catalogue succeeds in demonstrating not any essential affinity toward the tribal and modern or even a coherent modernist attitude toward the primitive but rather the restless desire and power of the modern West to collect the world." James Clifford, *The Predicament of Culture: Twentieth-Century Ethnography, Literature, and Art* (Cambridge: Harvard University Press, 1988), p. 196.

26. Yve-Alain Bois, "La pensée sauvage," *Art in America* 73 (April 1985): 184.

27. Marianne Torgovnick, "William Rubin," in *Perspectives Angles on African Art*, ed. Susan Vogel (New York: Abrams/Center for African Art, 1987), pp. 49−64.

28. Rasheed Araeen is among those critics who have commented on this ethnocentric bias; he particularly criticizes Rubin's tendency to categorize and evaluate primitive art. See Rasheed Araeen, "From Primitivism to Ethnic Arts," in *The Myth of Primitivism: Perspective on Art*, ed. Susan Hiller (London: Routledge, 1991), pp. 167, 172.

More recently, Gilane Tawadros also argued that the history of primitivism is an integral part of the history of European colonialism: "Far from disturbing the boundaries between Western and non-Western cultures, the discourse of so-called modern primitivism effectively reinforces the separation of spheres of the modern and the primitive which significantly can be traced to the Enlightenment." Gilane Tawadros, "Beyond the Boundary: The Work of Three Black Women Artists in Britain," in *Black British Cultural Studies; A Reader,* ed. Houston A. Baker, Jr., Manthia Diawara, and Ruth H. Lindeborg (Chicago: University of Chicago Press, 1996), p. 246.

29. Paul Guillaume and Thomas Munro, *Primitive Negro Sculpture* (New York: Harcourt, Brace & Co., 1926), p. 12.

30. Hal Foster, "The 'Primitive' Unconscious of Modern Art," *October* 34 (1985): 45.

31. Jack Flam, "A Continuing Presence: Western Artists/African Art," in Jack Flam and Daniel Shapiro, *Western Artists/African Art* (New York: Museum of African Art, 1994), p. 77.

32. Mary Schmitt-Campbell, David Driskell, David Levering Lewis, and Deborah Willis Ryan, *Harlem Renaissance: Art of Black America* (New York: Studio Museum and Harry N. Abrams, 1987), p. 27.

33. Edmund Barry Gaither, introduction to *The Life and Art of Loïs Mailou Jones,* ed. Tritobia Hayes Benjamin (New York: Pomegranate Artbooks, 1994), p. xvii.

34. Catherine Bernard, preface to *The Life and Art of Loïs Mailou Jones*, p. x.

35. Jane Carpenter, *Lois Mailou Jones: Prepatory Studies and Paintings from the African Series* (Washington, D.C.: Parish Gallery−Georgetown, 1995).

36. "Exhibition to Be Held of Work of Negro Artists," press release, January 4, 1930, HFP, Library of Congress.

37. "Negro Artists," editorial, *New York Amsterdam News*, January 8, 1930.

38. Richard J. Powell, *Homecoming: The Art and Life of William H. Johnson* (Washington, D.C.: National Museum of American Art, 1991), pp. 69, 78.

39. Alain Locke, foreword to *Contemporary Negro Art* (Baltimore: Baltimore Museum of Art, 1939).

40. Quoted in Lowery S. Sims and Mitchell D. Kahan, eds., *Robert Colescott: A Retrospective, 1975−1986* (San Jose: San Jose Museum of Art, 1987), p. 8.

41. Stuart Hall, "What Is 'Black' in Black Popular Culture?," in *Black Popular Culture*, ed. Gina Dent (Seattle: Bay Press, 1992), p. 23.

Chapter 3

1. U.S. Department of War, *Discovering Music*, Education Manual EM 603, 2nd ed. (Washington: American Book Company, 1944), pp. 7–8.

2. Gunther Schuller, *Early Jazz: Its Roots and Musical Development. The History of Jazz*, vol. 1 (New York: Oxford University Press, 1968), p. 27.

3. "Why 'Jazz' Sends Us Back to the Jungle," *Current Opinion* 65 (September 1918): 165.

4. "Condemns Age of Jazz," *New York Times*, January 27, 1925.
"Praises Broadway Music," *New York Times*, January 11, 1926.

5. Anne Shaw Faulkner, "Does Jazz Put the Sin in Syncopation?" *Ladies' Home Journal* 38 (August 1921): 16.

6. "Where Is Jazz Leading America," *Etude* 42 (August 1924): 520.

7. John R. McMahon, "Back to Pre-War Morals," *Ladies' Home Journal* 38 (November 1921): 13.

8. John R. McMahon, "The Jazz Path of Degradation," *Ladies' Home Journal* 26 (January 1922): 71

9. "What's the Matter with Jazz?" *Etude* 42 (January 1924): 6.

10. "Representatives of 2,000,000 Women Meet to Annihilate 'Jazz'," *Musical Courier* 86, (May 21, 1923).

11. Objecting to the "sensual stimulation of the abominable jazz orchestra with its voodoo born minors and its direct appeal to the sensory centers," Mr. Guyon's defamation of jazz is also based on the equation of Africa with sensuality. See John R. McMahon, "Unspeakable Jazz Must Go," *Ladies' Home Journal* (December 1921): 116.

12. See *New York Times*, January 30, 1922.

13. James Lincoln Collier, *Jazz: The American Theme Song* (New York: Oxford University Press, 1993), p. 23.

14. Morroe Berger, "Jazz: Resistance to the Diffusion of a Culture Pattern," *Journal of Negro History* 32 (1947): 461–494.

15. Neil Leonard, *Jazz and the White Americans: The Acceptance of a New Art Form* (Chicago: University of Chicago Press, 1962).

16. Alan P. Merriam, *The Anthropology of Music* (Chicago: University of Chicago Press, 1962) pp. 243, 242.

17. "Says Threatens Christian Civilization," *New York Times*, December 16, 1934.

18. James Lincoln Collier, *The Reception of Jazz in America: A New View*, I.S.A.M. Monographs, no. 27 (New York: Institute for Studies in American Music, 1988), p. 17.

19. Kathy J. Ogren, *The Jazz Revolution: Twenties America and the Meaning of Jazz* (New York: Oxford University Press, 1989), p. 159.

20. LeRoi Jones, *Blues People. Negro Music in White America* (New York: William Morrow & Co., 1963), p. 155.

21. Quoted in Iain Lang, *Jazz in Perspective: The Background of the Blues* (New York: Da Capo Press, 1976), p. 55.

22. Paul Whiteman and Mary Margaret McBride, *Jazz: Popular Culture in America 1800–1925* (New York: Arno Press, [1926] 1974), p. 155.

23. Quoted in Marshall W. Stearns, *The Story of Jazz* (New York: Oxford University Press, 1962), p. 110.

24. "Where Is Jazz Leading America?" *Etude*, pp. 517–518.

25. Quoted in Samuel Barclay Charters and Leonardt Kunstadt, *Jazz: A History of the New York Scene* (New York: Da Capo Press, 1981), p. 136.

26. *Vanity Fair* (March 1925): 46.

27. Arnold Shaw, *The Jazz Age: Popular Music in the 1920s* (New York: Oxford University Press, 1987), p. 142.

28. See Ole Brask, *Jazz People* (New York: Harry N. Abrams, 1976), p. 45.

29. Thomas A. DeLong, *Pops: Paul Whiteman, King of Jazz* (Piscataway, N.J.: New Century Publishers, 1983), p. ix.

30. Patricia Leighten, "The White Peril and L'Art Nègre: Picasso, Primitivism, and Anticolonialism," *Art Bulletin* 72, no 4 (December 1990): 609–629.

31. Abbe Niles, "Lady Jazz in the Vestibule," *New Republic* (December 23, 1925): 188.

32. Quoted in John Chilton, *Jazz* (Sevenoaks, Eng.: Hodder and Stoughton, 1979), p. 53.

33. Paul Whiteman, "The Progress of Jazz: Problems Which Confront the American Composer in His Search for a Musical Medium," *Vanity Fair* (January 1926): 52.

34. "Jazz Comes to Stay," *Current Opinion* 77 (September 1924): 337.

35. Quoted in David Ewen, *The Story of George Gershwin* (New York: Henry Holt and Company, 1943), p. 99.

36. Virgil Thompson, "The Cult of Jazz," *Vanity Fair* (June 1925): 54.

37. Virgil Thompson, "Enter: American-Made Music," *Vanity Fair* 25, no. 2 (October 1925): 71, 124.

38. Edmund Wilson, "The Jazz Problem," *New Republic* (January 13, 1926).

39. Ernest Newman, "Summing Up Music's Case Against Jazz," *New York Times Magazine* (March 6, 1927): 3.

40. Samuel Chotzinoff, "Jazz: A Brief History. A Consideration of Negro Harmonies and Modern Dance Music," *Vanity Fair* 20, no. 4 (June 1923): 69, 104.

41. Leopold Stokowski quoted in *The New Negro*, ed. Locke, pp. 221–222.

42. Irvin Berlin prophesies: "When commuters no longer rush for trains, when taxicabs pause at corners, when businessmen take afternoon siestas, then perhaps jazz will pass." Ogren, *Jazz Revolution*, p. 144.

43. Rogers, "Jazz at Home," in *The New Negro*, ed. Locke, pp. 223–224.

44. "Primitive Savage Animalism, Preacher's Analysis of Jazz," *New York Times*, March 3, 1922.

45. Frederick Lewis Allen, *Only Yesterday. An Informational History of the 1920's* (New York: Harper & Row, [1931] 1964).

46. Scott Fitzgerald, "Echoes of the Jazz Age," *Crack Up* (New York: New Directions Paperbook, 1945), p. 16.

47. *Chicago Defender*, June 2, 1923.

48. *Chicago Defender*, May 7, 1921.

49. *Journal and Guide*, January 15, 1921. The record company used advertisement slogans that stressed their racial background, for example, claiming to be "The Only Genuine Colored Record. Others Are Only Passing for Colored."

50. *Talking Machine World* 20 (April 1924): 168.

51. Edward Brooks, *The Bessie Smith Companion: A Critical and Detailed Appreciation of the Recordings* (New York: Da Capo Press, 1982), p. XVIII.

52. Richard Hadlock, *Jazz Masters of the Twenties* (New York: Macmillan, 1965), p. 223.

53. Chris Albertson, *Bessie Smith: Empress of the Blues* (New York: Macmillan, 1974), p. 10.

54. Ekkehard Jost, *Sozialgeschichte des Jazz in den USA* (Frankfurt: Fischer Verlag, 1991), p. 74.

55. Paul Oliver, *Blues Fell This Morning: Meaning in the Blues* (Cambridge: Cambridge University Press, [1960] 1994), p. 2. See also Robert M. W. Dixon and John Dodrich, *Recording the Blues* (New York: Stein and Day, 1970), p. 104.

56. Ibid., pp. 43, 48. See also "Columbia Buys OKey-Odeon Record Division of General Phonograph Corp.," *Talking Machine World* 22 (October 1926): 18.

57. Ronald Clifford Foreman, Jr., *Jazz and Race Records, 1920–32; Their Origins and Their Significance for the Record Industry and Society*, Ph.D. diss. (Urbana: University of Illinois, 1968), p. 83.

58. Marshall Stearns, *The Story of Jazz* (New York: Oxford University Press, 1958), p. 168.

59. Richard Wright, foreword to *Blues Fell This Morning: Meaning in the Blues*, by Paul Oliver (Cambridge: Cambridge University Press, 1994), p. xv.

60. Langston Hughes and Milton Meltzer, *Black Magic: A Pictorial History of Black Entertainers in America* (New York: Bonanza Books, 1967), p. 80.

61. Bruce Kellner, ed. *The Harlem Renaissance: A Historical Dictionary for the Era* (New York: Methuen, 1987), p. 415.

62. James Weldon Johnson, *Black Manhattan* (New York: A Da Capo Press, [1930] 1991), pp. 224, 225.

63. Steven Watson, *The Harlem Renaissance: The Hub of African-American Culture, 1920–1930* (New York: Pantheon Books, 1995), p. 128.

64. Quoted in David Leverings Lewis, *When Harlem Was in Vogue* (New York: Oxford University Press, 1989), p. 170.

65. Langston Hughes, "When the Negro Was in Vogue," in *The Big Sea: An Autobiography*, by Langston Hughes (New York: Hill and Wang, [1940] 1993), p. 225.

66. Quoted in Allon Schoener, ed., *Harlem on My Mind: Cultural Capital of Black America 1900–1968* (New York: Random House, 1968), p. 80.

67. Mary Ross, "Negro City in Harlem Is a Race Capital," *New York Times*, March 1, 1925.

68. Beverly Smith, "Harlem—Negro City," *New York Herald Tribune*, February 10, 1930.

69. A. Clayton Powell, Jr., "Powell Says Rent Too High," *New York Post*, March 28, 1935, in *Harlem on My Mind*, ed. Schoener, pp. 138, 139.

70. "Congestion Causes High Mortality," *New York Times*, October 24, 1929, in *Harlem on My Mind*, ed. Schoener, p. 81.

71. "Population Rises Steadfastly: Illness Takes Heavy Toll; Unemployment and Low Wages Result from Race Prejudice," *New York Herald Tribune*, February 10, 1930, in *Harlem on My Mind*, ed. Schoener, p. 125.

72. Gilbert Osofsky, *Harlem: The Making of a Ghetto. Negro New York 1890–1930* (New York: Harper Press, 1968), p. 151.

73. In the 1920s, Aldous Huxley argued, "having a good time" meant to eat well, to drink, to dance and to drive around in a car. He concluded that the leisure class suffered from boredom and tried desperately "to fill the intolerable vacuum of unlaborious existence." If this was the case, it is not surprising that so many Americans would find Harlem compelling. Harlem offered a kind of diversion that was both deviant and eccentric. See Aldous Huxley, "The Horrors of Society.

The Unutterable Boredom Involved in the 'Diversions' of the Leisured Classes,"
Vanity Fair (June 1925): 46.

74. "Jazz for the Nerves," *New York Times*, March 21, 1930.

75. Guy C. McElroy, *Facing History: The Black Image in American Art 1710–1940* (San Francisco: Bedford Arts, 1990), pp. xxii, 121.

76. Alain Locke, "Toward a Critique of Negro Music," *Opportunity* (December 1934): 367.

77. Alain Locke, *The Negro and His Music* (New York: Arno Press, [1936] 1968), p. 130.

78. Dave Peyton, "The Musical Bunch," *Chicago Defender*, January 30, 1927.

79. "Hayes Modestly Receives Medal," *Amsterdam News*, April 15, 1925.

80. "The 'Charleston'," editorial, *Opportunity* (July 1926).

81. Rudolph Fisher, "The Causasian Storms Harlem," *American Mercury* 11 (August 1927): 81.

82. "Chocolate Kiddies Company Sails for Germany," *Pittsburgh Courier*, May 16, 1925. Björn Englund, "Chocolate Kiddies: The Show That Brought Jazz to Europe and Russia in 1925," *Storyville* 62 (December 1975–January 1976): 44–50. Bernhard H. Behncke, "Sam Wooding and the Chocolate Kiddies at the Thalia-Theater in Hamburg 28, July 1925 to 24 August 1925," *Storyville* 60 (August–September 1975): 214–219.

83. The lyrics to "Jig Walk" are as follows:
"There's a funny twisting step makes others a joke. All you steppers gather round and make your footsies smoke. You don't need no big brass band. Don't need no song. Everybody put your hands. Get going strong. Jig Walk. Come on and do the Jig Walk. And do a little Charleston, Charleston with a pat-de-pat pat-de-pat. Jog Walk. Come make your funny feet talk. And when you do the Charleston you'll start them to rave. Show these kind folk New York's dancing craze. It has got that big Broadway ablaze Jig Walk."

84. "Jazz Bitterly Opposed in Germany," *New York Times* , March 11, 1928.

85. T. R. Ybarra, "Berlin Operettas Praised for 'Snap'," *New York Times*, March 11, 1928.

86. Darius Milhaud, "The Jazz Band and Negro Music," *Living Age* (October 18, 1924): 172.

87. Jaap Kool, "The Triumph of the Jungle," *Living Age* (January 3, 1925), vol. 324 No. 4200, pp. 339, 343.

88. Robert Goffin, *Jazz: From the Congo to the Metropolitan* (New York: Doubleday, 1944), p. 124.

89. Hugues Panassié, *The Real Jazz* (New York: A. S. Barnes, 1942), p. 36.

90. Ted Giola, *The Imperfect Art: Reflections on Jazz and Modern Culture* (New York: Oxford University Press, 1988), p. 31.

91. Martin Cooper, "Revolution in Musical Taste," in *The Impact of America on European Culture,* ed. Bertram Russell and John Lehmann (Boston: Beacon Press, 1951), p. 72.

Chapter 4

1. "Josephine nous quitte. La rapide carriere et les projects de la belle vedette noir," editorial, *Paris Midi*, January 29, 1928.

2. The number of people who would ultimately take credit for Baker's discovery is legion. Jacques Charles, the choreographer of *La Revue Nègre*, declared, "I invented her," and Paul Colin insisted, "I'm the one who invented her." See Jean-Claude Baker and Chris Chase, *Josephine: The Hungry Heart* (New York: Random House, 1993), pp. 109, 114.

3. Carol-Bérard, *Revue International de Musique et de Danse* (April 19, 1927).

4. e.e. cummings, *Vanity Fair* (September 1926): 114. Since there remains little footage of her appearance—some of it is included in the 1987 production, "Chasing a Rainbow," and in the HBO production "The Josephine Baker Story," starring Lynn Whitfield—we shall rely mostly on firsthand accounts published in the contemporary press to come to understand Baker's allure.

5. Nancy Cunard, "Josephine Baker," in *Negro Anthology*, ed. Cunard (New York: Negro University Press, [1934] 1969), p. 329.

6. André Levinson, *La danse d'aujourd'hui* (May 5, 1929), quoted in Pepito Abatino, *Josephine Baker Vue Par la Presse Francaise* (Paris: Les Editions Isis, 1931), p. 37.

7. Janet Flanner, *Paris Was Yesterday 1925–1939* (New York: Popular Library, [1934] 1972), p. xx.

8. See Sander L. Gilman, "Black Bodies, White Bodies," in *"Race," Writing and Difference,* ed. Henry Louis Gates, Jr. (Chicago: University of Chicago Press, 1986), pp. 223–261.

9. Nineteenth-century medical discourse posited that black women were transmitters of sexual diseases. "Medical" authorities argued that syphilis had originated in Africa and that syphilitic sores had turned human skin black. One widespread conviction—that sexual intercourse with black women inevitably led to infections—was "confirmed" by numerous medical treaties. Dr. Madison Tylor, for example, asserted that blacks were disproportionately infected by gonorrhea, tuberculosis, and insanity. Another widespread belief was that blacks were promiscuous. Dr. Murrel, for example, asserted that, for blacks, morality is "almost a joke, adultery and fornication are not regarded as a sin." Murrel concludes: "the average Negro is all slum." See Malgorzata Irek, *European Roots of the Harlem Renaissance.* Berliner Amerikanische Beiträge (Berlin: Akademie-Verlag, 1995), p. 118.

10. "Le 'secret' de Joséphine Baker," *Volonté* (December 10, 1929).

11. Marcel Sauvage, *Les Mémoires de Joséphine Baker* (Paris: Éditions Kra, 1927), pp. 99–100.

12. "Josephine Baker Is a St. Louis Washerwoman's Daughter," *Time* (February 10, 1936).

13. "Much Publicity for Josephine Baker," *New York Times*, March 4, 1928.

14. "Vienna Bars Negro Dancer," *New York Times*, February 4, 1928; "Josephine Baker's Dances Forbidden,"*New York Times*, April 14, 1929; "Missiles Hurled at Josephine Baker," *New York Times*, April 12, 1929.

15. "Crowd Demands Refund When Neither Josephine Baker nor Al Sherman Appears," *New York Times* , December 5, 1928.

16. "Josephine Baker, Sensation of Paris, Returns Home," *Boston Herald*, December 8, 1935.

17. Editorial in *Crisis* 33, no. 4 (February 1927): 204.

18. "Josephine Baker," *Crisis,* 34, no. 3 (May 1927): 86.

19. "From the Slums of St. Louis to the Toast of Gay Paris an Idol of the Silver Screen," *Pittsburgh Courier*, November 16, 1929.

20. "Josephine Baker, of Harlem, Adds a Noble Husband to Conquests Abroad," *New York World*, June 21, 1927.

21. While the *Washington Eagle* was skeptical about Abatino's title and claimed that the Abatino family was not registered on the official "nobility list," the *Chicago Defender* believed the claim. The paper responded with the following dispatch: "The Albertini [sic] family comes from Sicily and is of an old line of nobility." An op-ed piece in the *Washington Eagle* reluctantly conceded: "Let her have her count." See "Josephine Baker, Countess for a Day, Discounted," *Washington Eagle*, June 24, 1927; "Count's Father Glad His Son Chose Josephine as Bride; Is Proud of Her," *Chicago Defender*, July 2, 1927; "Count Right On," *Washington Eagle*, June 24, 1927.

22. "The New Countess," *Amsterdam News*, July 6, 1927.

23. "J.A. Rogers First to Interview Countess Pepito di Albertini," *Amsterdam News*, July 6, 1927.

24. "Josephine Baker Is the Rage at the Casino de Paris," *Crisis* 39, no. 2 (February 1931): 55.

25. Roi Ottley, "Hectic Harlem," *Amsterdam News*, March 28, 1936.

26. Bryan Hammond and Patrick O'Connor, *Josephine Baker* (London: Bulfinch Press, 1988), p. 90.

27. Kariamu Welsh Asante, "Baker," in *Black Women in America: An Historical Encyclopedia,* ed. Darlene Clark Hine (New York: Carlson Publishing Inc., 1993), p. 75.

28. Phyllis Rose, *Jazz Cleopatra: Josephine Baker in Her Time* (New York: Vintage Books, 1989), p. 18.

29. Mindy Aloff, "An American from Paris," *New York Times Book Review* (January 30, 1994): 1, 29, 30.

30. Mindy Aloff, "Josephine Baker's Jaunty Jiggle Makes a Comeback: Jazz Age Princess," *Dance Magazine* (July 1989): 32.

31. W. A. Roberts, *The Dance* (May 1929), quoted in Marshall Stearns and Jean Stearns, *Jazz Dance: The Story of American Vernacular Dance* (New York: Da Capo Press, [1968] 1994), p. 183.

32. Elizabeth Kendall, *Where She Danced* (New York: Alfred A. Knopf, 1979), p. 199.

33. Lynn Haley, *Naked at the Feast: A Biography of Josephine Baker* (New York: Dodd, Mead, 1981), p. 67.

34. I. de Rudbeck, "Une demi-heure intime avec Joséphine Baker et sa panthere 'Chichita,'" *Marseille Matin,* September 20, 1933.

35. Later in her life, Baker was also to become part of the civil rights movement's integrationist attempts. In 1963, just before Martin Luther King, Jr., was to deliver his "I have a dream" speech Baker was asked to say a few words. Looking at the crowd that had gathered for the March on Washington, she said: "You are on the eve of a complete victory. You can't go wrong. The world is behind you." She added: "Salt and pepper. Just what it should be." And in her personal life, Baker attempted to realize her own dream of universal brotherhood by adopting twelve children from different races who would live peacefully under one roof to demonstrate that interracial brotherhood was possible.

36. The italics are taken from the original. Joséphine Baker, Félix de la Camara, and Pepito Abatino, *Mon sang dans tes veines. Roman d'Apres une Idée de Joséphine Baker* (Paris: Editions Isis, 1931), p. 178.

37. Dr. Charles Drew, an expert in blood plasma who was awarded a medal be-

cause of his outstanding medical research, pointed out the folly of this policy of segregating blood: "I feel the recent ruling of the United States Army and Navy regarding the refusal of colored blood donors is an indefensible one from any point of view. As you know, there is no scientific basis for the separation of the bloods of different races except on the basis of the individual blood types or groups." "Along the N.A.C.P. Battlefront," *The Crisis* 51, no. 5 (1951), 166.

Dr. Drew, himself an African American, criticized the commonly accepted separation of blood into two types, black and white. This Jim Crow policy remained the practice of the blood bank of the American Red Cross, whose director Dr. Drew became in 1941, until 1951, when the American National Red Cross officially announced that it would eliminate racial designation of donors to its blood banks. "Race Tag Removed from Blood," editorial, *The Crisis* 57, no. 4 (1951), 714.

The Virginia Blood Bank, however, still segregated its blood in 1951 as the *Pittsburgh Courier* reported: "'white' blood is kept on the top shelf of the refrigerator, with one color label, while the 'black' blood is kept on the bottom shelf, with another color label. The 'white' blood costs $25 a pint, the 'black' blood $1." D. Walker, "Blood for Sale—Jim-crowed!," *Pittsburgh Courier*, April 19, 1957. This image of keeping black blood on the lower, white blood on the upper shelf and valuing the latter twenty-five times more than the former, reflects the hierarchical racial order in American social institutions.

38. Charles Darwin, for example, believed that "crossing obliterates character." Kant and Darwin quoted in Alfred P. Schultz, *Race or Mongrel* (New York: Arno Press, [1908] 1977), p. 146.

39. John Campbell, *Negro Mania Being an Examination of the Falsely Assumed Equality of the Various Races of Men* (Philadelphia: Campbell & Power, 1851), p. 214.

40. Walter Benjamin, *Gesammelte Schriften* (Frankfurt: Suhrkamp Verlag, 1972).

Chapter 5

1. Ray Stannard Baker, *Following the Color Line: American Negro Citizenship in the Progressive Era* (New York: Harper & Row, [1908] 1964), p. 248.

2. "A Negro Renaissance," editorial, *Opportunity* (June 1925): 187.

3. Henry Louis Gates, Jr., "The Trope of a New Negro and the Reconstruction of the Image of the Black," *Representations* 24 (Fall 1988): 129–155.

4. W. E. B. Du Bois, "The Conservation of Races," in *W. E. B. Du Bois Speaks: Speeches and Addresses, 1890–1919,* ed. Philip S. Foner (New York, [1897] 1970), p. 81.

5. Barnes claims that "the renascence of Negro art is one of the events of our age which no seeker for beauty can afford to overlook." His high esteem of Negro art resulted in the fact that the Barnes Foundation held one of the biggest selections of African art in America. Barnes's interest in black art can not be separated from his childhood memories; he fondly remembered playing with children of slaves. See Peter Plagens and Daniel Glick, "Is the Barnes Noble?" *Newsweek* (May 3, 1993): 60–61.

6. Alain Locke, *Harlem: Mecca of the New Negro, Survey Graphic* 6, no. 6 (March 1925): 630.

7. Locke writes that the American Negro "meets them [the various forms of "ancestral" African arts] in as alienated and misunderstanding an attitude as the

average European Westerner" Conceding that the Negroes' bond to Africa is constructed, Locke points to the benefits that can be gained from claiming this heritage: "This [African] art can scarcely have less influence upon the blood descendants, bound to it by a sense of direct cultural kinship, than upon those who inherit by tradition only, and through the channels of an exotic curiosity and interest." Curiously enough, he never resolves this contradiction, on the one hand he tries to avoid essentialist claims, but on the other hand he suggests that black Americans are closer to African art than Europeans. Locke, *New Negro*, pp. 255, 256.

8. See Amritjit Singh and William S. Shiver, eds., *The Harlem Renaissance: Revaluations* (New York: Garland Press, 1989). Cary D. Wintz, *Black Culture and the Harlem Renaissance* (Houston: Rice University, 1988).

9. Paul Guillaume, "The Triumph of Ancient Negro Art," *Opportunity* (May 1926): 147.

10. James Weldon Johnson, "Harlem: The Culture Capital," in *The New Negro*, ed. Locke, pp. 310, 311.

11. Jeffrey C. Stewart, *To Color America: Portraits by Winold Reiss* (Washington, D.C.: Smithsonian Institution Press, 1989), pp. 60, 38.

12. See Ralph D. Story, "Patronage and the Harlem Renaissance: You Get What You Pay For," *CAL* 32 (March 1989): 284–295.

13. See Jeffrey C. Steward, "Black Modernism and White Patronage," *International Review of African American Art* 11, no. 3 (1994): 43–46.

14. W. E. B. Du Bois, "Our Book Shelf," *Crisis* 31 (January 1926): 141.

15. Hugh Ford, ed., *Negro: An Anthology Collected and Edited by Nancy Cunard* (New York: Frederick Ungar, 1970), p. xvii.

16. Nancy Cunard, ed., *Negro Anthology* (New York: Negro University Press, [1934] 1969), p. iii.

17. V. F. Calverton, "The Growth of Negro Literature," in *Negro Anthology*, ed. Cunard, pp. 105–106.

18. Nancy Cunard, "Harlem Reviewed," in *Negro Anthology*, ed. Cunard, pp. 69, 70.

19. Rudolph Fisher, "The Caucasian Storms Harlem," *American Mercury* Vol 11 (August 1927).

20. Nancy Cunard, *Grand Man: Memories of Norman Douglas* (London: Secker and Warburg, 1954), p. 140.

21. Ernst Bloch, "Diskussion über Expressionismus"; George Lukács, "Es geht um den Realismus," in *Das Wort* (1938), quoted in Ronald Taylor, *Aesthetics and Politics* (London: Verso, 1977), pp. 53, 54.

22. Nancy Cunard, "Black Man and White Ladyship," in Hugh Ford ed., pp. 103–109.

23. Henry Lee Moon, "'Negro' Arrives at Last in Nancy Cunard's Anthology Found Invaluable Document," *Amsterdam News* (April 7, 1934): 1.

24. Henry Lee Moon, "Negro in the Western World," *The New Republic*, October 24, 1934: 316–317, p. 317.

25. Alain Locke, "The Eleventh Hour of Nordicism," ed., Jeffrey Stuart, *Alain Locke's Critical Temper*, 228–232, p. 231.

26. Alain Locke, *Negro Art: Past and Present*, Bronze Booklet Number 3 (Albany: The J.B. Lyon Press, 1936), p. 70.

Conclusion

1. Françoise Lionnet, *Autobiographical Voices; Race, Gender, Self-Portraiture* (Ithaca: Cornell University, 1989).

2. Virgil Thomson, "The Future of American Music," *Vanity Fair* (September 1925): 62.

3. Thomas Docherty, introduction to *Postmodernism: A Reader* (London: Harvester Wheatsheaf, 1993), pp. 26, 27.

4. Hal Foster, "The 'Primitive' Unconscious of Modern Art," *October* 34 (1985): p. 47.

5. W. E. B. Du Bois, "The Conservation of Races," in *W. E. B. Du Bois Speaks*, ed. Philip S. Foner (New York, [1897] 1970), p. 84.

6. Anthony Appiah, "The Uncompleted Argument: Du Bois and the Illusion of Race," in *"Race," Writing and Difference*, ed. Henry Louis Gates, Jr. Chicago: University of Chicago Press, 1986), pp. 21–37.

7. Steven Connor, *Postmodernist Culture: An Introduction to Theories of the Contemporary* (Oxford: Basil Blackwell, 1992), pp. 9, 10.

8. Theodor W. Adorno, *Der Positivismusstreit in der deutschen Soziologie* (Darmstadt: Luchterhand Verlag, 1976).

▣ BIBLIOGRAPHY

Abatino, Pepito. *Josephine Baker Vue Par la Presse Francaise*. Paris: Editions ISIS, 1931.

Adorno, Theodor W. *Aesthetic Theory*. Translated by C. Lenhardt. London: Routledge and Kegan Paul, 1984.

Allen, Frederick Lewis. *Only Yesterday: An Informational History of the 1920's*. New York: Harper, [1931] 1964.

Aloff, Mindy. "Josephine Baker's Jaunty Jiggle Makes a Comeback: Jazz Age Princess." *Dance Magazine* (July 1989): 32–34.

———. "An American from Paris." *New York Times Book Review* (January 30, 1994): 1, 29, 30.

Appiah, Anthony. "The Uncompleted Argument: Du Bois and the Illusion of Race." In *"Race," Writing and Difference*. Edited by Henry Louis Gates, Jr. Chicago: University of Chicago Press, 1986.

Arnold, A. James. *Modernism and Negritude*. Cambridge: Harvard University Press, 1981.

Asante, Kariamu Welsh. "Baker." In *Black Women in America: An Historical Encyclopedia*. Edited by Darlene Clark Hine. New York: Carlson Publishing Inc., 1993, 75–78.

Ashton, Dore. "On an Epoch of Paradox: Primitivism at the Museum of Modern Art." *Arts Magazine* 59 (November 1984): 76-79.

Baker, Houston A., Jr. *Modernism and the Harlem Renaissance*. Chicago: University of Chicago Press, 1987.

Baker, Jean-Claude, and Chris Chase. *Josephine: The Hungry Heart*. New York: Random House, 1993.

Baker, Josephine, de la Camara, and Pepito Abatino. *Mon sang dans tes veines: Roman d'Apres une Idée de Joséphine Baker*. Paris: Editions Isis, 1931.

Baker, Ray Stannard. *Following the Color Line: American Negro Citizenship in the Progressive Era*. New York: Harper, [1908] 1964.

Barnes, Albert C. "Negro Art: Past and Present." *Opportunity* (May 1926): 148–169.

Barr, Alfred H. "Letter." *College Art Journal* 10, no. 1 (1950): 59.

Barth, John. "The Literature of Exhaustion." *Atlantic Monthly* (August 1967): 29–34.

Baumann, Zygmut. *Modernity and Ambivalence*. Ithaca: Cornell University Press, 1991.

Berger, Morroe. "Jazz: Resistance to the Diffusion of a Culture Pattern." *Journal of Negro History* 32 (1947): 461–494.

Berman, Art. *Preface to Modernism*. Urbana: University of Illinois Press, 1994.

Berman, Marshall. *All That Is Solid Melts into Air: The Experience of Modernity*. London: Verso, 1982.

Boas, Franz. *Primitive Art*. New York: Dover Press, 1927.

Bois, Yve-Alain. "La Pensée Sauvage."*Art in America* 73 (April 1985): 178–189.

Boone, Danielle. *Picasso*. London: Studio Editions, 1989.

Bowness, A. *Post-Impressionism: Cross Currents in European Painting*. Royal Academy of Arts Catalog. London: Royal Academy of Arts, 1979.

Bürger, Peter. *Theory of the Avant-Garde*. Translated by Michael Shaw. Minneapolis: University of Minneapolis Press, 1984.

Burgess, Gelett. "The Wild Men of Paris," *The Architectural Record* (New York), vol. 27, no. 5 (May 1910): 401–414.

Calinescu, Matei. *Faces of Modernity: Avant-Garde, Decadence, Kitsch*. Bloomington: Indiana University Press, 1977.

Campbell, John. *Negro-Mania Being an Examination of the Falsely Assumed Equality of the Various Races of Men*. Philadelphia: Campbell & Power, 1851.

Charters, Samuel B., and Leonard Kunstadt. *Jazz: A History of the New York Scene*. New York: Da Capo Press, 1981.

Chilton, John. *Jazz*. Sevenoaks, England: Hodder and Stoughton Press, 1979.

Chotzinoff, Samuel. "Jazz: A Brief History. A Consideration of Negro Harmonies and Modern Dance Music." *Vanity Fair* 20, no. 4 (June 1923): 69–106.

Clifford, James. "Histories of the Tribal and the Modern." *Art in America* 73, no. 4 (1985): 164–215.

———. *The Predicament of Culture: Twentieth-Century Ethnography, Literature, and Art*. Cambridge: Harvard University Press, 1986.

———. "Of Other Peoples: Beyond the Salvage Paradigm." In *Discussions in Contemporary Culture. Number One*. Edited by Hal Foster. Seattle: Bay Press, 1987.

———. "Art-Value, Cultural Value." In *Theory and Cultural Value*. Edited by Steven Connor. Oxford: Basil Blackwell, 1992.

Collier, James Lincoln. *Jazz: the American Theme Song*. New York: Oxford University Press, 1993.

———. *The Reception of Jazz in America: A New View*. I.S.A.M. Monographs. No 27. New York: Institute for Studies in American Music, 1988.

Collier, Peter, and Judy Davies, eds. *Modernism and the European Unconscious*. New York: St. Martin's, 1990.

Connor, Steven. *Postmodernist Culture: An Introduction to Theories of the Contemporary*. Oxford: Basil Blackwell, 1992.

Constantin, M. M. "Brancusi:A Summary of Many Conversaions." *The Arts* 4, no. 1 (July 1923): 15–17.

Cooley, John R. *Savages and Naturals: Black Portraits by White Writers in Modern American Literature*. Newark: University of Delaware Press, 1982.

Cooper, Martin. "Revolution in Musical Taste." In *The Impact of America on European Culture*. Edited by Bertram Russell and John Lehmann. Boston: Beacon Press, 1951.

Cowley, Malcolm. *After the Genteel Tradition*. New York: W. W. Norton, 1937.

Cruse, Harold. *The Crisis of the Negro Intellectual*. New York: William Morrow, 1967.

Cunard, Nancy. *Grand Man: Memories of Norman Douglas*. London: Secker and Warburg, 1954.

Cunard, Nancy, ed. *Negro Anthology*. New York: Negro Universities Press, [1934] 1969.

Daix, Pierre. *Picasso and the Cubist Years*. Boston: Beacon Hill Press, 1979.

Damasse, Jacques. *Les Follies du Music Hall*. Paris: Editions Spectacles, 1960.

Davies, Hilary. *Modern and Primitive Art*. New York: Phaidon, 1978.

de Jongh, James. *Vicious Modernism: Black Harlem and the Literary Imagination*. New York: Cambridge University Press, 1990.

DeLong, Thomas A. *Pops: Paul Whiteman, King of Jazz*. Piscataway, N.J.: New Century Publishers, 1983.

Dent, Gina, ed. *Black Popular Culture*. Dia Center for the Arts. Discussions in Contemporary Culture. No 8. Seattle: Bay Press, 1992.

Devereux, George, and Edwin M. Loeb. "Antagonist Acculturation." *American Sociological Review* (April 1943): 133–147.

Dewitte, Philippe. *Les Mouvements Nègres en France*. Paris: Editions L'Harmattan, 1985.

Docherty, Thomas. *Postmodernism: A Reader*. London: Harvester Wheatsheaf Press, 1993.

Douglas, Ann. *Terrible Honesty: Mongrel Manhattan in the 1920s*. New York: Farrar, Strauss and Giroux, 1995.

Du Bois, W. E. B. "The Conversation of Races," In *W. E. B. Du Bois Speaks: Speeches and Addresses 1890–1919*. Edited by Philip S. Foner. New York, [1897] 1970, 73–85.

————. *The World and Africa*. Millwood, NY: Kraus-Thomson Organization Ltd., 1976.

Einstein, Carl. *Carl Einstein. Werke 1908–1918*. Edited by Peter Baacke. Berlin: Medusa Verlag Wolk & Schmid, 1980.

Ellison, Ralph. *Invisible Man*. New York: Vintage Books, [1947] 1952.

Ellman, Richard and Charles Fedelson, Jr., eds. *The Modern Tradition: Backgrounds of Modern Literature*. New York: Oxford University Press, 1965.

Esman, Aaron H. "Jazz—A Study in Cultural Conflict." *American Imago* (June 1951): 219–226.

Evans, Walker. *African Negro Art: A Corpus of Photographs by Walker Evans*. New York: Museum of Modern Art, 1935.

Ewen, David. *The Story of George Gershwin*. New York: Henry Holt, 1943.

Eysteinsson, Astradur. *The Concept of Modernism*. Ithaca: Cornell University Press, 1990.

Fairchild, Hoxie Neale. *The Noble Savage: A Study in Romantic Naturalism*. New York: Columbia University Press, 1928.

Faulkner, Peter. *Modernism*. London: Meuthen; New York: Harper & Row, 1977.

Ferguson, Russell, et al., eds. *Out There: Marginalization and Contemporary Cultures*. Cambridge: MIT Press, 1990.

Fisher, Rudolph, "The Caucasian Storms Harlem." *American Mercury* (1927). In *Voices From the Harlem Renaissance*. Edited by Nathan Irvin Huggins. New York: Oxford University Press, 1995, 74–82.

Fisher-Fishkin, Shelley. *Was Huck Black? Mark Twain and African-American Voices*. New York: Oxford University Press, 1993.

Fitzgerald, Scott, "Echoes of the Jazz Age," In *Crack Up*. New York: New Directions Paperbook, 1945, 13–22.

Flam, Jack D. *Matisse on Art*. London: Phaidon, 1972.

———— and Daniel Shapiro. *Western Artists/African Art*. New York: Museum of African Art, 1994.

Flanner, Janet. *Paris Was Yesterday 1925–1939*. New York: Popular Library, 1972.

Floyd, Samuel A. Jr. *Black Music in the Harlem Renaissance*. New York: Oxford University Press, 1990.

Fluck, Winfried. "Emergence or Collapse of Cultural Hierarchy?" *Popular Culture in the United States*. Edited by Peter Freese and Michael Porsche. Essen: Verlag Die Blaue Eule, 1994.

Ford, Hugh, ed. *Negro Anthology*. New York: Frederick Ungar, 1970.

Foreman, Ronald Clifford, Jr. *Jazz and Race Records, 1920–32: Their Origins and Their Significance for the Record Industry and Society*, Ph.D. diss. (Urbana: University of Illinois, 1968).

Foster, Hal. "The 'Primitive' Unconscious of Modern Art." *October* 34 (1985): 45–70.

Franc, Helen M. *An Invitation to See*. New York: Museum of Modern Art, 1992.

Frey, Edward F. *Cubism*. New York: McGraw-Hill, 1966.

Gaither, Barry Edmund. Introduction to *The Life and Art of Loïs Mailou Jones*. Edited by Tritobia Hayes Benjamin. New York: Studio Museum and Harry N. Abrams, 1987, xv–xvii.

Gates, Henry Louis, Jr. "The Trope of A New Negro and the Reconstruction of the Image of the Black." *Representations* 24 (Fall 1988): 129–155.

————, ed. *"Race," Writing and Difference*. Chicago: University of Chicago Press, 1986.

Gilman, Sander. "Black Bodies, White Bodies." *"Race," Writing and Difference*. Edited by Henry Louis Gates, Jr. Chicago: University of Chicago Press, 1985.

Gilot, Françoise, and Carlton Lake. *Life with Picasso*. New York: McGraw-Hill, 1964.

Gilroy, Paul. *The Black Atlantic, Modernity and Double Consciousness*. Cambridge: Harvard University Press, 1993.

Giola, Ted. *The Imperfect Art: Reflections on Jazz and Modern Culture*. New York: Oxford University Press, 1988.

Goffin, Robert. *Jazz: From the Congo to the Metropolitan*. New York: Doubleday, 1944.

Goldwater, Robert. *Primitivism in Modern Art*. Cambridge: Harvard University Press, Belknap Press, [1938] 1986.

Greenberg, Clement. "Modernist Painting." In *The New Art: A Critical Anthology*. Edited by Gregory Battock. New York: Dutton, 1966.

Greenblatt, Stephen Jay. *Renaissance Self-Fashioning: From Moore to Shakespeare*. Chicago: University of Chicago Press, 1980.

Gross, Seymour L., and John Edward Hardy, eds. *Images of the Negro in American Literature*. Chicago: University of Chicago Press, 1966.

Guillaume, Paul. "The Triumph of Ancient Negro Art." *Opportunity* (May 1924): 140–142.

———— and Thomas Munro. *Primitive Negro Sculpture*. New York: Harcourt, Brace & Co., 1926.

Haley, Lynn. *Naked at the Feast: A Biography of Josephine Baker*. New York: Dodd, Mead, 1981.

Hall, Stuart. "What Is 'Black' in Black Popular Culture? In *Black Popular Culture*. Edited by Gina Dent. Seattle: Bay Press, 1992: 21–33.

Harper, Philip Brian. *Framing the Margins: The Social Logic of Postmodern Culture*. New York: Oxford University Press, 1994.

Harrison, Charles. *Primitivism, Cubism, Abstraction: The Early Twentieth Century*. New Haven: Yale University Press, 1993.

Harvey, David. *The Condition of Postmodernity*. Oxford: Basil Blackwell, 1989.

Heinrichs, Hans-Jürgen.*Wilde Künstler; über Primitivismus, art brut und die Trugbilder der Identität*. Hamburg: Europäische Verlagsanstalt, 1995.

Hiller, Susan, ed. *The Myth of Primitivism: Perspectives on Art*. London: Routledge, 1991.

Hirsch, Joachim, and Roland Roth. *Das neue Gesicht des Kapitalismus. Vom Fordismus zum Post-Fordismus*. Hamburg: VSA-Verlag, 1986.

Hoffman, Frederick J. *The Modern Novel in America: 1900–1950*. Chicago: Regenery Press, 1951.

Howe, Irving. *The Decline of the New*. New York: Harcourt Brace Jovanovich, 1963.

———, ed. *The Idea of the Modern in Literature and the Arts*. New York: Horizon Press, 1967.

Huggins, Nathan Irvin. *Harlem Renaissance*. New York: Oxford University Press, 1971.

Hughes, Langston. "When the Negro was in Vogue." In *The Big Sea. An Autobiography by Langston Hughes*. New York: Hill and Wang, [1940] 1993.

Hughes, Langston and Milton Meltzer. *Black Magic:A Pictorial History of Black Entertainers in America*. New York: Bonanza Books, 1967.

Hutchinson, George. *The Harlem Renaissance in Black and White*. Cambridge: The Belknap Press for Harvard University Press, 1995.

Huxley, Aldous. "What, Exactly, Is Modern?" *Vanity Fair* (May 1925): 73, 94.

Huyssen, Andreas. *After the Great Divide: Modernism, Mass Culture, Postmodernism*. Bloomington: Indiana University Press, 1986.

Irek, Malgorzata. *European Roots of the Harlem Renaissance*. Berliner Amerikanische Beiträge. Berlin: Akademie-Verlag, 1995.

Iser, Wolfgang. *The Implied Reader: Patterns of Communication in Prose Fiction from Bunyan to Beckett*. Baltimore: Johns Hopkins University Press, 1974.

———. "Negativität als tertium quid von Darstellung und Rezeption Positionen der Negativität." *Poetik und Hermeneutik* VIII. Edited by Harald Weinrich. Munich: Wilhelm Fink, 1975.

Jameson, Frederic. "Reflections in Conclusion." In *Aesthetics and Politics*. Edited by Ronald Taylor. London: Verso, 1977.

———. "The Politics of Theory: Ideological Positions in the Postmodernism Debate." *New German Critique* 33 (Fall 1984): 53–65.

Jones, LeRoi. *Blues People: Negro Music in White America*. New York: Wiliam Morrow & Co., 1963.

Jost, Ekkehard. *Sozialgeschichte des Jazz in den USA*. Frankfurt: Fischer Verlag, 1991.

Jung, Carl G. "Your Negroid and Indian Behavior." *Forum* 83, no. 4 (April 1930): 193–199.

Kaes, Anton, Edward Dimendberg, and Martin Jay, eds. *The Weimar Sourcebook*. Berkeley: University of California Press, 1994.

Kalaidjian, Walter. *American Culture between the Wars. Revisionary Modernism & Postmodern Critique*. New York: Columbia University Press, 1993.

Kellner, Bruce, ed. *The Harlem Renaissance: A History Dictionary for the Era*. New York: Methuen Press, 1987.

Kendall, Elizabeth. *Where She Danced*. New York: Alfred A. Knopf, 1979.

Kiely, Robert, ed. *Modernism Reconsidered*. Cambridge: Harvard University Press, 1983.

King, Anthony D., ed. *Culture, Globalization and the World-System: Contemporary Conditions for the Representation of Identity*. Binghampton: Department of Art and Art History, 1991.

Knapp, James F. "Primitivism and the Modern." *Boundary* 2 (Fall/Winter 1986–1987).

Kramer, Hilton. "The 'Primitivism' Conundrum." *New Criterion* (December 1984).

Kraus, Rosalind. "Giacometti." In *"Primitivism" in 20th Century Art: Affinity of the Tribal and the Modern*. Edited by William Rubin. New York: Museum of Modern Art, 1984, 503–635.

———. "Preying on Primitivism," *Art & Text* 17 (April 1985): 58–62.

Krupat, Arnold. *Ethnocriticism: Ethnography. History. Literature*. Berkeley: University of California Press, 1992.

Kuna, Franz. "The Janus-faced Novel: Conrad, Musil, Kafka, Mann." In *Modernism: 1890–1930*. Edited by Malcolm Bradbury and James McFarlane. Harmondsworth: Penguin, 1976: 443–452.

Lang, Iain. *Jazz in Perspective: The Background of the Blues*. New York: Da Capo Press, 1976.

Lauter, Paul, et al., eds. *The Modern Period 1910–1945. The Heath Anthology of American Literature*. Washington, D.C.: Heath Press, 1990.

Lears, T. J. Jackson. *No Place of Grace: Antimodernism and the Transformation of American Culture*. New York: Pantheon Press, 1981.

———. "Uneasy Courtship: Modern Art and Modern Advertising." *American Quarterly* 39, no. 1 (1987): 133–154

Leighten, Patricia. "The White Peril and L'Art Nègre: Picasso, Primitivism, and Anticolonialism." *Art Bulletin* (December 1990): 609–629.

Leiris, Michel. *Brisées: Broken Branches*. Translated by Lydia Davis. San Francisco: North Point Press, [1929] 1989.

Leonard, Neil. *Jazz and the White Americans: The Acceptance of a New Art Form*. Chicago: University of Chicago Press, 1962.

Levin, Gail. "American Art." In *"Primitivism" in 20th Century Art: Affinity of the Tribal and the Modern*. Edited by William Rubin. New York: Museum of Modern Art, 1984, 453–474.

———. "Primitivism in American Art: Some Literary Parallels of the 1910s and 1920s." *Arts Magazine* 59 (November 1984): 101–105.

Levin, Harry. *Refractions: Essays in Comparative Literature*. New York: Oxford University Press, 1966.

Levine, Lawrence. *Black Culture and Black Consciousness: Afro-American Folk Thought from Slavery to Freedom*. New York: Oxford University Press, 1977.

Lewis, David Levering. *When Harlem Was in Vogue*. New York: Oxford University Press, 1989.

Lewis, Wyndham. *Paleface: The Philosophy of the Melting Pot*. London: Chatto & Windus, 1929.

Lionnet, Françoise. *Autobiographical Voices: Race, Gender, Self-Portraiture*. Ithaca: Cornell University Press, 1989.

Lloyd, Jill. *German Expressionsim, Primitivism and Modernity*. New Haven: Yale University Press, 1991.

Locke, Alain Leroy. "A Collection of Congo Art." *Arts* 2 (February 1927): 50–51.

————. "The Eleventh Hour of Nordicism." In *The Critical Temper of Alain Locke.* Edited by Jeffrey Stuart. New York: Garland, 1983, 228–232.

————, ed. *Harlem: Mecca of the New Negro Survey Graphic* 6, no. 6 (March 1925): 625–697.

————. *The Negro and His Music.* New York: Arno Press, [1936] 1968.

————, ed. *The New Negro.* New York: Atheneum, [1925] 1992.

————. *Contemporary Negro Art.* Baltimore: Baltimore Museum Art, 1939.

————. *Negro Art: Past and Present.* Bronze Booklet Number 3. Albany: The J.B. Lyon Press, 1936.

Locke, Alain. "Toward a Critique of Negro Music," *Opportunity* (November 1934): 328–331; (December 1934): 365–367.

Lovejoy, A. O., and George Boas. *Primitivism and Related Ideas in Antiquity.* New York: Octagon, [1938] 1965.

Lukács, Georg. *Essays über Realismus.* Neuwied and Berlin: Luchterhand Verlag, 1971.

Lyotard, Jean-Francis. *The Postmodern Condition: A Report on Knowledge.* Minneapolis: University of Minnesota Press, 1984.

Malraux, André. *Picasso's Mask.* Translated by June and Gauchos Guicharnaud. New York: Holt, Rinehart, and Winston, 1976.

Margolis, Norman M. "A Theory on the Psychology of Jazz." *American Imago* 11, no. 3 (Fall 1954): 263–291.

McElroy, Guy C. *Facing History: The Black Image in America Art 1710–1940.* San Francisco: Bedford Arts, 1990.

McEvilley, Thomas. "Doctor, Lawyer, Indian Chief." *Artforum* (November 1984).

McMahon, John R. "Back to Pre-War Morals." *Ladies' Home Journal* (November 1921): 12–13

————. "Unspeakable Jazz Must Go." *Ladies' Home Journal* (December 1921): 34.

————. "The Jazz Path of Degredation." *Ladies' Home Journal* (January 1922): 26.

Melville J. Herskovits. *The Myth of the Negro Past.* Boston: Beacon Press, 1989.

Mennicken, Peter. *Anti-Ford oder von der Würde der Menschheit.* Aachen: Die Kuppel Verlag, 1925.

Merriam, Alan P. *The Anthropology of Music.* Chicago: University of Chicago Press, 1962.

Milhaud, Darius. "The Jazz Band and Negro Music." *Living Age* (18 October 1924): 169–173.

Moon, Henry Lee. "Negro in the Western World." *New Republic* (24 October 1934): 27.

Morrison, Toni. *Playing in the Dark: Whiteness and the Literary Imagination.* Cambridge: Harvard University Press, 1992.

Nielsen, Aldon Lynn. *Reading Race: White American Poets and the Racial Discourse in the Twentieth Century.* Athens: University of Georgia Press, 1988.

North, Michael. *The Dialect of Modernism: Race, Language, and Twentieth-Century Literature.* New York: Oxford University Press, 1994.

O'Connor, Patrick, and Bryan Hammond, eds. *Josephine Baker.* London: Bulfinch, 1988.

Ogren, Kathy J. *The Jazz Revolution: Twenties America and the Meaning of Jazz.* New York: Oxford University Press, 1989.

Orvell, Miles. *The Real Thing: Imitation and Authenticity in American Culture, 1880–1940.* Chapel Hill: University of North Carolina Press, 1989.

Osofsky, Gilbert. *Harlem: The Making of a Ghetto. Negro New York 1890–1930.* New York: Harper Press, 1968.

Palmié, Stephan. "The Other Within: American Anthropology and the Study of Ethnic Minorities in the 1920's." In *Ethnic Cultures in the 1920's in North America.* Edited by Wolfgang Binder. Frankfurt: Peter Lang, 1993.

Panassié, Hugues. *The Real Jazz.* New York: A. S. Barnes, 1942.

Perry, Gillian. *Primitivism and the Modern: Primitivism, Cubism, Abstraction.* New Haven and London: Charles Harrison, 1993.

Peterkin, Julia. "The Negro in Art: How Shall He Be Portrayed, A Symposium." *Crisis* (September 1926): 238–239.

Platt, Susan Noyes. *Modernism in the 1920s: Interpretations of Modern Art in New York from Expressionism to Constructivism.* Ann Arbor: UMI Research Press, 1985.

Poggoli, Renato. *The Theory of the Avant-Garde.* Translated Gerald Fitzgerald. Cambridge: Harvard University Press, 1968

Powell, Richard J. *Black Art and Culture in the 20th Century.* London: Thames and Hudson, 1997.

———. *The Blues Aesthetic: Black Culture and Modernism.* Washington, D.C.: Washington Project for the Arts, 1989.

———. *Homecoming: The Art and Life of William H. Johnson.* Washington, D.C.: National Museum of American Art, 1991.

Price, Sally. *Primitive Art in Civilized Places.* Chicago: University of Chicago Press, 1989.

Reiss, Timothy J. *The Discourse of Modernism.* Ithaca: Cornell University Press, 1982.

Rhodes, Colin. *Primitivism and Modern Art.* New York: Thames & Hudson Press, 1994.

Robertson, Roland. "After Nostalgia." In *Theories of Modernity.* Edited by Bryan S. Turner. London: Sage, 1992.

Robinson, Lillian S., and Lise Vogel. "Modernism and History." *New Literary History* 3 (1971): 177–199.

Rose, Phyllis. *Jazz Cleopatra: Josephine Baker in Her Time.* New York: Vintage Press, 1989.

Rubin, William, ed. *"Primitivism" in 20th Century Art: Affinity of the Tribal and the Modern.* New York: Museum of Modern Art, 1984.

Said, Edward W. *Orientalism.* New York: Vintage, 1979.

Saldivar, Jose David. *The Dialectics of Our America: Genealogy, Cultural Critique, and Literary History.* Durham: Duke University Press, 1991.

Samaltanos, Katia. *Apollinaire.* Ann Arbor: UMI Research Press, 1981.

Sauvage, Marcel. *Les Mémoires de Joséphine Baker.* Paris: Éditions Kra, 1927.

Schneider, Helmut. *Exotische Welten: Europäische Phantasien.* Stuttgart: Editions Cantz, 1987.

Schoener, Allon, ed. *Harlem on My Mind: Cultural Capital of Black America 1900–1968.* New York: Random House, 1968.

Schuller, Gunther. *Early Jazz; Its Roots and Musical Development. The History of Jazz.* Vol. I. New York: Oxford University Press, 1968.

Schultz, Alfred. *Race or Mongrel.* New York: Arno, [1908] 1977.

Seckel, Hélène. "Anthology of Early Commentary on Les Demoiselles d'Avignon." In *Les Demoiselles d'Avignon.* Studies in Modern Art 3. Edited by William

Rubin, Hélène Seckel, and Judith Cousins. New York: Museum of Modern Art, 1995, 213–257.

Sims, Lowery S. and Mitchell D. Kahan, eds. *Robert Colescott: A Retrospective, 1975–1986.* San Jose: San Jose Museum of Art, 1987.

Singal, Daniel Joseph. "Towards a Definition of American Modernism." *American Quarterly* 39, no.1 (1987): 7–26.

Singh, Amritjit, and William S. Shiver, eds. *The Harlem Renaissance: Revaluations.* New York: Garland Press, 1989.

Smith, Terry. *Making the Modern: Industry, Art, and Design in America.* Chicago: Chicago University Press, 1993.

Smuda, Manfred. *Der Gegenstand in der Bildenden Kunst und Literatur: typologische Untersuchungen zur Theorie des ästhetischen Gegenstands.* Munich: Wilhelm Fink Verlag, 1979.

Solano, Solita. *Nancy Cunard: Brave Poet, Indomitable Rebel 1896–1965.* Philadelphia: Chilton Press, 1968.

Sollors, Werner. *Beyond Ethnicity.* New York: Oxford University Press, 1986.

Stearns, Marshall W. *The Story of Jazz.* New York: Oxford University Press, 1962.

——— and Jean Stearns. *Jazz Dance: The Story of American Vernacular Dance.* New York: Da Capo Press, [1968] 1994.

Stein, Leo. *Appreciation: Painting, Poetry and Prose.* New York: Crown, 1947.

Stewart, Jeffrey C. *To Color America: Portraits by Winold Reiss.* Washington, D.C.: Smithsonian Institution, 1989.

Story, Ralph D. "Patronage and the Harlem Renaissance: You Get What You Pay For." *CAL* 32 (March 1989): 284–295.

Sundquist, Eric J. *To Wake the Nations: Race in the Making of American Literature.* Cambridge: Harvard University Press, 1993.

Taylor, Ronald. *Aesthetics and Politics.* London: Verso, 1977.

Torgovnick, Marianne. "William Rubin." In *Perspectives: Angles on African Art.* Edited by Susan Vogel. New York: Abrams/Center for African Art, 1987.

———. *Gone Primitive: Savage Intellects, Modern Lives.* Chicago: University of Chicago Press, 1990.

Trilling, Lionel. *Beyond Culture: Essays on Literature and Learning.* New York: Harcourt Brace Jovanovich, 1965.

U.S. Department of War. *Discovering Music.* Education Manual EM 603. 2nd Edition. Washington: American Press, 1944.

Varnedoe, Kirk. *A Fine Disregard: What Makes Modern Art Modern.* New York: Harry N. Abrams, 1992.

Vogel, Susan, ed. *Perspectives: Angles on African Art.* New York: Abrams/Center for African Art, 1987.

von Luschan, Felix. "Die Neger in den Vereinigten Staaten." *Koloniale Rundschau* (1915): 504–540.

Wallace, Michele. "Modernism, Postmodernism and the Problem of the Visual in Afro-American Culture." In *Out There: Marginalization and Contemporary Cultures.* Edited by Russell Ferguson et al. Cambridge: MIT Press, 1990.

Warren, Kenneth Wayne. *Black and White Strangers: Race and American Literary Realism.* Chicago: University of Chicago Press, 1993.

Watson, Steven. *The Harlem Renaissance: The Hub of African-American Culture, 1920–1930.* New York: Pantheon Books, 1995.

Whiteman, Paul. "The Progress of Jazz: Problems Which Confront the American Composer in His Search for a Musical Medium." *Vanity Fair* (January 1926): 52–98.

—— and Mary Margaret McBride. *Jazz.* Popular Culture in America 1800–1925. New York: Arno Press, [1926] 1974.

Williams, Raymond. *The Politics of Modernism: Against the New Conformists.* New York: Verso, 1989.

Wilson, Edmund. "The Jazz Problem." *New Republic* (January 13, 1926): 217–219

Wintz, Cary D. *Black Culture and the Harlem Renaissance.* Houston: Rice University Press, 1988.

Woolf, Virginia. *To the Lighthouse.* New York: Harcourt Brace & Company, [1927] 1989.

Young, Robert J. C. *Colonial Desire: Hybridity in Theory, Culture and Race.* New York: Routledge, 1995.

Zervos, Christian. "Notes sur la Sculpture Contemporaire." *Cahiers d'art.* 10 (1929): 465–476.

☑ INDEX